JOURNAL FOR STAR WISDOM 2010

JOURNAL FOR STAR WISDOM

2010

Edited by Robert Powell

EDITORIAL BOARD

William Bento
Brian Gray
Robert Schiappacasse
David Tresemer

STEINERBOOKS
An Imprint of Anthroposophic Press, Inc.
610 Main Street, Suite 1
Great Barrington, MA, 01230
www.steinerbooks.org

Journal for Star Wisdom 2010 © 2009 by Robert Powell.
All contributions are used by permission of the authors.
All rights reserved. No part of this publication may be reproduced,
stored in a retrieval system, or transmitted in any form or by
any means, electronic, mechanical, photocopying, recording, or
otherwise without the prior written permission of the publisher.

With grateful acknowledgment to Peter Treadgold (1943–2005), who wrote
the Astrofire program (available from the Sophia Foundation), with which
the ephemeris pages in the *Journal for Star Wisdom* are computed each year.

COVER AND INTERIOR DESIGN: WILLIAM JENS JENSEN

ISBN-13: 978-0-88010-713-6
ISSN: 1949-8233

CONTENTS

PREFACE 7

THE ROSE OF THE WORLD
Daniel Andreev 12

EDITORIAL FOREWORD
Robert Powell 14

IN MEMORY OF WILLI SUCHER (1902–1985)
Robert Powell 17

SUN ON THE GALACTIC CENTER
David Tresemer 27

KYOT AND THE STELLAR SCRIPT OF PARSIFAL
Ellen Schalk 31

SIGNATURE OF JUPITER IN THE EVENTS OF JESUS CHRIST'S LIFE
David Tresemer, with Robert Schiappacasse and William Bento 35

CONTEMPLATIONS ON THE JUPITER–URANUS CONJUNCTION
William Bento 44

WORLD PENTECOST
Robert Powell 53

COMMENTARIES AND EPHEMERIDES: JANUARY–DECEMBER 2010
William Bento, David Tresemer, Claudia McLaren Lainson, and Sally Nurney 66

EPITAPH: THOUGH MY SOUL MAY SET IN DARKNESS
Words attributed to Galileo | Music by Joseph Haydn 103

ABOUT THE CONTRIBUTORS 104

ASTROSOPHY

The Sophia Foundation of North America was founded and exists to help usher in the new Age of Sophia and the corresponding Sophianic culture, the Rose of the World, prophesied by Daniel Andreev and other spiritual teachers. Part of the work of the Sophia Foundation is the cultivation of a new star wisdom, *Astro-Sophia* (Astrosophy), now arising in our time in response to the descent of Sophia, who is the bearer of Divine Wisdom, just as Christ (the Logos, or the Lamb) is the bearer of Divine Love. Like the star wisdom of antiquity, Astrosophy is sidereal, which means "of the stars." Astrosophy, inspired by Divine Sophia, descending from stellar heights, directs our consciousness toward the glory and majesty of the starry heavens, to encompass the entire celestial sphere of our cosmos and, beyond this, to the galactic realm—the realm that Daniel Andreev referred to as "the heights of our universe"—from which Sophia has descended on her path of approach into our cosmos. Sophia draws our attention not only to the star mysteries of the heights, but also to the cosmic mysteries connected with Christ's deeds of redemption wrought two thousand years ago. To penetrate these mysteries is the purpose of the yearly *Journal for Star Wisdom*.

☆ ☆ ☆

For information about Astrosophy/Choreocosmos/Cosmic Dance workshops
Contact the Sophia Foundation of North America:
3143 Avalon Court, Palo Alto, California 94306
Phone: 650-494-9900
Email: sophia@sophiafoundation.org
Website: www.sophiafoundation.org

PREFACE

Robert Powell

This is the first edition of the *Journal for Star Wisdom*, which is intended as a help to all people interested in the new star wisdom of Astrosophy and in the cosmic dimension of Christianity, which began with the star of the magi. The calendar comprises an ephemeris page for each month of the year, computed with the help of Peter Treadgold's *Astrofire* computer program, and a monthly commentary by David Tresemer (together with Claudia McLaren Lainson and Sally Nurney) for January to August, and by William Bento for September to December. The monthly commentary relates the geocentric and heliocentric planetary movements to events in the life of Jesus Christ.

Jesus Christ united the levels of the earthly personality (geocentric = Earth-centered) and the higher self (heliocentric = Sun-centered) insofar as he was the most highly evolved earthly personality (Jesus) embodying the Higher Self (Christ) of all existence, the Divine "I AM." To see the life of Jesus Christ in relation to the world of stars opens the door to a profound experience of the cosmos, giving rise to a new star wisdom (Astrosophy), the spiritual science of Cosmic Christianity.

The *Journal for Star Wisdom* is scientific, resting upon a solid mathematical-astronomical foundation and also upon a secure chronology of the life of Jesus Christ, and at the same time it is spiritual, aspiring to the higher dimension of existence that is expressed outwardly in the world of stars. The scientific and the spiritual come together in the sidereal zodiac that originated with the Babylonians and was used by the three magi who beheld the star of Bethlehem and came to pay homage to Jesus a few months after his birth. In continuity of spirit with the origins of Cosmic Christianity with the three magi, the sidereal zodiac is the frame of reference used for the computation of the geocentric and heliocentric planetary movements that are commented upon in the light of the life of Jesus Christ in the *Journal for Star Wisdom*.

Thus, all zodiacal longitudes indicated in the text and presented in the following calendar are in terms of the sidereal zodiac, which has to be distinguished from the tropical zodiac in widespread use in contemporary astrology in the West. The tropical zodiac was introduced into astrology in the middle of the second century C.E. by the Greek astronomer Claudius Ptolemy. Prior to this, the sidereal zodiac was in use. Such was the influence of Ptolemy upon the Western astrological tradition that the tropical zodiac came to replace the sidereal zodiac used by the Babylonian, Egyptian, and early Greek astrologers. Yet the astrological tradition in India was not influenced by Ptolemy, and so the sidereal zodiac is still used to this day by Hindu astrologers.

The sidereal zodiac originated with the Babylonians in the sixth to fifth centuries B.C.E., and was defined by them in relation to certain bright stars. For example, Aldebaran ("the Bull's eye") is located in the middle of the sidereal sign/constellation of the Bull at 15° Taurus, and Antares ("the Scorpion's heart") is in the middle of the sidereal sign/constellation of the Scorpion at 15° Scorpio. The sidereal signs, each 30° long, coincide closely with the twelve astronomical zodiacal constellations of the same name, whereas the signs of the tropical zodiac, since they are defined in relation to the vernal point, now have little or no relationship to the corresponding zodiacal constellations.

This is because the vernal point, the zodiacal location of the Sun on March 20/21, shifts slowly backward through the sidereal zodiac at a rate of one degree in seventy-two years ("the precession of the equinoxes"). When Ptolemy introduced the tropical zodiac into astrology, there was an almost exact coincidence between the tropical and the sidereal zodiac, as the vernal point, which is defined to be 0° Aries in the tropical zodiac, was at 1° Aries in the sidereal zodiac in the middle of the second century C.E. Thus, there was only one degree difference between the two zodiacs. So, it made hardly any difference to Ptolemy or his contemporaries to use the tropical zodiac instead of the sidereal zodiac. But now (the vernal point, on account of precession, having shifted back from 1° Aries to 5° Pisces), there is a 25° difference, and so there is virtually no correspondence between the two. Without going into further detail concerning the complex issue of the zodiac, as shown in the *Hermetic Astrology* trilogy, the sidereal zodiac is the zodiac used by the three magi, who were the last representatives of the true star wisdom of antiquity. For this reason the sidereal zodiac is used throughout the *Journal for Star Wisdom*.

Readers interested in exploring the scientific (astronomical and chronological) foundations of Cosmic Christianity are referred to the following works listed under "Literature." For example, *Chronicle of the Living Christ: Foundations of Cosmic Christianity* is an indispensable source of reference (abbreviated: Chron.) for the *Journal for Star Wisdom*, as also are the four Gospels: Matthew = Mt.; Mark = Mk; Luke = Lk.; John = Jn. The chronology of the life of Jesus Christ rests upon the description of his daily life by Anne Catherine Emmerich in her 4-volume work *The Life of Jesus Christ* (abbreviated: LJC). Further details concerning the *Journal for Star Wisdom* and how to work with it on a daily basis are to be found in the *General Introduction to the Christian Star Calendar*. The *General Introduction* explains all the features of the *Journal for Star Wisdom* and how to work with it on a daily basis. The new edition, published 2003, includes sections on the mega stars (stars of great luminosity) and on the thirty-six decans (10-degree subdivisions of the twelve signs of the zodiac) in relation to their planetary rulers and to the extra-zodiacal constellations, those constellations above or below the circle of the twelve constellations/signs of the zodiac. Further material on the decans, including examples of historical personalities born in the various decans, and also a wealth of other material on the signs of the sidereal zodiac, is to be found in *Cosmic Dances of the Zodiac* listed below. Also foundational is *History of the Zodiac* published by Sophia Academic Press, listed under "Astrosophic Works by Robert Powell."

LITERATURE

General Introduction to the Christian Star Calendar: A Key to Understanding, new edition: Sophia Foundation of North America: Palo Alto, CA, 2003.

Bento, William, Robert Schiappacasse & David Tresemer, *Signs in the Heavens: A Message for our Time*. Available from www.TheStarHouse.org or StarHouse, PO Box 2180, Boulder, CO 80306 (2000).

Emmerich, Anne Catherine, *The Life of Jesus Christ*, 4 vols., 2004. TAN Books, PO Box 410487, Charlotte, NC 28241.

Paul, Lacquanna & Robert Powell, *Cosmic Dances of the Planets*. Sophia Foundation Press, San Rafael, CA, 2007.

———, *Cosmic Dances of the Zodiac*. Sophia Foundation Press, San Rafael, CA, 2007.

Smith, Edward Reaugh, *The Burning Bush: An Anthroposophical Commentary on the Bible*, vol. I. SteinerBooks, Great Barrington, MA, 1997.

Steiner, Rudolf, *The Spiritual Guidance of the Individual and Humanity*. SteinerBooks: Great Barrington, MA, 1992.

Sucher, Willi, *Cosmic Christianity and the Changing Countenance of Cosmology*. SteinerBooks: Gt. Barrington, MA, 1993. *Isis Sophia* and other works by Willi Sucher are available from the Astrosophy Research Center, PO Box 13, Meadow Vista, CA 95722.

Tidball Charles S. & Robert Powell, *Jesus, Lazarus, and the Messiah: Unveiling Three Christian Mysteries*. SteinerBooks: Great Barrington, MA, 2005. This book offers a penetrating study of the Christ mysteries against the background of *Chronicle of the Living Christ* and contains two chapters—*The John Mystery* and *The Johannine Tradition*—by Robert Powell concerning the biographies of the Apostle John and John the Evangelist (Lazarus).

Tresemer, David and Robert Schiappacasse, *Star Wisdom & Rudolf Steiner: A Life Seen through the Oracle of the Solar Cross*. SteinerBooks: Great Barrington, MA, 2007. In this introduction to Astrosophy, David Tresemer shows how the patterns written in the heavens influence a person's life, taking as an example the remarkable life of Rudolf Steiner.

Astrosophic works by Robert Powell, Ph.D.

Published by SteinerBooks, PO Box 960, Herndon, VA 20172, www.steinerbooks.org.

Christian Hermetic Astrology: The Star of the Magi and the Life of Christ, 1998. Consists of twenty-five discourses, set in the "Temple of the Sun," where Hermes and his pupils gather to meditate on the Birth, the Miracles, and the Passion of Jesus Christ. The discourses offer a series of meditative contemplations on the deeds of Christ in relation to the mysteries of the cosmos. They are an expression of the age-old hermetic mystery wisdom of the ancient Egyptian sage, Hermes Trismegistus. This book offers a meditative approach to the cosmic correspondences between major events in the life of Christ and the heavenly configurations at that time two thousand years ago.

Chronicle of the Living Christ: Foundations of Cosmic Christianity, 1996. An account of the life of Christ day-by-day throughout most of the 3½ years of his ministry, including the horoscopes of conception, birth, and death of Jesus, Mary and John the Baptist, together with a wealth of material relating to a new star wisdom focused on the life of Christ. This work provides the chronological basis for the *Journal for Star Wisdom*.

Elijah Come Again: A Prophet for Our Time: A Scientific Approach to Reincarnation, 2009. Presents a scientific approach toward the foundation of a new "science of the stars" as the "science of karma," unveiling the mystery of human destiny and the fulfillment of Elijah's mission at this time, for Earth and humanity, in the next step underlying our spiritual evolution. Explores biographically the various incarnations of the Elijah–John the Baptist–Raphael–Novalis individuality against the background of their conception, birth, and death horoscopes, from incarnation to incarnation, scientifically revealing the foundations of Astrosophy.

Journal for Star Wisdom

Journal for Star Wisdom. Edited by Robert Powell and others in the StarFire research group: A guide to the correspondences of Christ in the stellar and etheric world. Includes articles of interest, a complete sidereal ephemeris and aspectarian, geocentric and heliocentric. Published yearly in the fall for the coming new year. According to Rudolf Steiner, every step taken by Christ during his ministry between the Baptism in the Jordan and the Resurrection was in harmony with—and an expression of—the cosmos. The *Journal for Star Wisdom* is concerned with these heavenly correspondences during the life of Christ. It is intended to help provide a foundation for Cosmic Christianity, the cosmic dimension of Christianity. It is this dimension that has been missing from Christianity in its two-thousand-year history. A starting point is to contemplate the movements of the Sun, Moon and planets against the background of the zodiacal constellations (sidereal signs) today in relation to corresponding stellar events during the life of Christ. Thereby the possibility is opened of attuning to the life of Christ in the etheric cosmos in a living way.

Published by Sophia Foundation Press | Sophia Academic Press, PO Box 151011, San Rafael, CA 94915, USA. Tel: 707-789-9062. Email: jameswetmore@mac.com

History of the Zodiac, 2007. Book version of Robert Powell's PhD thesis on the history of the zodiac. This penetrating study of the history of the zodiac restores the sidereal zodiac to its rightful place as the original zodiac, tracing it back to the Babylonians in the fifth century B.C.E. Available in paperback and hard cover.

Hermetic Astrology, Vol. I: Astrology and Reincarnation, 2007. Hermetic astrology seeks to give the ancient science of the stars a scientific basis. This new foundation for astrology is opened up through research into reincarnation and karma (destiny), the primary focus of this volume. It includes numerous reincarnation examples, the study of which reveals the existence of certain astrological "laws" of reincarnation. On the basis of these "laws" it is evident that the ancient sidereal zodiac is the authentic astrological zodiac, and the heliocentric movements of the planets are of great significance. Foundational for the new star wisdom of Astrosophy.

Hermetic Astrology, Vol. II: Astrological Biography, 2007. Volume 2 is concerned with karmic relationships and with the unfolding of destiny in seven-year periods through the course of life. The seven-year rhythm underlies the human being's astrological biography, which can be studied in relation to the movements of the Sun, Moon and planets around the sidereal zodiac during the time between conception and birth. The "rule of Hermes" is used to determine the moment of conception.

Sign of the Son of Man in the Heavens: Sophia and the New Star Wisdom, 2008. This new edition has been revised and expanded with new material. Concerned with a new wisdom of the stars in the light of Divine Sophia, this book is intended as a help in the present time when humanity is called upon to be extremely wakeful in the period leading up to the end of the Mayan calendar in the year 2012.

Cosmic Dances of the Zodiac, 2007, by Lacquanna Paul and Robert Powell. Study material describing the twelve signs of the zodiac and their forms and gestures in cosmic dance, with diagrams, including a wealth of information on the twelve signs and the 36 decans (the subdivision of the signs into decans or 10-degree sectors corresponding to constellations above and below the zodiac).

Cosmic Dances of the Planets, 2007, by Lacquanna Paul and Robert Powell. Study material describing the seven classical planets and their forms and gestures in cosmic dance, with diagrams, including a wealth of information on the planets.

Published by Starcrafts (formerly Astro Communications Services, or ACS), PO Box 446, Exeter, NH 03833. Tel: 603-734-4300 or from the toll-free number: 866-953-8458; Email: mariasimms@comcast.net; website: www.astrocom.com. These three works are in the ACS "All About Astrology" series:

The Zodiac: A Historical Survey, 1984.
History of the Planets, 1989.
History of the Houses, 1997.

Published by the American Federation of Astrologers (AFA), PO Box 22040, Tempe, AZ 85285.

The Sidereal Zodiac (written with Peter Treadgold), 1985. A history of the zodiac—sidereal, tropical, Hindu, astronomical—and a formal definition of the sidereal zodiac with the star Aldebaran ("the Bull's Eye") at 15° Taurus. This is an abbreviated version of *History of the Zodiac* (see above).

Published by Rudolf Steiner College Press, 9200 Fair Oaks Blvd., Fair Oaks, CA 95628.

The Christ Mystery: Reflections on the Second Coming, 1999. The fruit of many years of reflection on the Second Coming and its cosmological aspects. This work looks at the approaching trial of humanity and the challenges of living in apocalyptic times, against the background of "great signs in the heavens."

The Sophia Foundation of North America, 3143 Avalon Court, Palo Alto, CA 94306, distributes many of the above books and also other works by Robert Powell. Tel/Fax: 650-494-9900; Email: sophia@sophiafoundation.org; website: www.sophiafoundation.org.

Computer Program for Charts and Ephemerides

With grateful acknowledgment to Peter Treadgold, who has written the computer program *Astrofire* (with research module, star catalog of over 4000 stars, and database of birth and death charts of historical personalities) capable of printing out geocentric and heliocentric/hermetic sidereal charts and ephemerides throughout history. (The hermetic charts, based on the astronomical system of the Danish astronomer Tycho Brahe, are referred to as Tychonic charts in the *Astrofire* program.)

With this program one can:
- compute birth charts in a large variety of systems (tropical, sidereal, geocentric, heliocentric, hermetic)
- calculate conception charts using the hermetic rule, in turn applying it for correction of the birth time
- produce charts for the period between conception and birth
- print out an "astrological biography" for the whole of lifework with the geocentric, heliocentric (and even lemniscatory) planetary system
- work with the sidereal zodiac according to the definition of your choice (Babylonian sidereal, Indian sidereal, unequal-division astronomical, etc.)
- work with planetary aspects with orbs of your choice.

Included are eight house systems and a variety of chart formats. The program also includes an ephemeris program with a search facility. The geocentric/heliocentric sidereal ephemeris pages in the yearly *Christian Star Calendar* are produced by *Astrofire*. This program runs under Microsoft Windows.

If you are interested in *Astrofire*, please contact the Sophia Foundation of North America (see above).

For an example printout of a horoscope produced by the Astrofire program, see below.

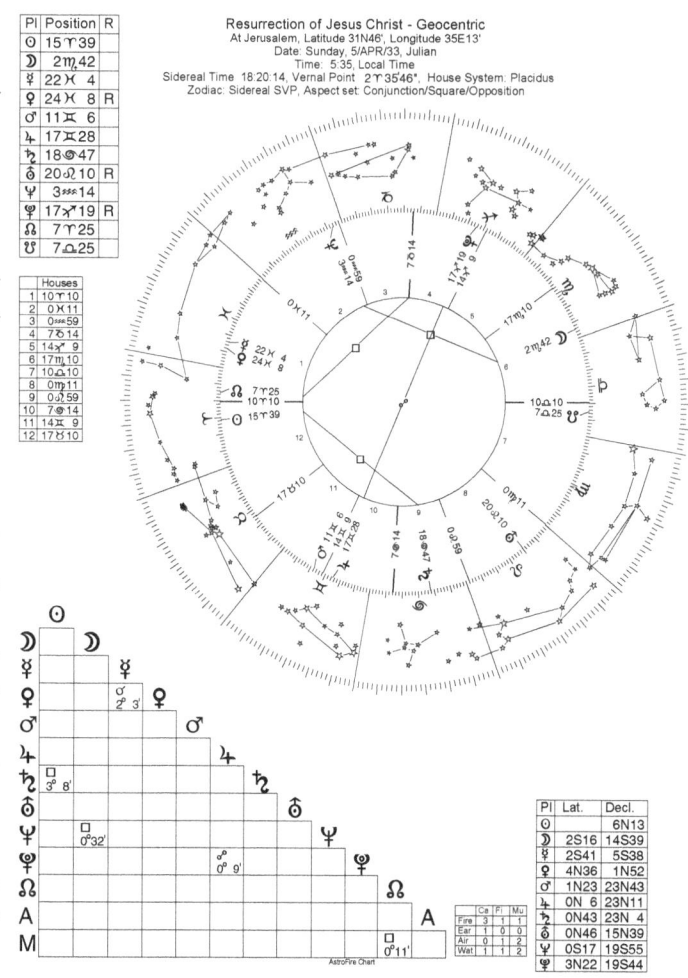

THE ROSE OF THE WORLD

Daniel Andreev

By warning about the coming Antichrist, and pointing him out and unmasking him when he appears, by cultivating unshakeable faith within human hearts and a grasp of the meta-historical perspectives and global spiritual prospects within human minds... [we help Sophia bring to birth the new culture of love and wisdom called by Daniel Andreev "The Rose of the World"]... [Sophia's] birth in one of the zatomis will be mirrored not only by the Rose of the World. Feminine power and its role in contemporary life is increasing everywhere. It is that circumstance above all that is giving rise to worldwide peace movements, an abhorrence of bloodshed, disillusion over coercive methods of change, an increase in woman's role in society proper, an ever-growing tenderness and concern for children, and a burning hunger for beauty and love. We are entering an age when the female soul will become ever purer and broader, when an ever greater number of women will become profound inspirers, sensitive mothers, wise counselors and far-sighted leaders. It will be an age when the feminine in humanity will manifest itself with unprecedented strength, striking a perfect balance with masculine impulses. See, you who have eyes.

— DANIEL ANDREEV,
The Rose of the World, p. 358 [1]

---

1 Words in brackets in this chapter added by Robert Powell.

The preceding words are those of Daniel Andreev, the great prophet of the coming Age of Sophia and the corresponding Sophianic culture that he called "The Rose of the World." In the above quote, "zatomis" refers to a heavenly realm within the Earth's etheric aura. Andreev refers to Sophia as "Zventa-Sventana," meaning "the Holiest of the Holy."

> A mysterious event is taking place in the meta-history of contemporary times: new divine-creative energy is emanating into our cosmos. Since ancient times the loftiest hearts and most subtle minds have anticipated this event that is now taking place. The first link in the chain of events—events so important that they can only be compared to the incarnation of the Logos—occurred at the turn of the nineteenth century. This was an emanation of the energy of the Virgin Mother, an emanation that was not amorphous, as it had been before in human history [at Pentecost, when there was an emanation of Sophia into the Virgin Mary], but incomparably intensified by the personal aspect it assumed. A great God-born monad descended from the heights of the universe into our cosmos. (ibid., p. 356)

The words of the great Russian seer, Daniel Andreev, are prophetic words. As I have indicated in *The Most Holy Trinosophia and the New Revelation of the Divine Feminine* (SteinerBooks, 2000), he points to the descent of Sophia and the resulting Sophianic world culture, the Rose of the World, in a most inspiring way:

She is to be born in a body of enlightened ether... There She is, our hope and joy, Light and Divine Beauty! For Her birth will be mirrored in our history as something that our grandchildren and great-grandchildren will witness: the founding of the Rose of the World, its spread throughout the world, and ... the assumption by the Rose of the World of supreme authority over the entire Earth. (ibid., p. 357)

The Sophia Foundation of North America was founded and exists to help usher in the new Age of Sophia and the corresponding Sophianic culture, the Rose of the World, prophesied by Daniel Andreev and other spiritual teachers.

✶ ✶ ✶

WORKING WITH THE *JOURNAL FOR STAR WISDOM*

The listing of major planetary events each month is intended as a stimulus toward attunement with the Universal Christ, the Logos, whose Being encompasses the entire galaxy. The deeds of the historical Christ wrought two thousand years ago are of eternal significance—inscribed into the cosmos—and they resonate with the movements of the heavenly bodies, especially when certain alignments or planetary configurations occur bearing a resemblance with those prevailing at the time of events in the life of Jesus Christ. With the rare astronomical event of the transit of Venus across the face of the Sun that took place on June 8, 2004 at exactly the zodiacal degree (23° Taurus) where the Sun stood at Christ's Ascension, a new impulse was given from divine-spiritual realms for the further unfolding of star wisdom, *Astro-Sophia*.

Indications regarding the similarity of contemporary planetary configurations with those at events in the life of Christ are given in the lower part of the monthly commentaries, and the upper part gives a commentary on the notable astronomical occurrences each month. Unless otherwise stated, all astronomical indications regarding visibility mean "visible to the naked eye"—see note concerning *Time* on page 66 of this journal, preceding the monthly commentaries.

With this jurnal, astronomy and astrology, which were a unity in the ancient star wisdom of the Egyptians and Babylonians, are reunited again, providing a foundation for Astrosophy, the all-encompassing star wisdom, *Astro-Sophia*, which is an expression of Sophia, referred to in John's Revelation as the "Bride of the Lamb."

The Russian poet and mystic Daniel Andreev also had a vision of the Holy Grail in the starry heavens and revealed its name:

"I remember seeing a glowing mist of stunning majesty, as though the creative heart of our universe had revealed itself to me in visible form for the first time. It was Astrofire, the great center of our galaxy."

—DANIEL ANDREEV, *The Rose of the World*, p.198

EDITORIAL FOREWORD

The *Journal for Star Wisdom* (formerly *Christian Star Calendar*) has appeared every year since 1991. From the beginning, the central feature has been the calendar comprising the monthly ephemeris pages together with commentaries drawing attention to the Christ events remembered by the ongoing cosmic events. The significance of following the Christ events in relation to daily astronomical events is an important foundation for the new star wisdom of Astrosophy.[1] This new star wisdom is arising in our time in response to the second coming of Christ—known as his return in the *etheric realm* of life forces—as a path of communing with Christ in his *life body* (*ether body*). It should also be mentioned that, with the onset of the second coming of Christ during the course of the twentieth century, Christ is now the Lord of Karma, and this is important to take into consideration in the development of a new relationship of humanity to the stars in our time, particularly with respect to the horoscope as an expression of human karma, or destiny.

The events of Christ's life lived two thousand years ago are inscribed into his ether body, and to meditate upon these events at times when they are cosmically remembered is a way of drawing near to Christ. The recently updated version of my article "Subnature and the Second Coming" in the new book *The Inner Life of the Earth*[2] outlines the background to contemporary events as a confrontation between good and evil in relation to Christ's descent at this time through the subearthly realms and also gives an overview of the various cosmic rhythms unfolding in relation to his second coming, including the thirty-three-and-one-third-year rhythm of his ether body.

The *Journal for Star Wisdom* encourages the reader to engage in the practice of star-gazing. The activity of star-gazing, as described on my website www.Astrogeographia.org (see "A Modern Path of the Magi" in the section on "The Star of the Magi"), is also fundamental to the development of the new star wisdom of Astrosophy. One of the foundations of Astrosophy lies in the science of astronomy, providing the new star wisdom with a secure scientific foundation, which moreover, can be brought into the realm of experience through the practice of star-gazing. In Astrosophy there is no longer a separation between astronomy and astrology. For example, when in the *Journal for Star Wisdom* it is indicated that currently Mars in the heavens is at 15° Taurus then, assuming that Mars is visible, the red planet can be seen in conjunction with Aldebaran marking the Bull's eye

---

1. There are many different approaches to Astrosophy and not all use the equal-division sidereal zodiac that forms the basis of the approach followed in the *Journal for Star Wisdom*. All references to the zodiac and to planetary positions in the zodiac in the *Journal for Star Wisdom* are in terms of the sidereal zodiac as defined in my book *History of the Zodiac* (San Rafael, CA: Sophia Academic Press, 2007). Moreover, in Astrosophy there are different chronologies of the life of Christ, and the chronology that forms the basis of the approach followed in the *Journal for Star Wisdom* is set forth in my book *Chronicle of the Living Christ*. Thus, all references to planetary positions at the Christ events in the *Journal for Star Wisdom* are in terms of the scientifically established chronology of the life of Christ set forth in my book *Chronicle of the Living Christ* (Hudson, NY: Anthroposophic Press, 1996).

2. P. V. O'Leary (editor), Christopher Bamford, Dennis Klocek, David S. Mitchell, Marko Pogacnik, Robert Powell, Rachel C. Ross, *The Inner Life of the Earth: Exploring the Mysteries of Nature, Subnature, and Supranature* (Great Barrington, MA: Steiner Books, 2008), pp. 69–141.

at the center of the constellation of Taurus, whose longitude, as the central star in this constellation, is 15° Taurus. In Astrosophy, the astrological fact of Mars at 15° Taurus is identical with the astronomical reality of the location of Mars at the center of the constellation of Taurus. Astrosophy thus relates to sense-perceptible reality and to the Divine "background of existence" (the spiritual hierarchies)[3] underlying this reality, whereas astrology is generally practiced in such a way that there is a split between astrology and astronomy (in this example, modern astrology, which uses the tropical zodiac rather than the equal-division sidereal zodiac used in Astrosophy, would say that Mars is "in Gemini"). The historical background as to how this separation between astronomy and astrology arose is described in my book *History of the Zodiac*.[4]

The present issue of the *Journal for Star Wisdom* is the twentieth, but is the first published under the new title, as all previous issues were published under the title *Christian Star Calendar*. By way of explanation concerning the new title: this publication is intended as an outreach from the StarFire research group (an Astrosophy group) that meets yearly in Boulder, Colorado (sometimes in Fair Oaks, California)—see the website www.StarWisdom.org. (Other related websites concerned with the new star wisdom of Astrosophy are www.sophiafoundation.org and www.astrogeographia.org). The *Journal for Star Wisdom* is intended as an organ for the development of the new star wisdom of Astrosophy. This was also the purpose of the *Christian Star Calendar*. However, there the focus, at least, initially, was primarily on the calendar—the monthly ephemeris and commentaries. In the course of time, more and more research articles on the new star wisdom of Astrosophy came to be published in the *Christian Star Calendar*. A point was reached where it became clear that the publication is more of a journal than a calendar, although the calendar continues to play an important role. It is therefore a natural transition from the *Christian Star Calendar* to the *Journal for Star Wisdom*.

Another important reason for the change of title is that the editorial board of the *Journal for Star Wisdom*, drawn from members of the StarFire research group, acknowledge their debt to the pioneer of the new star wisdom of Astrosophy, Willi Sucher (1902–1985), who from 1965 to 1972 published his research findings in the regularly appearing *Star Journal*. The change of name emphasizes the line of continuity from the *Star Journal* to the *Mercury Star Journal*, which I edited during the years 1974 to 1981. The *Christian Star Calendar* (1991–2009) was also in this same line of continuation from Willi Sucher's original *Star Journal*, however without the line of continuity being explicitly indicated by way of the title.

A major change, this year, is that the *Journal for Star Wisdom* is published by SteinerBooks, our new publisher. From 2006 to 2009, issues of the *Christian Star Calendar* were published by the Sophia Foundation Press. Another major change is that, whereas I compiled the monthly commentaries for all nineteen issues of the *Christian Star Calendar*, the monthly commentaries for the *Journal for Star Wisdom* are compiled by a team of contributors: David Tresemer assisted by Claudia McLaren Lainson and Sally Nurney for the months January to August 2010, and William Bento for the months September–December 2010.

Astrosophically, the year 2010 is an extraordinary year. Three times this year (January 14/15, July 7/8, November 17) Pluto crosses the exact position (8°55' Sagittarius) where it was located at the third temptation of Jesus in the wilderness,

---

3. According to Rudolf Steiner, the constellations are the abode of the first hierarchy, called Seraphim, Cherubim, and Thrones. The movement of the planets takes place against the background of the zodiacal constellations, which—considered as the abode of the first hierarchy—form the Divine "background of existence" in the heavens. "Suppose you wanted to point to some particular [group of] Thrones, Cherubim and Seraphim, one denotes them by a particular constellation. It is like a signpost. In that direction over there are the [group of] Thrones, Cherubim and Seraphim known as the Twins, over there [the group of Thrones, Cherubim and Seraphim known as] the Lion, etc." (Rudolf Steiner, *The Spiritual Hierarchies*, New York, Anthroposophic Press, 1970, p. 99; words in brackets [ ] added by R. Powell).
4. Robert Powell, *History of the Zodiac* (San Rafael/CA: Sophia Academic Press, 2007).

at which time Pluto was in conjunction with the Sun, symbolizing the encounter between Satan/Ahriman (the lord of the underworld) and Christ, the Spiritual Sun. Then, on December 26/27, 2010 the conjunction of the Sun and Pluto takes place at 10° Sagittarius.[5] By way of analogy, the Sun represents Christ together with the forces of light in his service, and Pluto, at least in its manifestation as Pluto-Hades,[6] is a symbol for the dark forces of opposition to Christ. It is a matter of focusing upon "the light shining in the darkness" (John 1:5) as the primary focus, whereas the darkness itself—one has to be aware of its existence, otherwise one would be living in illusion—is secondary, simply a counterpart to the light.

In conclusion I would like to express gratitude to our publisher, Gene Gollogly of SteinerBooks, and to the able assistance of Jens Jensen of SteinerBooks, for making this first issue of the *Journal for Star Wisdom* available, and to all those who have contributed to make this issue possible, in particular to our authors for presenting their research articles as contributions to the foundations of the new star wisdom of Astrosophy, and to all our readers who ultimately are the reason for the existence of the *Journal for Star Wisdom*.

Please note that for economy of space, the valuable research article "Signature of Jupiter" by David Tresemer (with help from Robert Schiappacasse and William Bento) has been shortened. The full-length version of this article on Jupiter can be found at www.StarWisdom.org/JupiterSignature.html.

---

5. Robert Powell & Kevin Dann, *Christ & the Maya Calendar: 2010 and the Coming of the Antichrist* (Great Barrington, MA: SteinerBooks, 2009), pp. 230–234 discusses the significance of the third temptation of Christ in the wilderness and the Sun-Pluto conjunction of 2010.

6. Robert Powell, "Pluto-Hades and Pluto-Phanes": www.sophiafoundation.org/articles—this article, written with the help of Krista Kösters, describes the dark and the light side of Pluto.

> *Experience Fire—*
> *You unite with the Being of the Sun.*
> *Experience Air—*
> *You unite with the Light of the Sun.*
> *Experience Water—*
> *You unite with the Force of the Sun.*
> *Experience Earth—*
> *You unite with the Life of the Sun.*
>
> —Rudolf Steiner

IN MEMORY OF WILLI SUCHER
(1902–1985)

Robert Powell

May 21, 2010, commemorates the twenty-fifth anniversary of Willi Sucher's death in California. The original intention was to publish a lengthy article here to honor Willi's life and achievement as the founder of Astrosophy. The friend who wrote the article withdrew it, however, for reasons that I respect and understand.[1] And so this article is a short tribute to Willi, in place of a much longer one. This short article is not intended as a biography of Willi Sucher.[2] Rather, it is a reflection on a little known aspect of his work. It is understandable that this aspect of his work is not generally known, for it was discussed with me by Willi in a private conversation—as I had the privilege of having many private discussions with him during two stays with him as a guest at his home in Meadow Vista, California, in the foothills of the Sierra Nevada mountains, first for six weeks during the summer of 1977, and then for four weeks during the summer of 1982. These visits, where I came over to California from England, were decisive for me in terms of committing my life to deepening into the development of a new star wisdom (Astrosophy) appropriate for our time.

I had already been a student of astrology since 1969, when I encountered the work of Willi Sucher on the same day (February 29, 1972) as I came across the work of Rudolf Steiner in a bookstore in Museum Street, London, opposite the British Museum where, in the great library there, I was in the preparatory stages of starting work on my Ph.D. thesis at that time. My first meeting with Willi then took place at a workshop at Hawkwood College in the west of England in 1973. At that time, I offered to organize two one-week Astrosophy workshops in England, with Willi as presenter if he wanted to return from California to England in the summer of 1974, to which he agreed. During the course of these workshops, he and I agreed in a discussion that I would bring out a quarterly star journal, to which he would contribute. Subsequently the first issue of the *Mercury Star Journal* appeared at Christmas 1974, with a contribution by Willi entitled "Towards a New Star Wisdom." As stated in my introductory article in the first issue of the *Mercury Star Journal*:

> The spiritual impulse out of which Astrosophy has evolved may be traced back to Rudolf Steiner, the founder of Anthroposophy. Those individuals associated with the cultivation of esoteric star knowledge in the twentieth century found in Anthroposophy an impulse toward the renewal of ancient star wisdom—however, in a modern form. One such person was the Dutch astronomer Elisabeth Vreede, who was Rudolf Steiner's choice to head the Mathematical-Astronomical Section of the University for Spiritual Science (*Freie*

---

1. Instead, the article "Perspectives Inspired by the Death of Willi Sucher in California in the Early Hours of May 21, 1985," by Charles Lawrie is published in the 2009 Advent issue of *Starlight*, the newsletter of the Sophia Foundation of North America.

2. There is an excellent biography compiled by Jonathan Hilton, originally published in Willi Sucher, *Cosmic Christianity & the Changing Countenance of Cosmology: An Introduction to Astrosophy: A New Wisdom of the Stars* (Hudson, NY: Anthroposophic Press, 1993), pp. 9–24 (now available online at http://Astrosophycenter.com/inv/bio.htm).

Hochschule für Geisteswissenschaft) that he founded at the Goetheanum, Dornach, Switzerland in 1924. Elisabeth Vreede devoted her life to the study of the stars and developed the basic elements of Astrosophy. Her work, a star wisdom embracing both astronomy and astrology as well, is summarized in her book *Astronomy and Spiritual Science*.[3] Elisabeth Vreede's work was taken up by Willi Sucher and under her guidance it was developed further. Building upon the basic elements described by Elisabeth Vreede and guided by the shining beacon of Rudolf Steiner's wisdom, Willi Sucher labored to found Astrosophy as a spiritual stream in the West. The final outcome of his endeavors was the *Star Journal* (subsequently *Star Letters*) that made its first appearance toward the end of 1965. For more than seven years the *Star Journal* (*Star Letters*) continued to present many great and far-reaching ideas on the human being's relationship to the starry worlds. The contents of this publication, representing the culmination of a lifetime's study of the stars, embody a completely new approach to star wisdom, breaking away from previous astrological traditions. In a sense, it may be said that after a long embryonic period (Willi Sucher began his studies around 1920), Astrosophy was born in 1965 and developed through a seven-year period with the publication of the *Star Journal* (*Star Letters*) as the ripe fruit of Willi's lifelong studies. The *Mercury Star Journal* is intended as a vehicle for star wisdom following on quite naturally from the original *Star Journal*. The work of Willi Sucher will continue to contribute, and others as well, so that in this way the work of developing Astrosophy can go forward with the *Mercury Star Journal* as a focus for expression.

The *Mercury Star Journal* appeared quarterly (except for the final issue, which came out in the format of a yearly journal) from 1974 to 1981—again, as with Willi's *Star Journal* (*Star Letters*), for a period of seven years. Circumstances of destiny meant that the publication of the *Mercury Star Journal* was discontinued in 1981. However, ten years later, as a "spiritual successor" to the *Mercury Star Journal*, the annual *Christian Star Calendar* was published from 1991 to 2009.[4] Now, in 2010, the work of focusing a new star wisdom (Astrosophy) is continuing with the yearly *Journal for Star Wisdom* in the line of succession: *Star Journal* (*Star Letters*) (1965–1972), *Mercury Star Journal* (1974–1981), *Christian Star Calendar* (1991–2009), *Journal for Star Wisdom* (from 2010).

It is important to note that no exclusivity is intended here with the foregoing depiction of this journal's genesis. The editor and the editorial board of this journal recognize that there are different approaches to the star wisdom of Astrosophy, each valid in its own way, and the gesture of this journal is one of openness and acknowledgment of such approaches.[5] It is our hope that everyone who is interested in star wisdom will find something of

---

3. Elisabeth Vreede, *Astronomy and Spiritual Science: The Astronomical Letters of Elizabeth Vreede* (Great Barrington, MA: SteinerBooks, 2007). "At the living center of this book lies the mystery of the future relationship between the human being and the stars" (from the foreword by Norman Davison).

4. In the ten years between 1981 and 1991, I carried out research into dating the life of Christ, and in 1985 I "struck gold" while reading *The Life of Jesus Christ* by Anne Catherine Emmerich, realizing that it contained the key to an exact chronology of Christ's life. Through her four-volume work I was able to find the dates later published in *Chronicle of the Living Christ*, which provides a scientific foundation for Cosmic Christianity, since, on the basis of these dates it was possible to compute the horoscopes of events in Christ's life, as discussed in *Christian Hermetic Astrology: The Star of the Magi and the Life of Christ*. Having found the true and exact dates of most of the events in Christ's life, it was possible to bring out the *Christian Star Calendar*, enabling the day-by-day correspondence of the life of Christ with the starry heavens to be followed with scientific exactness—as continued, now, in the calendar/ephemeris section of the *Journal for Star Wisdom*.

5. Without listing all the wonderful contributions throughout the world to the ongoing stream of Astrosophy, particular acknowledgment and gratitude is due to the Astrosophy Center, P.O. Box 13, Meadow Vista, California 95722; phone (530) 878-2673; website: http://astrosophycenter.com for the invaluable work of publishing Willi Sucher's books and study materials and continuing to represent his impulse in the world.

value in this journal, and those engaged in astrosophical research are warmly invited to contribute the results of their research findings. For the editor and the editorial board, there are three pillars upon which our star wisdom research rests: Anthroposophy, Esoteric Christianity, and Astrosophy.[6] These are the three areas that are represented in this journal.

* * *

Having elucidated this background, I would like to return now to the little-known aspect of Willi Sucher's work mentioned at the start of this article. The reason for focusing upon this here is that it entails a prophecy that is relevant to our time now. First, some background is needed to understand the importance of this prophecy.

According to Rudolf Steiner, just as Christ incarnated into Jesus at the baptism in the River Jordan two thousand years ago, Ahriman/Satan will also incarnate into a human being, mimicking the baptism of Jesus, and this will take place not long after the start of the third millennium, soon after the year 2000.[7] This is known in Christian tradition as *the coming of the Antichrist*, an event considered in light of various prophecies and traditions in *Christ & the Maya Calendar: 2012 and the Coming of the Antichrist*.[8] Here it should be noted that *Ahriman* is the name for the prince of darkness in the ancient Persian religion of Zoroastrianism, whereas in the Hebrew tradition, *Satan* is the name for this same being. There are several prophecies concerning the coming of the Antichrist (the incarnated Ahriman/Satan), derived mostly from Christ's own words:

> So when you see the abomination of desolation spoken of by the prophet Daniel, standing in the holy place...then there will be great tribulation, such as has not been from the beginning of the world until now, no, and never will be. And if those days had not been shortened, no human being would be saved; but for the sake of the elect those days will be shortened. Then if anyone says to you, "Lo, here is the Christ!" or "There he is!" do not believe it. For false Christs and false prophets will arise and show great signs and wonders, so as to lead astray, if possible, even the elect. (Matt. 24:15, 21–24)

The reference to the prophet Daniel is connected with his prophecy concerning the city of Jerusalem (the "holy place"), where Daniel speaks of "a prince who is to come [who] shall destroy the city and the sanctuary...desolations are decreed" (Daniel 9:26). Here Daniel refers to the "prince of this world" (Ahriman/Satan).

In Vladimir Solovyov's inspired work *A Short Story of the Antichrist*,[9] originally published in Russia at Easter 1900, he describes the false Christ (Antichrist), who, in league with a false prophet (the magician Apollyon), becomes emperor of the world and establishes his residence in Jerusalem. Among Apollyon's magical powers is the ability to make fire come down from heaven. This is a clear allusion to the two-horned beast referred to in the thirteenth chapter of the book of Revelation. In fact, it is in Revelation that we find an account of the reign of the Antichrist (referred to there simply as "the beast"), who is aided by the two-horned beast:

> The two-horned beast exercises all the authority of the first beast in its presence, and makes the earth and its inhabitants worship the [first beast].... Men worshipped the first beast, saying, "Who is

---

6. The website www.StarWisdom.org came about through the initiative of David Tresemer, the founder of StarHouse, a beautiful twelve-sided building surrounded by twelve standing stones relating to the zodiacal signs, located in the Rocky Mountains a few miles from Boulder, Colorado. See David Tresemer and Robert Schiappacasse, *Star Wisdom & Rudolf Steiner: A Life Seen through the Oracle of the Solar Cross* (SteinerBooks, 2007); and William Bento, Robert Schiappacasse, and David Tresemer, *Signs in the Heavens: A Message for Our Time* (StarHouse, 2000), which is dedicated to Willi Sucher.

7. Rudolf Steiner, *The Incarnation of Ahriman: The Embodiment of Evil on Earth* (London: Rudolf Steiner Press, 2006), p. 37.

8. Robert Powell & Kevin Dann, *Christ & the Maya Calendar: 2012 and the Coming of the Antichrist* (Great Barrington, MA: SteinerBooks, 2009).

9. Vladimir Solovyov, *War, Progress, and the End of History: Three Conversations Including a Short Story of the Antichrist* (Hudson, NY: Lindisfarne Press, 1990).

like the beast, and who can fight against it?" And the beast was given a mouth uttering haughty and blasphemous words, and it was allowed to exercise authority for forty-two months. (Revelation 13:12, 4–5)

It is precisely the meeting with the Antichrist that is depicted in the thirteenth chapter of the Revelation. Satan, the dragon (the first beast), gives his authority to the beast—that is, he incarnates in human form and becomes the beast, known traditionally as the *Antichrist*. The beast is allowed to exercise authority for forty-two months, which can be interpreted as signifying that the Antichrist is allowed to gain world dominion (as emperor or "prince of this world") and, for a certain period of time ("forty-two months"), is allowed to tempt humanity into accepting him as the Messiah. Here it should be noted that the length of Christ's ministry was forty-two months,[10] and it is this same period allotted to the Antichrist for his work of perdition. According to the account in Revelation, the Antichrist is aided by the two-horned beast, whose number is 666.

This special number, stemming from the Apocalypse of St. John, is given a unique interpretation by Rudolf Steiner. In his lectures published as *The Apocalypse of St. John*,[11] Rudolf Steiner refers to 666 as the number of the Sun Demon Sorath. In Hebrew, *Sorath* is spelled with the characters Samech, Vau, Resh, Tau, which have the numerical value 60 + 6 + 200 + 400 = 666. Steiner describes the Sun Demon Sorath as the one who inspires black magic. In Solovyov's account of the reign of the Antichrist, the beast is helped by the magician Apollyon, who wields magical powers. In other words, just as one particular human being will emerge as the Antichrist (the beast) by becoming a vehicle for the incarnated Ahriman/Satan, so another human being will act under the inspiration of Sorath as a wielder of black magic "to make the earth and its inhabitants worship the first beast." This second human being is "the false prophet who in its [the beast's] presence had worked the signs by which he deceived those who had received the mark of the beast" (Revelation 19:20).

Discussing the influence of Sorath in a lecture on September 12, 1924, Rudolf Steiner refers to the historical intervention of the Sun Demon at rhythmic intervals of 666 years. He mentions the first intervention around the year 666, the second around 1332 (2 x 666), and the third around 1998 (3 x 666), which leads to the present time. He spoke of "the arrival of the Sun Demon before this century [the twentieth] comes to an end."[12] The year 1998 is only an approximate indication, yet there can be no doubt that around this time (which includes the first part of the twenty-first century) a remarkable individual is destined to appear on the world stage as a fulfilment of the prophecy in Revelation of the coming of the prophet of the beast.[13]

This signifies a great trial for humanity, first through the emergence of the prophet of the beast, and then through the appearance of the beast himself, the Antichrist, as the "world emperor." In light of Rudolf Steiner's indication concerning 1998 (3 x 666), if this is brought into connection with the emergence on the world stage of the human being who is the prophet of the beast, inspired by Sorath to prepare the way for the coming of the Antichrist, it is clear that these two human beings must have been born before 2000. In fact, a definite date for the birth of the Antichrist was communicated by the American clairvoyant Jeane Dixon in her book *My Life and Prophecies*,[14] where she refers to a vision in which she saw the birth of the Antichrist at sunrise on February 5, 1962, at a place in the Middle East—a matter of only five

---

10. Robert Powell, *Chronicle of the Living Christ* (Hudson, NY: Anthroposophic Press, 1996), p. 424.

11. *The Apocalypse of St. John: Lectures on the Book of Revelation* (Hudson, NY: Anthroposophic Press, 1993), 12 lectures, Nuremberg, June 17–30, 1908.

12. Rudolf Steiner, *The Book of Revelation: And the Work of the Priest* (London: Rudolf Steiner Press, 1998), 18 lectures, Dornach, September 1924, p. 119.

13. See the chapter on the rhythm of 666 years in Robert Powell & Kevin Dann, *Christ & the Maya Calendar: 2012*, pp. 96–112, especially p. 109.

14. Jeane Dixon & Rene Noorbergen, *Jeane Dixon: My Life and Prophecies* (New York: William Morrow, 1969). For some background concerning Jeane Dixon and her prophecies, see Robert Powell & Kevin Dann, *Christ & the Maya Calendar*.

hours after a total eclipse of the Sun in the sidereal sign of Capricorn. There was indeed a most spectacular alignment of planets in Capricorn at this time of the birth of the Antichrist as indicated by Jeane Dixon, with Saturn, Jupiter, Mars, Venus, the Sun, Mercury, and the Moon aligned with the Moon's Node in Capricorn. The most recent previous occurrence of such a grand conjunction of the seven visible planets took place in 1524. If the future "world president" was actually born on this date in 1962, then he was born with the most powerful horoscope imaginable—an *imperial horoscope*, to use the terminology of Roman astrologers who cast horoscopes for members of the emperor's family. Those astrologers credited imperial power to the horoscopes of those born with two or more planets in proximity to the Ascendant. In the 1962 horoscope, all seven classical planets are close to the Ascendant (see figure below). If the Antichrist was indeed born on February 5, 1962, he will be forty-eight years old in 2010, signifying an important time in the unfolding of his destiny—a time having to do with the start of a new Jupiter cycle in his life. Note that 48 = 4 x 12, which is four times the twelve-year rhythm of Jupiter's orbital period around the zodiac, a rhythm associated with "immense spiritual adjustments"[15] as exemplified in the life of Jesus, who went through a profound transition at the age of twelve in the temple in Jerusalem. If Jeane Dixon's vision is true, the Antichrist's fourth "Jupiter birthday," at the age of forty-eight, might signify the *coming to power* on an inner level, and perhaps coming out into the public arena on an outer level, although it is also possible that this figure may for the time being prefer to work from behind the scenes.

Let us return now to the content of the private conversation with Willi Sucher previously mentioned. In this conversation, Willi indicated to me that he had done research into Jeane Dixon's vision and that he had found it plausible. Based on his own inner perception, he had even identified Tobruk, Libya, as the birthplace of the individual born on February 5, 1962. This enabled him to cast the horoscope (see figure on next page, showing the planetary alignment in Capricorn close to the Ascendant in Capricorn). When asked about the significance of the planetary alignment in Capricorn, he replied:

> In antiquity, Capricorn was called the "gateway to the gods," and what better moment could the Antichrist choose to be born than when all the planets are aligned in front of Capricorn, blocking the gateway to the spiritual world, in order to establish his rulership in a world of materialism, cutting off humanity from all spirituality.[16]

Whether Jeane Dixon's vision comes true or not remains to be seen. What is striking for me is the confirmation of her vision by Willi Sucher, who even determined the place of birth of the individual born on February 5, 1962, and who spent time contemplating the horoscope of that birth. As I learned from a friend who was present at some of Willi's workshops at Hawkwood College in England in the 1970s, Willi had already spoken about this prophecy by Jeane Dixon on one occasion then.[17] However, as far as I know he did not speak about the prophecy in subsequent lectures. This could indicate that he had some reservation about the prophecy. However, in his conversation with me about it in California, he positively affirmed the validity of Jeane Dixon's vision and even added to it a geographical location (Tobruk) from his own perception. On the other hand, the fact that he did not speak about it more often subsequently in public lectures might indicate that he was well aware of the unsettling nature of this prophecy, which, in any case, he knew would not really be relevant until after the start of the new millennium, as he was certainly aware of Rudolf Steiner's words: "Before only a part of the third millennium of the post-Christian era has elapsed, there will be

---

15. William Bryant, *The Veiled Pulse of Time: Life Cycles and Destiny* (Great Barrington, MA: Lindisfarne Books, 1996), p. 146.

16. Robert Powell, *The Christ Mystery: Reflections on the Second Coming* (Fair Oaks, CA: Rudolf Steiner College Press, 1999), p. 65.

17. This friend recently informed me that he distinctly remembers Willi saying the word "Tobruk".

Journal for Star Wisdom 2010

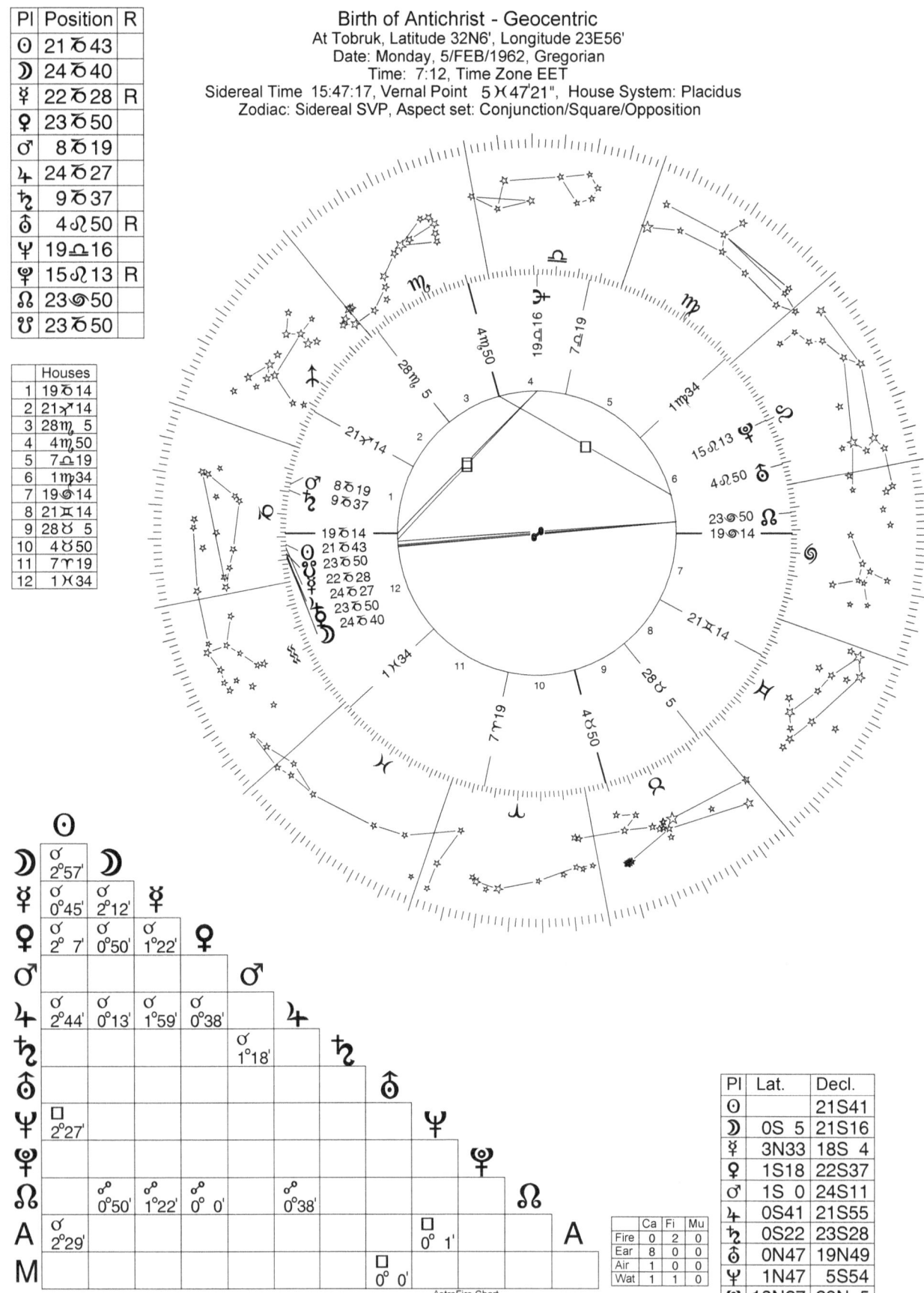

in the West an actual incarnation of Ahriman—Ahriman in the flesh."[18]

Given the relevance to our present time (about ten years into the new millennium), it is now appropriate to give Rudolf Steiner's prophecy serious consideration, and this is precisely the reason for this consideration of the content of the private conversation with Willi Sucher about this matter. Evidently, during Willi's lifetime, he exercised restraint in speaking about this matter. Now, however—a quarter of a century after his death—world events have moved ahead rapidly, and given the reality of the current world situation, we cannot ignore the possibly imminent appearance of such individuals as the Antichrist and his prophet on the world stage.

In the space of this article, it is not possible to go into details concerning the symptomatology of contemporary world affairs (this has been attempted in the book, *Christ & the Maya Calendar,* mentioned earlier). It is important, however, to understand that the appearance of the Antichrist is a trial for humanity, and that this initiation trial, if passed successfully, leads directly to what is spoken of in my article in this journal, "World Pentecost." In other words, there is a process through which humanity is passing that will culminate with humanity as a whole crossing the threshold, leading to the World Pentecost.

What does "crossing the threshold" mean? Each of us crosses the threshold at the moment of death. The veil of appearances is lifted, and we become aware that we are spiritual beings who belong to *the great chain of being,* which comprises all the spiritual hierarchies, from the angels and archangels to the cherubim and seraphim and beyond, to the Godhead, the Creator, the Ultimate Source of existence. Crossing the threshold is also possible during earthly life, prior to death, and this is called *initiation.*

Rudolf Steiner prophesied the event in which humanity *as a whole* will cross the threshold, whereby humankind *as a whole* encounters the Guardian of the Threshold,[19] who reveals to humankind the sum of humanity's negative karma. The encounter with the Antichrist is none other than this meeting with the whole of humankind's negative karma. The Antichrist thus represents the "double of humanity" to be met with in a courageous and morally upright way in order to cross the threshold into the spiritual world.

In his book *How to Know Higher Worlds,*[20] Rudolf Steiner depicts the Guardian of the Threshold as Christ. Elsewhere, he characterizes the Archangel Michael, at the right-hand of Christ, as the Lesser Guardian of the Threshold. The crossing of the threshold is thus a twofold event. On the one hand, it is the meeting with the Guardian of the Threshold (Christ) or with the Lesser Guardian of the Threshold (Archangel Michael). On the other hand, in the course of this encounter, one is shown one's own double through the Guardian of the Threshold, the sum of one's negative karma accumulated through all of one's incarnations. Since the double is an entity generated by the human individual, one must assume responsibility for it.[21] This is the admonishment of the Guardian of the Threshold, constituting the prerequisite for crossing the threshold. Not until one takes responsibility for one's negative karma in the shape of the double is the individual allowed to cross the threshold. For humanity as a whole, crossing the threshold—under the guidance of Christ or the Archangel Michael—means beholding the *double of humanity,* which embodies the sum of humankind's negative karma as represented by the Antichrist.

Expressed another way, the figure of the Antichrist (representing the sum of humanity's negative karma) is the entity to be faced by humanity as a whole in crossing the threshold to the spiritual

---

18. Rudolf Steiner, *The Incarnation of Ahriman: The Embodiment of Evil on Earth* (London: Rudolf Steiner Press, 2006), p. 37.

19. Rudolf Steiner, "The Crossing of the Threshold and the Social Organism," lecture of September 12, 1919 (from CW 193); available from the Rudolf Steiner Library, Ghent, NY. "Humanity passes through this crossing of the threshold in such a way that the spheres of thought, feeling and will become separated."

20. Rudolf Steiner, *How to Know Higher Worlds: A Modern Path of Initiation* (Great Barrington, MA: Anthroposophic Press, 1994).

21. Modern psychology has an inkling of this in referring to work upon "transforming one's shadow."

world, just as the double is the entity each individual must face and take responsibility for upon crossing the threshold. Crossing the threshold means opening up to, and becoming cognizant of, the Angelic realm. This is the first cosmic sphere that human beings enter subsequent to crossing the threshold at death while departing from the Earth. In this connection Rudolf Steiner made a specific prophecy concerning this event for humanity as a whole:

> When we're asleep to important events around us, we run great risk. That is, if humanity continues with its refusal to turn to the spirit, then at some point before the third millennium, the consequences of our stubborn resistance could descend upon us. It's really not long anymore to the third millennium, which begins in the year 2000. If the angels have to work with our sleeping body instead of being able to use our waking soul to accomplish their task, they would have to move all their work out of our astral body and immerse it in our etheric.... If the angels have to carry out their task in the etheric body, they can do so only if we're not there, because if we were there in our waking state, we would keep the angels from doing their work.[22]

Initiation is nothing other than crossing the threshold while still alive, and this is the event that leads to a conscious relationship with the angels that, according to Rudolf Steiner, should occur (or should already have occurred) for humanity as a whole around the beginning of the third millennium with the year 2000. At the same time, however, he clearly saw the grave negative potential presented if the formation of a relationship with the angelic hierarchy by human beings in a wide-awake (fully conscious) condition were not to occur early in the third millennium (or before), and he referred to this as a "great risk."

This is yet another pointer to our present time as one of enormous possibility through consciously crossing the threshold and thus forming a conscious relationship with angelic beings. Simultaneously, it is a time fraught with grave danger if the initiation trial entailed in crossing the threshold should fail. Humanity's encounter with the Antichrist is part of the initiation trial of humanity as a whole crossing the threshold.[23] The external aspect of this initiation trial is the meeting with the Antichrist embodying the whole of humanity's negative karma, *the double of humankind as a whole*. The inner aspect is the encounter with Christ or the Archangel Michael as the Guardian of the Threshold. The result of successfully passing through this initiation trial is opening up our conscious awareness of the Angelic realm. This is one aspect of the great event at the culmination of the process of humankind as a whole crossing the threshold. Another aspect of this culmination is depicted in my article "World Pentecost."

The New Age of angelic consciousness toward which humanity is moving will be a time of developing a new relationship with the world of stars, since the heavens are the outer aspect of the reality of weaving spiritual hierarchies in the work of creation and in tending the further unfolding of creation. It was toward this time of a new consciousness of the angelic realm that the lifework of Willi Sucher in pioneering Astrosophy was dedicated. Now, twenty-five years after his crossing the threshold of death, the time has come for the flowering of the seeds of Astrosophy that he so diligently sowed.

For me, as for many others who knew him, Willi Sucher lives on in our hearts and souls as a wonderful source of inspiration. Apart from being tremendously knowledgeable, he was also a deeply humble human being. He extended

---

22. Rudolf Steiner, *Death as Metamorphosis of Life: Including "What Does the Angel Do in Our Astral Body" and "How Do I Find Christ?"* 7 Lectures, various cities, Nov. 29, 1917–Oct. 16, 1918 (Great Barrington, MA: SteinerBooks, 2008), p. 120.

23. The grave danger presented if humanity fails the initiation trial of crossing the threshold is that humankind could be dragged down by the Antichrist into a subhuman level of existence of war, violence, torture, brutality, cruelty, sexual perversion, and so on, to name only some of the features of a world ruled by Ahriman. Humanity is faced with the choice: Christ or Antichrist?

warmth and a most gracious and generous hospitality during my two stays with him in Meadow Vista, California, making those times unforgettable. He will always be for me a radiant representative of humanity's striving for a new star wisdom as a metamorphosis of the star wisdom of antiquity. Expressed in words that he was fond of quoting:

> It became clearer and clearer to me—as the outcome of many years of research—that in our epoch there is really something like a resurrection of the astrology of the third epoch [the Egyptian-Babylonian period], but permeated now with the Christ impulse. Today, we must search among the stars in a way different from the old ways. The stellar script must once more become something that speaks to us.[24]

In conclusion, returning to our discussion of humanity's crossing the threshold and experiencing the angelic realm, I would like to add the following words of the Etheric Christ addressed recently (2009) to a dear (anonymous) Sophia friend. These words serve as a living example relevant to the encounter with the Guardian of the Threshold and the meeting with the angels as described in this article. They also relate to the coming great wave of love associated with World Pentecost as discussed in my other article in this journal:

> As I stood before Christ in the Etheric, He lifted me up so that we were hovering just above the Earth. He was like a fire, a purifying fire. He was glowing like the Sun. Upon His chest was a brilliant cross of light, with rays of blue-violet light emanating out from it. He spoke to me:
>
> *O child of light, I came to Earth that I might illuminate it with My love, and My love knows no bounds. I love all, and the light of My love shines upon all beings, both good and evil. And all those whom I love, who receive My love, receive illumination to their souls. And this illumination calls forth the darkness from their souls. The darkness is there because of pain. Those who let go of their darkness in My light receive the light of My love into their souls. And My light emanates from their souls and then illuminates others' souls. In this way, others awaken to My love, and also awaken to their darkness. I hold their darkness in My love, and call it forth that their hearts may be purified and prepared to receive Me. I am the light that shall lead you out of your darkness. Keep your eyes on Me.*
>
> *Remember the story of the prodigal son, and hold fast to the image of the great reunion that took place when the son returned to his father. When you become aware of the prodigal son that is within each person, which is the part of that person who has left the light to squander his gifts and talents and time in the darkness—remember the image of the great reunion when the prodigal son returned. And when you meet the prodigal son within others, hold for them the image of the glorious return as a prayer in your heart, instead of falling into judgment or anger or fear about the choices they have made. All have the possibility of redemption. I love the lost sheep. I go out after the ones who are lost. That is where I am; and you shall do this work with Me also, bringing the lost sheep home to Me, where they may be safely enfolded in My love.*
>
> *So when negative thoughts about others creep in, because you have become aware of their darkness, immediately turn your mind to the prayer of the glorious reunion that I am already preparing. I am already preparing the Feast. The Lamb has already been sacrificed. The table is spread before Me. The Angels are standing ready and waiting to rejoice with Me when the prodigal returns. The Music of*

---

24. Rudolf Steiner, *Christ and the Spiritual World: The Search for the Holy Grail* (London: Rudolf Steiner Press, 1983), 6 lectures, Leipzig, December 1913–January 1914, p. 106.

the Spheres already knows its harmonies, for everything with Me is one great Eternal Round. There is no beginning and no end. I am here and I am also there. Because of this, all beings you meet are truly divine, because they were and they shall be. This earthly existence and this point in time you call the present shall pass away. The time spent as a prodigal is only but a minute compared to the time spent as a divine being who is evolving. All who have come to this Earth choose to have opposing forces act upon them as part of the process of evolution. Many prodigals have returned to me already, and in this you may have a greater hope. Even My beloved brother Judas has returned to Me. And others who have been labeled by historians and locked in to the evil doings of the past in your history books—many of them have already turned toward Me and are coming to Me and serving Me. So as you look at people of the past, you must reserve judgment of them also, for they have moved on in their evolution. Not all, but many.

You experience the pain of knowing the darkness, and you have the courage and faith to withstand this. But as you strive to focus upon the good, the good shall indeed prevail. Let us stand together at the Feast I am preparing, and welcome all who are returning, and we shall rejoice together. Be at peace and be patient, for you cannot see or know the breadth and the depth of the human soul to the extent that I see and know—but have faith that I am working a mighty work in human souls. You may not see the results until further lifetimes, but be at peace knowing that I see and know all, and that I love each human soul, and have love for each soul as if it is My own child. This is where the glorious reunion takes place: within the human heart.

---

*To starry realms,
To the dwelling places of Gods,
Turns the Spirit gaze of my soul.*

*From starry realms,
From the dwelling places of Gods,
Streams Spirit power into my soul.*

*For starry realms,
For the dwelling places of Gods,
Lives my Spirit heart through my soul.*

—RUDOLF STEINER

SUN ON THE GALACTIC CENTER

David Tresemer, Ph.D.

www.StarWisdom.org

Many versions of "the Sun will intersect the Galactic Center on December 21, 2012!" are now being proclaimed. Let us separate some fact from fiction and play with the design of the cosmos.

For this discussion, let us accept a model that goes beyond our sensory experience: Our Earth orbits a Sun in an arm of a galaxy comprised of billions of stars, whose radius is approximately fifty thousand light years, our location being half way from the center. We cannot see the center of the galaxy among the other stars at night for all the interstellar dust between the center and us. This center was found some decades ago by sensitive instruments measuring radio waves, gamma rays and high energy X-rays outside of the visible range (even ultraviolet rays and low-energy X-rays will not penetrate the clouds). It was also known since ancient times in iconography suggesting that powers lurked in that section of the sky, what we would call (astronomically and sidereally) about 2° of The Archer, Sagittarius, an invisible power center toward which the Archer's arrow points. Taking our cues from observation of other galaxies, we can assume that the billions of stars in our galaxy tend to swirl about the center as a flat plane, or a plane with some thickness, and not as a sphere. That plane is indicated by the Milky Way, whose flowing river shows us the galactic plane. Imagine the Milky Way as a large dinner plate with the Galactic Center at the center of the plate. Our interest in the Galactic Center parallels our interest in the Sun—the Sun as the source of light, warmth, orientation and the Galactic Center as the immensely powerful source of creation itself.

We can ask how our solar system and our Earth relate to that location in the heavens. The Earth's orbit around the Sun defines a plane, which we call the ecliptic plane, for upon this plane eclipses can occur if something comes between the Sun and Earth. Imagine this plane as a small plate, with the Earth at the center of the small plate and the Sun traveling around it (it could be Sun at the center, but Earth at the center accords more with our actual experiences).

Then let us imagine several possibilities for the relation to the galactic plane (large plate) and the ecliptic plane (small plate).

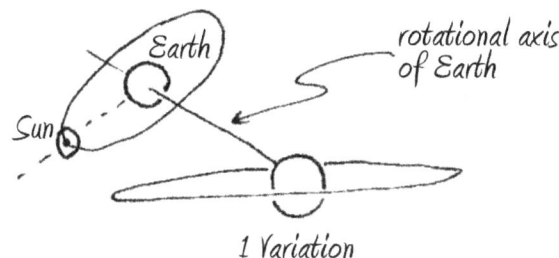

1) It might have been the case that the ecliptic plane (Earth and Sun) was at right angles to the galactic plane. (Set the large plate on a table top, and set the other plate up on edge, its face at right angles to the Galactic Center.) One version of this arrangement points the axis of the Earth's rotation, now centered on Polaris in the North, toward the Galactic Center.

Then this grand source of X-rays, radio waves, and other emanations (love, light…) would have beamed upon the Northern Hemisphere day and night. Moving to the Southern Hemisphere, one would have felt a diminishment of its influence. There would have been no change in this streaming of energy over periods of time, whether days, years, or longer.

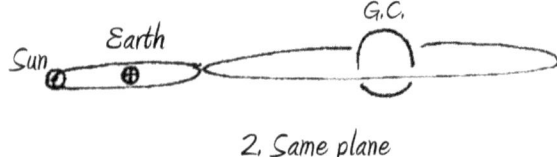

2. Same plane

2) The ecliptic plane might have been parallel to the galactic plane. (Lay the big plate on a table, and the little plate next to it, on the same table.) As the Sun-Earth dance is actually within the galaxy (about half way out from the center), we would have seen the Sun (and all the planets) moving along the Milky Way throughout the course of the year and every night the Sun's path would be illuminated by the Milky Way. The Milky Way would pour energy through the Sun every day of the year. From the point of view of the Earth, the Sun would have aligned with the Galactic Center once a year, while we would have received constant (and unremitting) influx from planetary conjunctions with billions of stars of immense power along the plane of their orientation (the galactic plane).

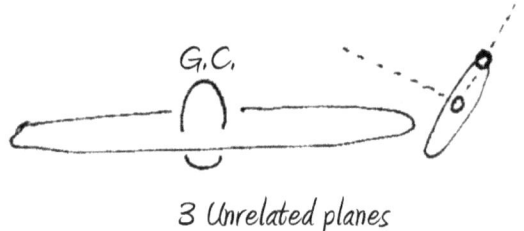

3 Unrelated planes

3) The ecliptic plane could have been tilted in an infinite number of ways so that the Galactic Center was somewhere halfway up in the sky. Neither pole (#1) nor Sun (#2) would have ever aligned with it, though the Sun (from the Earth's perspective) would have entered the domain of the Milky Way twice a year.

4) The present situation (nearly). Set both plates on the table and slide the little one off the edge of the table while keeping the two plates edge to edge (as in 2). While keeping the edge of the little plate touching the larger plate, twist the little plate. The ecliptic plane is tilted in relation to the galactic plane, approximately 60°. Once a year the Sun passes in front of the

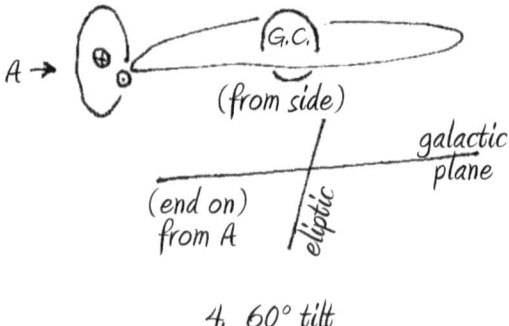

4. 60° tilt

Galactic Center thus stepping down the core energy of the Galactic Center to the Earth.

In this version, the Galactic Center lies on the galactic plane and on the ecliptic plane. From the Earth's perspective, the Sun traverses that place once a year (dates for this in a moment), and has done so since the Earth and Sun were created. There is no truth to the notion that the Sun-Earth line lines up with the Galactic Center as if for the first time in 2012; it happens every year. The Galactic Center is also touched by all our solar system's planets that orbit the Sun as they go past 2° of Sagittarius. We can observe or feel the Galactic Center each day rise at the eastern horizon, pass overhead, and set in the West along the path that the Sun travels. It is no rare stranger.

Were we to guess why the creators made it this way, we might consider that #1 above would have constituted a showering of blessings all the time, and an unchanging shadow in the southern hemisphere; this would not have led to wakefulness. In number 2), we likewise would have been showered with blessings from the Milky Way all the time, again with no prod to wakefulness. Number 3) would have been much less energized, though twice a year the Sun (and at other times the planets) would have stimulated our Earth by alignment with the Milky Way, and there would have been no amplification of the Galactic Center by Sun or planets.

In 4), our present situation, we are not stimulated by the powers in the Milky Way (through conjunction with Sun or planets) all the time (as in 2), but at certain times. And once a year, the Sun aligns with the Galactic Center for a boost.

Now for a bit more accuracy. Our situation is not exactly as in #4, where the Sun is conjunct the Galactic Center once a year. We have a bit of #3, as the Galactic Center lies just over 5° from the Sun's path, a couple of finger widths distance in your outstretched arm mapping the heavens, thus close, but not exact. The Archer's arrow points at it, just below the ecliptic. (Here shown via a drawing by Brian Gray, with the Galactic Center as a small cross just beyond the tip of the arrow, and the ecliptic as a dotted line above.)

The Sun crosses the Galactic Equator (or Galac-

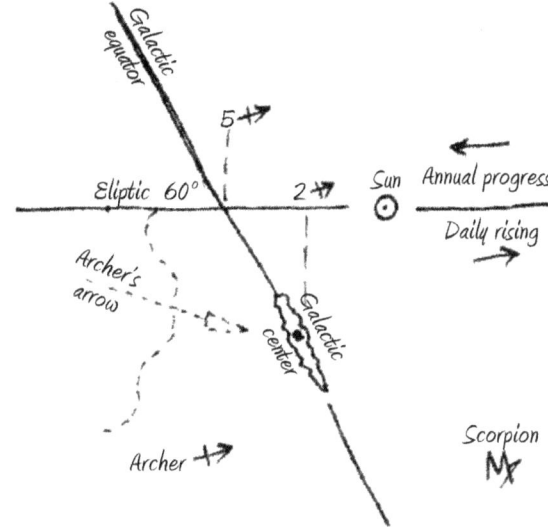

tic plane) twice a year, when the Sun is at 5° Sagittarius 17 and at its opposite when the Sun is at 5° Gemini 17. The Sun is a bit closer to the Galactic Center at 2° Sagittarius 6. (Though we specify a point location for the Galactic Center, X-ray maps show that its greatest intensity may extend for 2° or more along the Galactic Equator.) The Sun, always in the plane of the ecliptic, passes over the Galactic Equator every year, as well as past the point that is closest to the Galactic Center, while never actually being right on the point of the Galactic Center. Interestingly, the Moon can conjunct the Galactic Center exactly, but the Sun does not. The following schematic representation reveals all these interrelationships.

There is something to this tilt of the ecliptic plane in relation to the galactic plane (#4 in contrast to #2) that metes out energy and stimulation, not too little and not too much.

To understand this, we must mention a tilt and a wobble—the tilt of our planet's axis to the ecliptic plane (23 ½°) and the wobble in Earth's orbit whereby the axis of orientation of north and south moves slowly around a small circle of the heavens, taking 25,920 years to complete one wobble. The seasons exist because of this 23 ½° tilt. Without that tilt, the equatorial middle would be always hot and the poles always cold. With the tilt the weather transforms, people must respond to shifting situations, and consciousness strengthens as a result. The wobble slowly adjusts the seasonal date on which the Sun intersects the Galactic Equator. In Jesus Christ's time, the Sun intersected the Galactic Equator on November 26 (and was closest to the Galactic Center on November 23). Today it is December 21 (and December 18).

The tilt of the ecliptic plane in relation to the galactic plane may have the same effect, some kind of awakening (vs. the situations in #1, #2, and #3) that we also get in response to the seasons. Thus we can see the importance of a seasonal date, December 21, winter solstice in the Northern Hemisphere, in relation to the Sun's alignment with the Galactic Center. Even here we must sort the truth from the many claims. This alignment is not unique for the year 2012. As the Sun has a half-degree diameter, the Sun on December 21 has aligned with the Galactic Equator where it crosses the ecliptic plane (at 5° Sagittarius 07 at the present time) since 1980 and will do so until 2016. If you consider that the fiery disc of the Sun has its most active areas at the edges and going out into the corona, these years may actually be extended by another decade in either direction. 2012 is not a unique contact point.

The Sun comes closest to the Galactic Center (at 2 Sagittarius 6) once a year. It comes closest on December 21 between 2209 and 2245 (Robert Powell's estimates, while the astronomer Patrick Wallace gives 2201 to 2237). One could say that there is a special kind of closeness to connect with the path of a thing, even if you come closer to the thing itself in some future. The path is the Galactic Equator. In any case, these conjunctions occur over a span of years, and we could say that 1980 to 2245 marks the time when our solstice season interacts with the Galactic Center in a dynamic way.

Thus we can ask about our time right now, "How has the alignment of the Sun with the Galactic Equator on a date important to our seasonal sleep (winter solstice or shortest day in the Northern Hemisphere) and waking (summer solstice or longest day in the Southern Hemisphere) changed the way we experience the Sun's annual alignment with the Galactic Center?" We don't have to wait until 2012 to answer that question.

My personal experience was assisted by finding the date of the original Pentecost as May 24, 33 C.E., when the Sun lay directly opposite the Galactic Center (Sun—Earth—Galactic Center). A downpouring of spiritual fire revealed as sparks of spirit mediated by Mother Mary spread out to the twelve disciples, then to the seventy-two men and seventy-two women most connected to the teaching, then to three thousand people visiting Jerusalem, where the barrier of different languages was breached by the communication of love. These sparks were not intended for one day but for all days, though I experience them most intensely from June 18 (Sun nearest opposite to Galactic Center) to June 21 (Sun on Galactic Equator) and December 18 (Sun nearest Galactic Center) to December 21 (Sun on Galactic Equator). At the StarHouse in Boulder, we celebrate these as solstices, "Sun stands still," a seasonal punctuation mark to accentuate a celestial memory.

The linear alignment of the Pentecost downpouring of spirit becomes simply the line-up of Gemini—Earth—Sun—Sagittarius—Galactic Center, and in more detail as braided streams of life force connected as follows: 2° to 5° Gemini—Pentecost memory—Showers of spiritual sparks—Earth—Sun as magnifier— 2° to 5° Sagittarius—Galactic Center. We can experience this alignment as Earth-Sun on June 18 to 21 and as Sun-Earth on December 18 to 21.

* * *

Now let's ask anew, why pursue the Galactic Center, so grand, yet so distant and obscured from view? The Galactic Center—as swirls of heat, electricity, subatomic particles, and gravity forces all of immense size, even to the distortion and extinction of time and space as we know them, indeed as the disembodied and chaotic source of creation—has no meaning unless compared to the coagulated, embodied Earth, expressing itself in a version of time and space that we can call familiar, that is, part of our family. From our embodied selves on the embodied Earth, we can experience the immensity of spirit force in the Galactic Center through its regent and representative, the Sun. When we attune to the Sun in all its power, beyond the measures of light and warmth, we can begin to feel the intensity of love focused there, and then emanating ceaselessly for all.

Perhaps this is why the Galactic Center has been obscured from view, to point our attention closer to home. The Sun represents the power of love of the greater center, stepping down further to the heart of the Earth and the heart of the human being. I experience the source, what some call the Central Spiritual Sun, in the Sun and its center, and also in my heart and in the hearts of others. The alignment of Sun, Earth, and Galactic Center merely intensifies a relationship that is there always, represented by the regent—the Sun. That representative and the spiritual beings who reside there are with us always, not in some future time, but this very moment.

KYOT AND THE STELLAR SCRIPT OF PARSIFAL

Ellen Schalk

In the lecture cycle *Christ and the Spiritual World: The Search for the Holy Grail*, Rudolf Steiner makes an admission regarding his spiritual scientific research:

> If you follow up the various expositions in my books and lecture courses, and if you feel about it as I do, you will find, especially in the older ones, that what I have said in connection with the name of the Holy Grail is one of the least satisfying parts... [for] often, when I tried to trace the further course of this stream—when I tried to unravel the further occult development of Christianity in the West—then before my soul rose the admonition: "You must first read the name of Parsifal in its right place."[1]

In this search for the place where the name of Parsifal stands written, Rudolf Steiner was ever and again led astray by exoteric science, in that it deemed Kyot—Wolfram von Eschenbach's secret source—to be an invention of the poet. After following lengthy false trails, Rudolf Steiner is finally led onto the right path through the thought association "stellar script—Grail" that is inspired into him through Kyot's words, "a thing was called the Grail," and the reference to an oriental document by the star-sage Flegetanis. Inspired by Kyot, Rudolf Steiner found "the name Parsifal in wonderful letters of the occult script on the sickle of the Moon."

It is the great achievement of Werner Greub, today still scarcely appreciated, to have resolved the Kyot issue that for generations now has not been uncovered by science. Kyot is no invention of the poet. Wolfram von Eschenbach's *Willehalm* epic (the first of the trilogy *Willehalm–Parsifal–Titurel*) is the bridge to *Parsifal*. Indeed, Willehalm is identical with Wolfram's secret source Kyot, he is identical with Kyot of Katelangen, with Kyot of Provence, with Willehalm of Toulouse, with Saint Guilhem, and with Willehalm of Oransche.[2] Wolfram's secret source for *Willehalm* is Willehalm himself, since no one other than the historical Willehalm was in a position to produce an authentic report on the historical battle of Alischanz (in 818 C.E.). Kyot himself proves to be the author of the epics that through Wolfram are translated into Middle High German. He is a contemporary, a witness, and a co-organizer of the events of the ninth century. Wolfram also describes for us in *Parsifal* a bit of the family history of his secret source Willehalm, who like no secondary chronicler is in a position to inform Wolfram about every detail.

As Willehalm, Count of Toulouse, Kyot lands in Arabian captivity. There he learns the Arabic language and studies the ancient cultures. In a manuscript by the Baghdad scholar Th'âbit ben Sâlômôn he finds a reference to the Grail tradition, which the holy three kings have already pursued. In *Parsifal* it is reported of Kyot that he had found the Flegetanis document (which caught the attention of Rudolf Steiner). After Willehalm's escape from captivity, his teacher—Queen Arabel—accompanies him to Oransche and becomes his wife, Gyburc (she becomes a Christian). After

---

1. Rudolf Steiner, *Christ and the Spiritual World: The Search for the Holy Grail* (1983), pp. 97–98.

2. Note by translator: in English one can translate this name also as William of Orange, although this person is not to be confused with the other well-known William of Orange who was the liberator of the Netherlands.

Gyburc's death we find Willehalm as Duke of Katelangen in Montpellier. He applies himself as an urban planner, a creative artist, and a seeker of the Grail.

Finally, with the aid of the Flegetanis document, he discovers the house of the Grail and takes home as his bride the Grail-daughter, Schoysiane. She dies during the birth of their daughter, Sigune. Willehalm-Kyot now goes back to the hunting castle Le Verdus near Saint-Guilhem-le-Désert. From there, as Kyot of Katelangen he lends support to those of his relatives who are situated in official positions of authority. He delivers his daughter Sigune to his sister-in-law Herzeloyde in Kanvoleis for her upbringing. After the death of his brother Tampenteire, he provides support for his niece Condwiramur. After her marriage to Parsifal, he also has the opportunity to be Parsifal's teacher for sixteen months. Five years later, he accompanies Condwiramur to Munsalvaesche and returns to Montpellier with Kardeiz, whose education he takes over.

At the end of his richly active life, as Wolfram's secret source, he authors *Parsifal*. He commits his three epics to an oral tradition. Some 350 years later, Wolfram translates the French Kyot transmission into Middle High German. *Willehalm* is a portion of the biography of Kyot.

Let us return again to Rudolf Steiner's "admission." In this context, he describes how during the third post-Atlantean cultural epoch, when star wisdom influenced the human soul directly, the sibylline forces were justified, although they were no longer appropriate for soul development in the fourth cultural epoch.

> When the Christ impulse entered the evolution of humanity in the way known to us, one result was that the chaotic forces of the sibyls were thrust back for a time, as when a stream disappears below ground and reappears later on. These forces were indeed to reappear in another form, a form purified by the Christ impulse.[3]... "Yes, a time is coming when the old astrology will live again in a new form, a Christ-filled form, and then, if one can practice it properly, so that it will be permeated with the Christ impulse, one may venture to look up to the stars and question them about their spiritual script.[4]

At this point Rudolf Steiner introduces two personalities whose soul forces were transformed under the influence of the Christ impulse: the Maid of Orleans as a Christianized sibyl, and Johannes Kepler as the one who was able to read the new stellar script. We may regard it as our future task to practice for ourselves the mode of thinking infused with the Christ impulse as modeled for us by Kepler, and to learn to read the new stellar script.

Following upon this, Rudolf Steiner mentions an example from Wolfram's *Parsifal*—in order to make clear that at that time there was a searching for the spiritual stellar script: "What sort of time was it, then, when Parsifal entered the Castle where Amfortas lay wounded and on Parsifal's arrival suffered unceasing pain from his wound? What was this time? The saga itself tells us—it was Saturn time."[5] As it was on Good Friday that Parsifal had his conversations with Trevrizent, Wolfram notes in his review of this time: *"dö der Sterne Säturnus/wider an sin zil gestount, / daz wan uns bi der wunden kuont"* ("When the star Saturn had returned to the zenith, we knew it by the wound").[6]

With the above quotation regarding the star constellation, it is quite apparently not a matter of a spiritual scientific research result—since it indeed notes, "The saga tells." Whether the Wolfram text was correctly translated into New High German, is not discussed. The weight lies in the influence of the stars that stand in relation to the increased suffering of Amfortas. From this context one may not conclude from Steiner's quote that he has expressed himself in a spiritual scientific manner regarding the

---

3. Ibid., p. 94.
4. Ibid., p. 122.
5. Note in 1963 edition, p. 128: i.e., a period when the forces of Saturn work with particular strength.
6. From p. 286 in the 1961 Vintage Books edition (trans. Helen Mustard and Charles Passage). The scholarly reference P 489, 24–26 means "passage 489, verses 24–26."

Parsifal *chronology*, in the way that this has indeed occurred in the current year's edition of the *Sternkalendar* (1987).[7] Rudolf Steiner is quite simply reporting what the translator says when that translator expresses the opinion that *zil* (Middle High German) means "zenith."[8] The "zenith" misunderstanding comes from the fact that in regard to this passage, the translator (from Middle High German) and the publisher were always of the opinion that they had to 'clarify' Wolfram's text—even if they understood little of astronomy. Such text clarifications are by no means always "clarifying."

Thus it is said about these textual passages that Saturn has run its course, that it has again reached its zenith in the constellation of the Crab, and that it was situated there in conjunction with the Sun. Rudolf Steiner connected on to this accepted translation, without taking a position with regard to the chronology. With any examination he would have been able to reveal it as a further misdirection on the part of exoteric academic scholarship; meanwhile, this error has been duly corrected by Wilhelm Deinert.[9]

According to Kyot's astronomy, every planet has its goal. The term *zil* (the meaning of which is the issue at hand) is referred to in contemporary astrology as "domicile" or "house." Every planet has its home or its *zil* in a certain constellation of the zodiac; the return of the planet to its *zil* describes its entry into this constellation. (Saturn requires approximately thirty years for this; its *zil* is Capricorn.)

Whoever would nonetheless presume to see Rudolf Steiner's quote as the basis of a Parsifal chronology must quickly fail; for we know that on that Good Friday, Trevrizent can exactly determine when Parsifal was last at this place. Parsifal then took Taurian's spear along with him—which is an important fact for the chronology. The absent Trevrizent notices this taking in the psalter (the psalter serves as a "memorandum" for Trevrizent). Thus he is in a position to tell Parsifal exactly how long he has been straying: *"Fünfthalp jar un dri tage."*[10] In other words, five-and-a-half years and three days lay in between. When one reckons from Good Friday backward for this span of time, one never comes into midsummer (Crab), but rather into September (Virgo). The posthumous publication of the essay related to these matters in the current year's *Sternkalendar* (1987), on the occasion of the thirty-third anniversary of Joachim Schulz's death, may presumably not be something he would have wished for. If he had been certain of his competency in regard to this issue, he would indeed have taken care of getting it published back then.

Based on Wolfram's numerous indications regarding planetary constellations, the question thus arises as to whether he provides indications about chronological matters that allow us to determine with certainty the historical time of the Parsifal story. Upon precise examination, it becomes evident that it did not have its source in his poetic imagination, but rather that it corresponds to the facts. Wolfram never tires of repeatedly assuring us that what he presents is based on his secret source Kyot, whom he greatly venerates, and that he does not say anything other than what his master has spoken, and that he speaks the truth.

Wolfram's epics contain factual accounts from the eighth and ninth centuries, whereas in the Parsifal story of Chrétien de Troyes, one finds the thoughts of twelfth-century people regarding the Grail, but no factual accounts from the ninth century. Chrétien does not base himself on Kyot as Wolfram does. Out of devotion to Kyot, Wolfram finds it disconcerting that Chrétien does not mention Kyot and praises only Philip. "If Master Chrétien de Troyes did not do justice to this story, that may well vex Kyot, who furnished us the

---

7. This refers to an article written in 1947 by Joachim Schultz entitled "Parsifal and the Stellar Script," edited and published by Suso Vetter in the 1987/88 edition *Sternkalender* ("Star Calendar"), published by the Philosophisch-Anthroposophisch Verlag, Dornach.

8. *Höchstand* in New High German.

9. *Ritter und Kosmos im Parzival. Eine Untersuchung der Sternenkunde Wolframs von Eschenbach* ("Knights and the Cosmos in Parsifal: An Investigation of Woram von Eschenbach's Knowledge of the Stars"), by Wilhelm Deinert; Munich: Verlag Beck, 1960.

10. In the comparative text notation: 460, 22.

right story" (*Ob von Troys meister Christjan/diesem maere hat unreht getan/daz mac wol zürnen Kyot/der uns diu rehten maere enbot*).[11]

Wolfram does not depict the astronomy of the twelfth century, having drawn not from contemporary Arabic reports as has been hitherto presumed. Rather, he makes use of an astronomy as it was taught by Tebit at the time of Harun al-Rashid in late eighth-century Baghdad, whereby one must indeed recognize Wolfram's Flegetanis (*Flegetanis* means star sage).

If Wolfram's indications regarding the planets are correct, then these must have been given to him by a contemporary of the Grail events: by Kyot. This was the person who was astronomically schooled and had considered the planetary movements in the context of the fixed star background as something quite real—in terms of their location. We find with Wolfram four kinds of ancient astronomical knowledge: 1) the observation and calculation of the movement of the stars; 2) the knowledge of star influences, and thereby the qualitative effect of the planets upon the individual person, which are strengthened or weakened through the west–east course of the planets through the zodiac (Amfortas); 3) the art of reading the occult script in the stars. A fourth kind of star influence has to do with the sibyls, who experienced the star forces as they work from the organism of the Earth.

What is significant for the Parsifal chronology, above all, is the first of the four named kinds of astronomical knowledge. In the context of this essay, however, it would lead too far to interpret all of Wolfram's relevant indications regarding star constellations. Wolfram specifies these planetary positions because Kyot was capable of seeing certain correspondences between the occurrences in the sky and those on the Earth, which at that time were perceptible as real influences in a way that we are no longer capable of today. Wolfram presents the constellations in the manner conveyed to him by Kyot. In fact it seems that even Parsifal's contemporaries at the Grail castle were not educated enough to be accomplished astronomers; indeed no constellation is described as though it had been directly observed. In the Grail family one had drawn conclusions about the planetary constellations based on the health condition of Amfortas. Presumably in Christian Europe at that time no one was schooled in the Chaldean star wisdom of Flegetanis except for Kyot-Willehalm, who in his captivity went so far as to acquire the Eastern "heathen" schooling in addition to his Western education, and he learned "Chaldaic."

Kyot must have resolutely researched and energetically sought out the Grail family. Indeed he was the only Western person who knew of the prophetic cosmic revelation of the impending Grail events—as did once the wise men prior to the birth of the Solomon Jesus youth. Kyot's mission was to make sure that, in Munsalvaesche, people would also come to know the Eastern aspect of the Grail prophecy with which he was familiar, and that they would take the measures needed to ensure that, at the right moment, everything would happen accordingly. One can clearly recognize Kyot-Willehalm as the guiding spiritual force (*Spiritus rector*) in the background.

Ultimately, we have Rudolf Steiner to thank for the insight into these connections, as the one who found, via Kyot, the occult stellar script PARSIFAL in the bowl of the Moon. And then we have Kyot himself, who fulfilled his mission in the ninth century. Last, but not least, we have Wolfram von Eschenbach to thank for faithfully conveying this lore.

Translated by Richard Bloedon from an essay originally published in The Journal of Anthroposophical Work in Germany *(issue 160, 1987).*

---

11. In the comparative text notation: 827, 1–4.

SIGNATURE OF JUPITER IN THE EVENTS OF JESUS CHRIST'S LIFE

Historical Personalities and Modern World Events

David Tresemer, with Robert Schiappacasse and William Bento

How does Jupiter affect my life, empower me or overpower me? When people say, "I can't wait for Jupiter to come round to my birthday—then I'll win the lottery or something else really big will happen in my life." Or, "You are so expansive, so regal, so generous, so wise, so Jupiterian!" What are they talking about?

For the last few decades, astrology has emphasized key words as a way of simplifying the answer. What are these words for Jupiter? *Grand, generous, optimistic, philosophical, wise, kingly, queenly* for the positive view of Jupiter and, for the less developed, *inflated egotism, bombastic verbosity, puffing and blowing with big ideas and big plans, always taking charge.*

If Jupiter is a living being vast in power and extent, or a home to beings of great majesty, before whom we would bow in reverence were we to behold them, then perhaps we ought to meditate more deeply upon Jupiter's essential nature. We can approach a being as vast as Jupiter with stories—stories from the life and times of Yeshua, the Hebrew name for Jesus, during his ministry where he was the bearer of Christ consciousness during the last three and a half years of his life. We take our stories from the pictures given by evangelists and seers, extended through the authors' personal meditation. The stories are followed by commentaries to develop important themes. We look at the hard aspects between Jupiter and the Sun to see when these traits were at their maximum. We have done the same in the *Christian Star Calendar (CSC)* with Pluto for 2008 and for Saturn in 2009.

As Jupiter, owing in part to its inherent grandeur, led to such a grand study—far larger than an article for this journal—we include here only the first of several stories, and leave the rest for you to enjoy as they appear serially in the *Star Wisdom Monthly Newsletter*, which you can access via www.StarWisdom.org. You can sign up for the newsletter at that site.

Here is what will appear in the full series on Jupiter:

The methodology we use for finding the story material.

Stories such as the one below on different aspects of Jupiter in action, including an imagination of the cleansing of the seven energy centers of Mary Magdalene (which occurred during an important Jupiter transit).

Commentaries on each of the stories, seriously abridged for this story, and more complete.

How important Jupiter transits worked in the life of Rudolf Steiner.

Historical personalities who were born with prominent Jupiter positions, and our understanding of how this may have played out in their lives.

Enjoy this story as a way of understanding the great planet Jupiter.

Jupiter Imagination 1
Sun square Jupiter

The Globe of Light

Yeshua and the three young men who had accompanied him had been walking in the desert for days. In every direction they could see only an immensity of pebbles and sand, extending to the horizon. In the direction toward which they walked, a thin line of mountains rimmed the meeting of sand and sky, distant and never seeming closer. As they walked, the plane of the desert began to rise gently, bending itself from utterly flat into rolling hills. They began to see a few green shoots amid the desiccated sticks poking up between the little stones that carpeted the vastness. After two days walking, these became expanses of grass. They began to see flocks of animals far off to their right or left. Yeshua pressed on toward the mountains. The three youths followed. They came to a small collection of huts built of stacked pieces of grass sod, with grassy roofs. Somehow a message had been passed to the villagers, for a group had gathered at the edge of this huddle of huts to meet the strangers.

The men of the little village greeted their guests, gave them water immediately, and quickly ascertained that these were special people, not only for the miracle of finding their way across the grasslands to their remote village, but in a quality that they felt from all of them. In a short time, the men cut fresh squares of sod out of the ground with bone knives, and stacked them to make seats for their guests. They brought meat and yoghurt and cheese, all sourced from the animals that they kept, as well as some greens from plants that the women tended near the huts. The men, ready to eat, noticed that Yeshua and the three who accompanied him held their bowls, with their eyes closed, uttering words. The focus of this activity and its earnestness caused the men of the village to stop eating. A spokesman asked, "May we ask what you are doing?"

Yeshua responded, "We are blessing what has been given to us through you, that originated with God."

The men could sense something quite tangible about what Yeshua and his assistants were doing, and stopped their eating. The headman asked, "Could you teach us how to bless this food?"

Yeshua spoke words to them, only a few at a time, which the men repeated, the women in the background repeating these words also. After several phrases, Yeshua said, "Amin!" The people repeated, "Amin!," and waited to see what they should do next.

Yeshua smiled, "That is the last word, the seal on your blessing." Everyone nodded, waiting for the next instruction. Yeshua smiled broadly and lifted a mouthful, as in demonstrating the next activity, "The blessing is done. Now you eat." Everyone laughed and began to eat with enthusiasm.

After they finished, the headman asked, "Tell us how we can bless all of our food."

Yeshua said, "I will show you. Bring me bowls of your different foods." The women brought several serving bowls to him. From his robe Yeshua pulled out a small cloth parcel, which he unwrapped, revealing a pile of whitish powder. Yeshua took some of it and mixed it with the different foods, while speaking the prayer that he had just taught. "This preserves these foods, so that they will never go bad. Indeed, the mixture in this bowl has now become a source for preserving. A small bit of this mixture can be added to any other food of its kind, and it will be preserved for your nutrition. The blessing can extend itself in this way." The men and women stared, and began to understand what this meant for their economy, how times of plenty could now be extended to cover times of leanness, how children crying from lack of food would now be sustained and happy. They muttered to themselves, then each to his or her neighbor, and the hubbub increased until all were nodding, wide-eyed and smiling.

"Let me show you further about blessing." The men nodded, and then a series of events occurred very swiftly. Yeshua stepped away from the group, and then reached up his right hand toward the sky. All the rays of the Sun turned into a forest of long thin parallel filaments, each as thin as a spider's thread, each one gleaming, all pointing to the Sun. Color in every object disappeared, then as suddenly all objects disappeared. All that shown was the tightly packed forest of vertical dimly glowing strands, against which they saw Yeshua in silhouette picking out one of the filaments. Immediately all the other spider-thread filaments disappeared and the things of the world reappeared in full color. Yeshua carefully held this very thin shimmering filament with his right hand. The villagers exclaimed their amazement, laughing out loud at this work with light itself. "Amin!," they shouted, "Amin!" Thinking that the demonstration was over, they began to move forward to see the captured Sun's ray better. They stopped when they saw that the filament held by Yeshua was changing shape.

The light of the filament began to expand at the bottom, the light pooling down into it, forming a globe, which Yeshua suspended from his hand by the remaining short thread of light. The shimmering gleaming globe seemed to increase in size until it was two hand spans across, then four hand spans across, very large yet easily suspended by Yeshua's hand. They could see inside it, and enter it with their awareness. From inside it was as big as the world.

This in itself gave them cause for amazement. Yet within this globe, the shepherds began to perceive activity, as in pictures. Each could feel himself or herself inside the picture. Chaotic swirls congealed to darkness, and the viewers felt the sacredness of this darkness, not a frightening darkness but something full of potential. The globe then felt warm, a general heat that permeated all. Beings with intelligence could be felt, intelligence that had intention. These beings created light, a blinding light, that flashed and became a vibrating single strand of light going right through the middle of the globe, as if in memory of the trembling ray of sunlight. The tremors increased, sending out shocks as other lines of light going in various directions, as matched pairs, symmetrically moving from the single pulsing line. The emanating lines that flashed outward made triangles and pentagons, then expanded and vanished. Multiple lines intersected each other at slightly different angles making curves. The curves then moved, whirlpooling out and in, bending and twisting.

The vortices compounded one upon another, some subtle and fiery, some cool and dry like air. The air thickened and became water. The creators densified water further, making earth, which they separated from the water. The elements, once they were separated, combined to create landscapes. By millions of rapid manipulations, the creators fashioned plants, then animals, forms that the men and women knew and other forms that they had never seen or imagined. The creators made human beings, by taking from the periphery of the globe the original human beings, what the men and women recognized had been there since the very beginning, when in the original darkness full of potential. The plants and animals had been drawn from the same zone, as if they had been parts of the first human being that, because of their rigid forms, were pulled away from the first human. The template of the human being had been kept flexible and adaptable, and co-creative with the divine beings, until the time for humans to appear. The creators intentionally transformed potentials of different qualities into a vast array of shapes and colors and activities of plants and animals, and then human beings were given shape and color and activity.

The villagers expressed their astonishment with a series of gasps and exclamations of "ohh." Over and over again they observed the process of coalescing of a particular quality of colored mist, tighter and tighter, until it achieved a specific kind of leaf structure, a peculiar shape of flower, a distinctive chemical composition. The separate forms related to each other through the chemical commonalities in the air, the water, and the soil, all flowing from the one form to the other. Ceaseless movements interconnected everything, especially the activities of myriad small things, the insects, ants and bees, the worms and other earth-burrowing forms, and birds of all sizes and shapes and colors flowing in and around each other and all other forms. Minute organisms were magnified to the sight, numerous odd shapes flowing around and through the larger bodies.

They saw the forms of human beings densifying quickly, as if, gaining weight, they swiftly fell from realms of light, and lost their connections to the divine creators. Human beings were propelled at a faster rate than the others, and entered a darkness that did not have the sense of vast potential, but a darkness of loneliness and separation. The descent of human beings was not as joyful as the creators had intended it. Even though the human form could be seen in its beauty and brilliant design, something about the arrival of human beings felt tragic.

They then saw many scenes of life on the Earth and life in their village. They lived through occasions happiness and of sadness, generation after generation of living in the same way. They could see human beings with different colors of skin, different costumes, some in groups so large in number and in dwellings so immense and magnificent that they gasped.

Each could likewise see his or her own life in the globe, scenes that were familiar, and scenes that were not. Each could see his or her own life earlier, scenes quickly passing when he or she was a youngster. Each grew younger and younger, each with his or her beloved parents, seen in their youth again, and each as a small child under their care. Sounds of everyday life occurred, though muffled, and all on top of each other. They heard human voices sometimes singly, and sometimes many at the same time, settling into a murmur in the background.

Then each could feel the youngster become an infant, and somehow suddenly become an elder, in unfamiliar surroundings, a wise person supported by a community not familiar to them. Each watching thought inwardly, "That is myself. Though I do not recognize the body nor the other people around me nor the surroundings, I know that is me and I feel that I know that place." The elder grew younger and younger, then disappeared, and another elder appeared, in yet different surroundings. A panoply of lives streamed past, with whom each observer felt intimately linked. All this happened very quickly. Each could feel a sense of continuity of other lives with his or her inner being. Only some observing the globe wondered at how what they saw was so unique, yet familiar, and how this could be so for everyone present. The query quickly passed as each was gripped by the reality of so many life settings and experiences.

Sounds could be heard to accompany all of these revelations, talking and sounds of nature as if from a distance. Amidst many other sounds, the shepherds heard a number spoken by a deep grand voice, "Three-hundred-sixty-five." For an instant they saw the Earth before it tilted and spun, simply hanging in space. Then it began to move, giving the days, and it tilted, giving the different seasons. Through the other sounds that were merged with one another, that number was pronounced clearly. They heard confirmed the divine order in time and movement, and in the length of day and the changing of the seasons.

They saw their village in the present. Then they saw it change swiftly, first a few new sod huts joining the group and more animals grazing on the grasses, then the whole village abandoned, and eroded back into the desert. They saw scenes of strife, first known scenes of disagreement between those in their village. They saw conflicts between larger groups of people, shouting and flourishing weapons that they used against each other. Large groups of people hacked away at each other, spilling blood, severing limbs, something that they had never known and which horrified them. Smoke and fire and screams engulfed large areas. They saw explosions, and heard them too, not the beautiful expressions of creators creating, but explosions that destroyed things. Blood leaked out, and puddled, and ran in rivers, with the sound of shrieking and the moans of mourning. The destruction increased in intensity until the yearning of all peoples caused the creators to appear again, at first at the edges, and then into the center of human and world suffering. In the midst of this chaos of world despair and feeble hope, they saw a light that they recognized as the visitor who had drawn out a filament of sunlight from the sky. He stood within the globe, dispensing blessing in such a way that all learned to dispense this same blessing to others.

The villagers looked for Yeshua. Where he had been standing before them, they could perceive only brilliant light. Past amazement and past reaction, they were drawn back into the events within the globe where they recognized Yeshua as a being of light, overseeing all of humanity.

Each person could feel continuity in what he or she beheld, going with increasing rapidity from one frame to another, from the details of a day in their present life, to the growing of mountains and great movements of continents, to the great destructions, to the flood of peace that calmed the world. The villagers sensed that the series of bodies and lives that belonged to them increased in light. Each one found some one thing in what he or she had seen that entered as a spark into an inner recess, to be nurtured until later. One found an interest in how life forces expressed in the germination of plants. Another felt very curious about how stone and timber were fashioned and interconnected to make large structures for human habitation such as they had seen. Another wondered how the myriad forms of animals came to be, through complexities of the minutest parts of the body. Still another was attracted to how certain refined liquids interacted with other substances to make entirely new solutions. Each felt an inspiration arise about some specific part of what had been revealed. Each knew that the observation and the spark of interest in it were safely harbored deep inside, and each confirmed inwardly, "I will investigate this further, sometime in the future. I will probe this secret of nature."

In the sphere, the entire scene became suffused with light, light from within each life, and light from without. The light became brilliant, brighter than the Sun itself, without beginning or end. Each observer could look in any direction, seeing only brilliant light. But this did not frighten. All felt a sense of release, a sense of expansion into the whole, a sense of forgiveness for all the mistakes of the past, and a lifting up into pure love.

The light then retreated to the globe, which began to grow dim, and to shrink in size. Yeshua stretched it out with both hands, and it again became a filament of light. He lifted this solid ray up into the sky, placing it where he had found it. It joined the other rays and disappeared altogether. The shepherds, now aware of their own feet on familiar ground with familiar objects around them could not speak. A panic of loss gripped them. They had to have back the luminous globe, which they had not known an hour previously. The beauty and grandeur was gone and they had only their familiar hard life. It was more than they could bear, and they collapsed under the weight of the loss. The men and women swooned, moaning. They fainted and fell down upon the Earth. One began to weep, then another, each overwhelmed by the sorrow that welled up inside. They all wept—wept for the grandeur of creation, which they had beheld. They wept with gratitude for the new light that was within them, brightening their view of the world and its possibilities. They wept for the loss of the greater light that had departed. They wept with bitterness for the difficult trials of humanity behind and ahead. They wept with humility for the meanness and ignorance of their present lives. They wept with gratitude for the privilege to be in the presence of the one who would liberate them in the end, Yeshua. They also wept with the realization that they would have to explain what they had learned to their children and grandchildren as best they could, already feeling inadequate to do this.

Yeshua also lay down and wept with them. When the catharsis had passed through some of the village elders, they noticed that Yeshua had lain down in the dust. They jumped up to help Yeshua rise, to lift him up off the ground, to serve him. But Yeshua motioned to them not to interfere. He joined them fully in the release of human emotion faced with the enormity of true knowledge.

COMMENTARIES 1 (ABRIDGED)

Major Themes

Isolation from the world—as individuals trekking through the desert and as a community also removed in the vast expanses of sand and of grass; teaching about how one can bless one's food; preservation of food with some kind of extraordinary substance; the nature of light and what light holds as a secret; ability to pluck a sunbeam from the air; the movement of lines, and intersections of rapidly moving lines in such a way that curves are made; the knowledge of origins—cosmogony, anthropogenesis—and evolution—cultural development, wars and destruction, resolution in light; sorrow over loss of connection with the source of light; finding one's vocation for the future in what one feels attracted to; bearing the burden of knowledge into the future; bestowal of blessings and the reception of blessings.

A Ray of Light

We observe the catching of a sunbeam, and must ask about the nature of light. The argument about whether light is truly a particle or a wave has dominated physics for some decades, and research seems to have concluded that it acts as both. To begin with, examine what it means to be a particle, a photon. In this view, a photon has no mass and no electric charge, though it does have force. It takes many photons to make light as we know it, approximately a million quadrillion (10^{21}) photons striking every square meter every second from the Sun. Understood as a wave, a photon pulses at different frequencies or wavelengths depending on the energy that it holds and what color it is connected to. Either as particle or wave, a photon cannot be seen from the side. Photons elude definition as wave or particle, acting as both, sometimes interchangeably, sometimes interacting with an observer in a most elusive fashion.

In this story we find a third possibility: Light as a ray, a thin filament like a piece of spider's web, a strand, a straight long string of delicate nature.

It makes one yearn to go outside and try to catch a beam of light. Indeed, Elisabeth Haich has written that the high initiates in ancient Egypt had the capacity to pull out a strand of light from the air.[1] The iconography of Egypt, especially during Akhenaton's reign, showed rays of light streaming from the Sun disk, with little hands at the end, some also with ankhs at the end. This implies that Yeshua had those capacities, and perhaps it implies that he had the specific training given to the initiates of Egypt.

We discover from this vignette a fourth fact about light: The thin line of the ray of light has within itself as potential a sphere, that is, its opposite and complement. These realizations exceed the contrast of particle and wave. A filament includes more than a particle; it includes the path of the particle or at least part of the path. How long was this filament? Does the whole filament extend from the Sun to the object illumined on Earth, and did Yeshua then have to break off a part of the complete filament?

We have also a fifth discovery: Each beam of light carries within it the totality of the creation in picture form. All that has happened and will happen exists in each beam of light. Holograms have begun to show this quality of self-similarity of the small part to the big part—each piece of a hologram has an image of the whole within it. Yeshua's demonstration reveals the big within the small, a sense of Jupiter's immensity, bestowal of grace, joy and gratitude, all contained within a gesture. *The Course in Miracles* says repeatedly that there are no larger or smaller miracles. Thus Jupiter in its essence has less to do with bigness, and more to do with essential grace, even in a small gesture.

Contemplate the nature of light revealed in this Imagination, and how it reveals that the grandeur of creation exists in even the smallest light ray that occurs instantly, and then is gone, repeatedly and continuously in our every day. As Rudolf Steiner said repeatedly, "Wisdom lives in the light."[2]

Choice of Audience

Why did Yeshua choose this particular audience for this magical display? He presented nothing like this to the priests, intelligentsia, or city dwellers, not even to his own students. Those reading the prohibitions against the low forms of the supernatural, which they considered sub-natural, perhaps considered such magic in a negative light.[3] From this point of view, Yeshua presented

---

1. Elisabeth Haich, *Initiation* (Palo Alto, CA: Seed Center, 1974), p. 219. The physicist and anthroposophist Arthur Zajonc has written on this topic also, with a title that summarizes this part of our vignette: *Catching the Light* (New York: Oxford University Press, 1995). The theme of "catch a sunbeam" can be found in poetry through the ages.

2. Rudolf Steiner, "Occult Science and Occult Development," lecture 1, May 1, 1913, among many other times that he used that phrase.

3. Exodus 22:18: "You shall not permit a female sorcerer to live." Deuteronomy 18:10-12: "No one shall be found

to these country people precisely because they were isolated and very distant from Israel and the power center of Jerusalem.

Rudolf Steiner developed this reason in a series of lectures at the very end of 1924, a time that we shall visit again when we speak of Steiner's life. He said that materialistic concepts and over-abstract philosophies have paralyzed the soul of modern human beings. If one has had suprasensory thoughts—above the normal senses, imbued with spirit light, just as the shepherds experienced in this Imagination—then one can cross the threshold at death and return with one's thinking enhanced. However, if one has accepted the prison of modern abstract concepts of what life is all about, then one will cross the threshold and experience shock at what one finds there, later returning with a diminished power of thinking, indeed relying only on one's instinctual nature. He warned that, unless one broke free of stultifying concepts and embraced spiritual realities now, then one would become less and less accessible to spirit in succeeding incarnations.[4] This seems to be Yeshua's reason for choosing a group that was not encumbered by limiting concepts.

Rudolf Steiner gave a picture of brilliant celestial light revealed to nearby shepherds at the birth of the Nathan Jesus, a time also when Jupiter squared the Sun, though more widely than the rule we use for choosing our stories. The shepherds were awakened into an experience of the spiritual body of the Buddha, speaking through the many hosts of angels to humanity.[5]

In Steiner's view, the shepherd stream became the natural scientists, while the star gazing magi became the astronomers and mathematicians. In the present Jupiter Imagination of the shepherds in brilliant light, having observed the creation of life forms, the densification of mists of light into number, weight, and measure, the individualities awakened to these wonders might well look around them with an entirely different view to the wisdom innate in everything. Each one found a unique connection to what later would be zoology, chemistry, biology, physics of architecture, and indeed all the sciences.

In either case, one wonders who the men and women of this village have become in their subsequent lives. What became of these seeds of light planted into human beings that had stimulated their capacity for thinking?

Wisdom of the Earth Age—"365"

In our present age, the Earth age, when we have a physical Earth upon which to walk and ponder philosophy, we are tutored by divine beings who have ordered our life in ways that we slowly learn. Thus, the important fact, that the villagers heard the number 365, the number of days in a solar year. From this we can surmise that the number was not random, but the design of celestial beings, who have taken on the task of encouraging human beings to become more conscious and more loving. This story causes us to ponder the number 365, and to ponder the effect of the seasons on our soul development. The simplest counting unit is one day, marked

---

among you who makes a son or daughter pass through fire, or who practices divination, or is a soothsayer, or an auger, or a sorcerer, or one who casts spells, or who consults ghosts or spirits, or who seeks oracles from the dead. For whoever does these things is abhorrent to the Lord." Other references include 2 Kings 21:6 and 2 Chronicles 33:6. A special threat was leveled at "those who study the heavens...who gaze at the stars, and at each new Moon predict what shall befall you" (Isaiah 47:13-15). These passages counseled extreme measures against black magic. Positive references to the influence of the stars also exist, as well as positive versions of extraordinary skills of prophecy, but the point is that, among the intelligentsia in the cities, magical phenomena were suspected of being a pact with the devil.

4. Rudolf Steiner, *World History and the Mysteries in the Light of Anthroposophy* (London: Rudolf Steiner Press, 1997, originally 1923 and early 1924), especially the last lecture of January 1, 1924, for example, for those who have cultivated spiritual experience: "Thus when you return to the physical world, you will have enough strength to protect you from being paralyzed by the spectacle of the supersensible world" (p. 147).

5. At the birth of the Nathan Jesus (*Chron.* 149), the Sun (15° Sagittarius 4) squared Jupiter (12° Virgo 22), within less than 3°, not tight enough to warrant an Imagination story, yet exactly in line with our theme of the bestowing of revelation under the influence of Jupiter, whose effect is strengthened by the Sun. Steiner's picture appears in *According to Luke: The Gospel of Compassion and Love Revealed* (SteinerBooks, 2001).

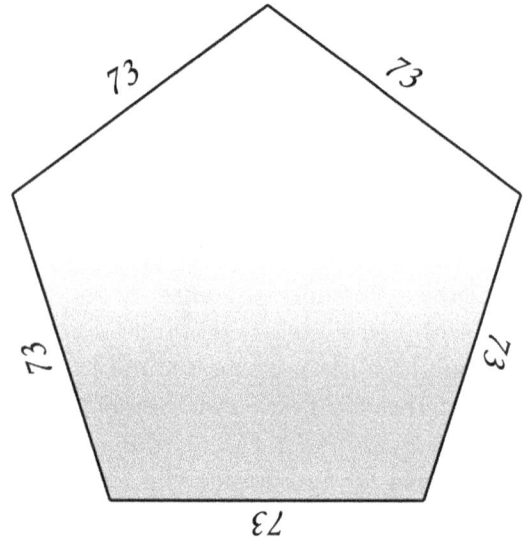
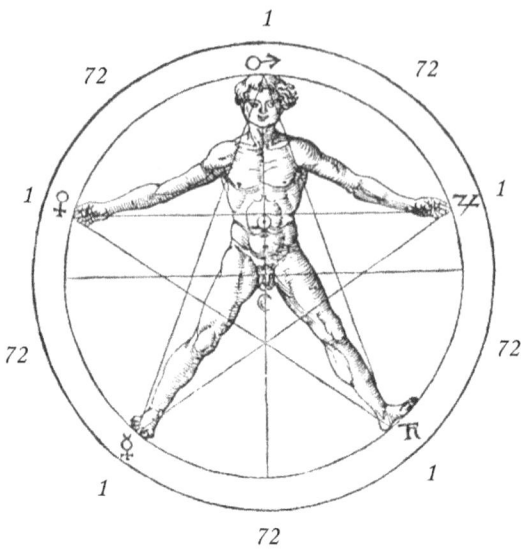

by the unmistakable rising and setting of the Sun—the rotation of the Earth in relation to the Sun. Speaking about 365 of these units refers to a time when the Earth orbited the Sun in relation to the stars beyond. The Sun appears in the same background of stars after 365 rotations. Because of the tilt of the Earth, we experience the four seasons during that orbit.

But why the number 365? Can we penetrate the wisdom of this number? It is a very odd number, and has only two factors 5 x 73. Were one to move along a 360° circle the distance of 73°, one would have gone just past the mark of the fifth of that circle, the quintile, at 72°. One can see 365 as (5 x 72) + 5. These are all fives, the "72" being the degrees in the angle of a fifth of a circle of 360°. One could break down the 72 into five smaller factors, as follows: 365 = (5 x 2 x 2 x 2 x 3 x 3) + 5. Fivefold geometry thrives here. The 72 relates to the average number of heart beats per minute, and the average number of breaths in four minutes. We breathe 25,920 times per day, which is the number of years in a Great Year, the completion of one cycle of precession of the equinoxes (from the Age of Aquarius back again to the Age of Aquarius). Seventy-two is thus the number of years to travel one degree of the 360° in the precession of equinoxes.[6]

The great teacher of Star Wisdom, Zaratos, divided the heavens into 12 (= 2 x 2 x 3) sections of 30° (= 2 x 3 x 5) each, totaling 360, and thus declared the extra five days holy days, time out of time. The orderliness of the universe was proclaimed plus "some extra." That "extra"—those five days—were treated with great respect.[7]

If we imagine a pentagon with 73 on each side, we can see an orderly progression through the course of a year. If we emphasize the orderliness of seventy-two, then the one holy day that makes seventy-three ought to come at points separated by seventy-two days. These points come at the extremities of the human body, as illustrated in this adaptation of the Vitruvian Man by Agrippa von Nettesheim, the pentagonal version of what Leonardo da Vinci gave as the human being within the circle and square. In Agrippa's version, the holy days come at the hands, feet, and head.[8]

---

6. In the esoteric system of the Kabbalah, it is quite common to add or subtract 1 from any number to understand its full significance, thus 73 and 72 are seen as the same.

7. The number of days in a year is actually 365.2425 days. The extra quarter of a day is added to the "extra" that one considers holy outside of the 360 ordered days. Or one could begin to see a kind of order in the following: 365 = (12 x 30) + 5 + 1/4 − 1/100 + 1/400, where each new character has its special significance in relation to the intention of the creators.

8. Leonardo da Vinci, born April 14 1452 (J) with Sun (16 Aries 32) sextile Jupiter (14 Aquarius 19). Da Vinci's diagram did not include the pentagram, as did Agrippa von Nettesheim's figures of human beings within geometries, born September 14, 1486 (J), with Sun (12 Virgo 37) square to Jupiter (15 Sagittarius 59). Some commentators have suggested taking da Vinci's common diagram of the human

Often, we think of the planet Venus having the fivefold signature, as it creates a five-petal flower in the heavens over a period of 8 (2 x 2 x 2) years. Here we entertain the relation of five to Jupiter, as well as to the number 73, which Robert Lawlor says is the controlling number of cycles of time.[9]

The reference to 365 may relate to other cycles of time from the ones that we know: "Thus all the days of Enoch were three hundred sixty-five years. Enoch walked with God; then he was no more, because God took him."[10] Instead of days, years were cited. Indeed, Hindu tradition sees a "divine year" as 365 human years.[11] In both cases, it makes 365 x 365. At that point something ends. Enoch disappears. A Hindu age ends. There is nothing left, challenging the notion of conservation of energy,[12] a theme that we will visit in other imaginations. In any case, 365 relates to all cycles of time, ordered by divine beings for purposes which we can slowly come to know.

Further commentaries, stories, and other Jupiter discoveries via the newsletter available at www.StarWisdom.org

---

being within the squared circle and connecting legs and arms to make three sides of a pentagram, implying the final point above the head to complete the pentagram.

9. In a personal conversation, Robert Lawlor, author of *Sacred Geometry* (London: Thames & Hudson, 1989), gave the following relation: yuga/Great Year :: 7/3. If you multiply the 73 by 100, you get the lengths of the five great sections of the millennium, "the key relations in the large cycles of the life and death of species." Robert Lawlor was born on August 11, 1938, with Sun (24 Cancer 25) widely opposed to Jupiter (4 Aquarius 37). 73 and 37 work together not only through inversion but as levels of a hexagon: beginning with six circles around a central circle, the sequence grows by adding new layers of circles, as follows: 1, 7, 19, 37, 73.

10. Genesis 5:23–24.
11. Vishnu Purana, true for both the devas and the pittris.
12. First law of thermodynamics, which seems contravened in Enoch's case.

---

*My head bears
The being of the resting stars.
My breast harbors
The life of the wandering stars.
My body lives and moves
Amidst the elements—
This am I.*
— RUDOLF STEINER

CONTEMPLATIONS ON THE JUPITER–URANUS CONJUNCTION

William Bento, Ph.D.

The major celestial event of 2010 is a threefold conjunction of Jupiter and Uranus in the sidereal sign of the Fishes. The dates are the following: June 8, 2010–September 19, 2010–January 4, 2011. Its approximate cycle is nearly every 14 years. The last threefold Jupiter and Uranus conjunction in the Fishes occurred between July 1926 and January 1927. In the span of time since the 1926/1927 conjunctions of these two planets there have been five other sets of Jupiter/Uranus conjunctions. The conjunctions have alternated between a water sign to being in an earth sign, thereby forming a hexagon pattern in the sky. This pattern can also be visualized as two interlocking triangles by connecting the water signs and the earth signs, or it can be viewed as the "Seal of Solomon."

Dates of the Jupiter & Uranus Conjunction	In the sign of the
7/15/1926, 8/11/1926, 1/25/1927	Fishes Pisces, a water sign
5/8/1941	Bull Taurus, an earth sign
10/7/1954, 1/7/1955, 5/10/1955	Crab Cancer, a water sign
12/11/1968, 3/11/1969, 7/20/1969	Virgin Virgo, an earth sign
2/18/1983, 5/14/1983, 9/25/1983	Scorpion Scorpio, a water sign
2/16/1997	Goat Capricorn, an earth sign
6/8/2010, 9/19/2010, 1/4/2011	Fishes Pisces, a water sign

A conjunction of planets begins a new cycle of development under the themes associated with the planets. We may discover the themes by combining the key concepts and influences of each planet. In the case of Jupiter and Uranus we may propose the following themes with the first word referring to Jupiter and the second word to Uranus. The list is by no means exhaustive and inclusive, but gives an example of how to read the language of Star Wisdom.

- Social Visionary Perspectives
- Community Revolution
- Cultural Freedom
- Educational Innovations
- Philosophical Metaphysics
- Expanding the Transpersonal
- Thinking into the Future

The themes are not fixed and immutable, but quite varied and contextual. Given the conditions of the time, the conjunctions will often reflect the historical development of both social situations and the needs of humanity's evolving consciousness. A comprehensive interpretation of these themes requires an understanding of three factors. The first requirement is to have a thorough grasp of the universal nature of the planets and the zodiac. Knowing its cosmological origins, the Spiritual Beings related to each planet and sign, and the characteristic attributes associated with each establishes a sound basis for understanding the deeper aspects of each theme signified by the planetary conjunction. The second requirement is to become as well informed as is possible about the history and current state of local, national, and world affairs. Lastly, there is a need to assess the stages of humanity's evolution of consciousness as objectively as one can, and then to deduce from it the probable challenges and gifts of the specific planetary conjunction under question.

Coming to terms with any interpretation given to a planetary conjunction is much more than an abstract conceptual notion. It is the result of a research effort. Although there are many research methods that could be employed to this end, I would postulate a three-pronged methodological approach involving aspects of historical heuristic, phenomenological, and intuitive inquiry practices. The heuristic method is about learning, discovering, and/or problem solving by conjecturing a series of experimental trial and error assumptions that coherently describes, rationally understands, and appreciates the subject at hand. When applied to historical events it allows one to see the patterns inscribed in the collective memory of humanity's psyche. The phenomenological method allows the researcher to read the phenomena as an unfolding story, whole unto itself. It is quite apropos for observing the events of the present and living with the questions of what the events are attempting to convey. The intuitive inquiry method is a transpersonal contemplative approach involving an awakened compassionate heart and an intention to live into the interior of the mystery subject under investigation (W. Braud & R. Anderson 1998). This approach demands a *presencing* of attention intent on receiving the stream of the future (Scharmer, O., 2008). In order to arrive at this state of *presencing* all attachments to the past must be let go.

The Historical Cycle of Jupiter–Uranus Conjunctions

In order to take the long view of Jupiter conjunct Uranus in the Fishes we must begin in July 1926. One of the most striking historical facts of this time was the founding of two Fascist youth organizations, the *Balilla* in Italy and the *Hitlerjugend* in Germany. Fascism became a mighty political force after World War I when right-wing parties throughout Europe campaigned on the message that they would restore the economy, re-establish moral order, and provide a renewed sense of purpose to their respective national communities. It appealed to the disenfranchised in various socio-economic groups, but particularly to the vulnerable and vital youth population seeking to identify with a facet of lost national pride. The Fascists promised the youth not only jobs and educational opportunities, but also a divine mission—to be leaders of a revolutionary movement that would reinvigorate and purify the nation. The Fascist doctrine professed that individuals owed primary allegiance to the state and that youth—not their elders—would shape the future. These two youth organizations, with their paramilitary training and supremacy ideology, became the core driving powers of the Italian/German alliance that unleashed the terrors of World War II.

One can see how the Jupiter/Uranus themes mentioned above can be found in this singular world-shaping historical fact. The aftermath of World War I lent itself to a need for new social visions, communities were astir with the feeling for a revolution, and a longing for cultural freedom was filled with youth oriented arts rejecting the ruling elite and traditional Catholic values. The Fascist parties were quite adept in convincing the people of its progressive education and philosophy that pivoted around mythical glory and were capable of giving every community member a transpersonal identity based on the idea of changing the world for the better. Much of this rhetoric can also be attributed to a worldview of psychism and an attitude of magnanimity connected to the sign of the Fishes, albeit somewhat distorted. The Fascists tapped into a worldview of psychism by creating symbols, resurrecting mythic heroes into cult figures, and encouraging a mystical relation with nature. These tactics catalyzed a great deal of unresolved collective unconscious psychic energy. Speeches were aimed at fostering hypnotic, trance-like effects. Under the Piscean virtue of magnanimity, youth were swept into the "quest" to change the world in accordance to Fascist ideology.

By the third Jupiter/Uranus conjunction in late January 1927 the Inter-Allied Military Control of Germany ended, giving the Fascist-Nazi party a sense of political victory. On May 13, 1927 "Black Friday" in Germany occurred. It was this severe economic system collapse that gave further opportunities for the Fascist party to raise its flag as the new dispensation and to co-opt businesses and schools for furthering its objectives. On the heels of this emerging political movement of the Nazi party arose two fascinating literary works. The first was Sigmund Freud's *The Future of an Illusion*, wherein he discussed religion as a mass wish on the part of people dictated by primitive instincts. He also addressed "the assertion made by certain nationalists that the *Indo-Germanic* race is the only one capable of civilization" as an illusion. The other classic published at this time was Martin Heidegger's *Being and Time*, the definitive work that shaped existential philosophy as a western world movement.

On May 8, 1941, a single conjunction of Jupiter and Uranus in the Bull occurred. The bitter harvest of the previous Jupiter/Uranus conjunction became painfully ever so present. World War II had gained momentum and the concerns to the western free world were at a peak. Within a week of this conjunction the following turning point events happened:

1. May 6: Joseph Stalin became premier of Russia.
2. May 7: The British Commonwealth voted for Winston Churchill 477 to 3.
3. May 9: The English Army broke the German Spy Code.
4. May 10: Adolf Hitler's Deputy, Rudolf Hess, parachuted into Scotland to broker a peace effort unauthorized by the Chancellor.
5. May 14: 3,600 Parisian Jews were arrested by the Nazis.

As if struck by a lightening bolt, the bulk of humanity awakened from a kind of slumber into an insane war. There was no doubt that a return to rational thinking was needed. This response to the tragedies taking place throughout Europe was accented by the Jupiter/Uranus conjunction in the Bull. From this sign streamed a resurrected worldview of rationalism and a call to the virtues of integrity, balance and progress. However, not all responses to the war were as rational as they may have been reactive. One of the most alarming during this time was the decision by those involved in the "Manhattan Project" to build the atomic bomb. It, too, could be seen as a turning point event.

Dark clouds of anger, paranoia, and viciousness pervaded the post-World-War-II era. By the time of the third set of Jupiter/Uranus conjunctions (October 7, 1954 to May 10, 1955) in the Crab, McCarthyism was sweeping the USA. Advertising campaigns sponsored by educational and religious organizations sought to raise fears about a communist takeover of America. Accusations of disloyalty, subversion, or treason were being made without proper regard for evidence. The primary targets of such suspicions were government employees, those in the entertainment industry, educators, and union activists. Anyone demonstrating free-thinking became subject to investigation by the House Committee on Un-American Activities. One can conceive of McCarthyism as a veiled form of the Fascist mentality that was unleashed in the 1926–1927 set of Jupiter/Uranus conjunctions.

Significant to this period of time was the beginning of the Mid-East turmoil. Jordan conducted raids on Israel that a year later ended with a United Nations truce and the United States sending huge aid to Israel in finances and military support. The seeds of this conflict remain with us today as one of the most worrisome threats to world peace. Given this conjunction was in the Crab it comes as no surprise to recognize that the issue of homeland became a major issue. Fueled by an insidious materialistic worldview and selfish interests, the Mid-East continues to be a hotbed for religious wars based on the notion of possessions of geography considered to be sacred by its peoples.

During the December 1968 first Jupiter/Uranus conjunction in the Virgin, the Apollo 8 spacecraft orbited around the Moon, heralding the Space Age! This event was a positive highlight amidst the peak of the Viet Nam War. The second conjunction in March 1969 witnessed the admission of two infamous assassins—Sirhan Sirhan, who killed presidential hopeful Robert F. Kennedy in Los Angeles, California, and James Earl Ray, who allegedly shot down Dr. Martin Luther King, Jr. in Memphis, Tennessee. Both of these slain men were representative voices for new social visions, for community non-violent revolutions, for cultural freedoms, for a compassionate and progressive America. Their loss deflated a counter-culture movement populated by the youth and political liberals. Yet, the movement did not altogether dissolve, for there were events like John Lennon and Yoko Ono's honeymoon "Bed-In for Peace" in the Amsterdam Hilton Hotel that captured the imagination of the world; and the safe landing of Apollo 9 after testing the Lunar Module on the surface of the Moon. Neil Armstrong and Edwin "Buzz" Aldrin punctuated the third conjunction on July 20, 1969 with the Apollo 11 landing on the Moon and their walking on the Moon. As Armstrong stated as he set foot on the Moon, "That is one small step for man and one giant leap for mankind." Weeks later the Woodstock celebration stunned the world with more than half a million people peacefully enjoying the folk and rock minstrels that had unleashed a musical revolution throughout the 1960s. Like the youth of the mid-twenties they felt a mission to change the world for the better; yet unlike the youth of the mid-twenties they detested the military approach to achieve its goals, and instead espoused a path of peace and nonviolence.

When these events are perceived through the lens of the sign of the Virgin, it becomes quite clear how the worldview associated with it (Phenomenology) dominated the landscape of the time. To use a hyperbole, the end of the 1960s was a phenomenal time! Cultural shifts in music, politics, education, science, religion, the media, spirituality and social activism were constant. It was the coming of age for "Baby Boomers." These souls deeply held a view for the need to change the prevailing paradigm from a masculine to a feminine orientation, from an aggressive competitive to a protective caring society.

As the fifth set of Jupiter/Uranus conjunctions in the Scorpion took place (February—September 1983) the Cold War had reached fever pitched contention between the USA and the Soviet Union. Ronald Reagan blatantly declared the Soviet Union an evil empire. Under this cloud of fear-based rhetoric he announced his Strategic Defense Initiative, known as the "Star Wars" program. Meanwhile the Soviets invaded Afghanistan. In the mainstream of culture the technological industry was exploding with such innovations as personal computers, the launching of Microsoft Word, and the innovation of the cellular communication system. Much of the international policies that were implemented in both the Bush administrations were created during this time. The latter indicates the character of the Scorpionic worldview of dynamism, or hidden forces at work in shaping social reality.

With the sixth Jupiter/Uranus conjunction that took place in the sign of the Goat in February 1997, three major newsworthy events broke forth. The first was the uncontested 10 billion dollar merger between Morgan Stanley and Dean Witter. The second was the Dow Jones Industrial Average closing at 7, 022, the first time ever over 7,000. The third event was the report from Roslin, Scotland, that scientists had successfully cloned an adult sheep named Dolly. Applying the heuristic approach to these events in the light of the worldview connected to the Goat—Spiritism or Spiritual Science—and the virtues and vices associated with it, we can see two dimensions opening up in human history. The first is the unregulated permissiveness given to societal institutions to amass wealth without regard for the public welfare. There is no question that this relates to a misuse of power and cowardice to confront such misuses, typical vices linked to the sign of the Goat. Secondly, we can correlate the cloning of the sheep Dolly to an expression of a spiritual science being applied in a realm that begs the question of human ethics.

This sixth in the cycle of Jupiter/Uranus conjunctions completes the hexagon pattern. From the upsurge of Fascist ideology to the breakthroughs of cloning and the breakdowns of economic regulation these conjunctions have marked significant and impactive events on the social conditions and consciousness of humanity. As we have entered into an era of global citizenship hardly anyone on the planet can be found who has not somehow been influenced by the historical events connected to this Jupiter/Uranus conjunction cycle.

Esoteric Dimensions of Jupiter Conjunct Uranus in the Fishes

There are many routes to discovering the esoteric dimensions innate to the planets and the zodiac. One route would be to penetrate Rudolf Steiner's *Outline of Esoteric Science,* published one hundred years ago. Willi Sucher's *Isis Sophia* is one splendid example of such a penetration. The anthroposophic cosmo-genesis, as interpreted by Willi Sucher, formed the foundations for Astrosophy, new star wisdom. However, I am selecting the route given in the book, *Meditations on the Tarot* (1967, 1985). The key to this journey is unlocking the associations between the 22 tarot cards with the 12 signs of the zodiac and the 10 planets. The association I shall apply to this intuitive inquiry into the esoteric dimensions comes from the tradition of Christian Hermeticism. As I do so, I urge the reader to abandon any fixed concept of keywords or classical astrological correlations to Jupiter, Uranus, and the sign of the Fishes. However helpful they may have been in gaining an understanding of the historical cycle presented in the first part of this article, they may pose more of an obstacle in attempting to grasp the esoteric dimensions. For this journey it is best to proceed with an open mind, an open heart, and a willingness to live in the imaginative realms.

Jupiter: The Emperor, letter iv in the *Meditations on the Tarot*

"*To be* something, *to know* something and *to be capable of* something is what endows a person with authority. One can also say a person has authority in proportion to what he unites within himself of the profundity of mysticism, the direct wisdom of gnosis and the productive power of magic. Whosoever has this to a certain degree can found a 'school.' Whosoever has this to a still higher degree can 'lay down the law.'"

The above words open up the meditation to the fourth letter. It addresses the true nature of Hermeticism. In cases of, "founding a school" and "laying down the law," a teaching is implied. However, it is not merely content that is being taught, but a transmission of a *way of being* that is being called for on the part of both teacher and student. Jupiter is both the archetypal teacher/student and the universal school. One who aspires to know how to become the author of his or her own biography sets foot on the path toward the sacred hallways of Jupiter. With each step an active renunciation must be enacted. In the letter this is described as a deliberate emptying out in order that there be space for the Divine to fill up and flow out as a genuine "state of consciousness where eternity and the present moment are one." Only in this state can the Emperor have a sense for spiritual comprehension. It is indeed another lucid example of the art of *presencing*.

It is not a fanciful notion to imagine the crown of the Emperor as symbolically being the crown chakra. Although the fontanel, which receives the imprint of the heavens at one's birth (Steiner, *The Spiritual Guidance of Humanity*, 1911), closes physically at approximately the age of three, it is capable of being opened etherically through contemplative study. The Emperor is a master at this practice. In knowing the thoughts of the Spiritual Beings inhabiting the heavenly world the Emperor must bear the "crown of thorns"; for he is bound to suffer the weight of responsibility of being a knower about the demands of the time.

So many of the intrinsic teachings about the Emperor concern the right relation one must have to revelation, truth and power. The distortion of this relationship leads to a worship of the idol of power as the source of true authority. Through our historical study above we see how both Benito Mussolini, who founded the Balilla, and Adolf Hitler, who founded the Hitlerjugend, assumed positions as the bearers of revelation, truth and supreme power. Both aspired to be masters or high priests. Each longed to be regarded by their followers as the future superman. There is only one master in the school of Christian Hermeticism that one can attribute the true source of authority to, and that is the being who taught, "I am the *way*, the *truth*, and the *life*." It is He who guides one toward initiation.

By adherence to the *way*, the Hermeticist develops an aptitude for acquiring esoteric knowledge when he or she needs it. As stated in the fourth letter, "The initiate is one who knows how to attain knowledge, i.e. who knows how to *ask, seek and put into practice* the appropriate means in order to succeed." In knowing the truths of one's existence the initiate can then enter into direct experiences with the spiritual beings at play in human evolution, thereby living into the divine upon the Earth.

In this context Jupiter can be understood as the wisdom of Hermetic Philosophy practiced in one's personal daily life and shared within the circle of community as a sacrament of humanization. Is there any greater schooling than to learn how to be human, to know the divine, and to be capable of being an instrument of God? The Spirits of Wisdom are guardians to this school. They bear the light of the Ancient Sun existence into the current orbit of Jupiter. Each circuit around the present Sun is twelve years, taking one year to pass through a zodiacal sign. As Jupiter moves through the vault of Heaven it sheds light on the nature of the logos, both as a divine being and as a capacity of human logic.

Uranus: The Tower of Destruction, letter XVI in *Meditations on the Tarot*

"So the sixteenth Arcanum is related to human evil, i.e., to evil that does not come from outside, but that certainly has its origin within the human soul." This is a very complex problem deserving serious attention. The seeds of this dilemma are found in the story of Genesis. The disregard of the one and only prohibition given to Adam and Eve—eating from the Tree of Knowledge of Good and Evil—resulted in the consequences of toil, suffering and death. It is the fate of every incarnation to undergo these experiences. Such is the price we all pay for "the sin of presumptuous audacity or impudent curiosity." Expulsion from Paradise marks the beginning of the human quest toward freedom. It is fundamentally a moral issue of cosmic proportion. Whether the eating of the Tree of Knowledge of Good and Evil is to be considered a violation of the laws of development as conceived by the divine order (a premature act) or is to be regarded as a foreordained act in order to emancipate the human being from an infantile state of dependency, the fact remains—freedom comes at a cost. This first stage of the "Fall" is based on the desire to have our eyes opened and to be as gods, knowing good and evil (Genesis 2:5).

In letter sixteen the author writes of three subsequent stages of the "Fall" and the emergence of human evil. Cain's fratricide of his brother Abel is the second stage of the "Fall," leaving the deep imprint of murderer in the psyche of every human being. Each person is capable of doing what Cain did, yet each person has the choice not to do it. Giving sway to the instinct and planning to commit fratricide has become the primordial archetype for war. The third stage is referred to as the generation of giants. In this aspect of the Genesis story we are shown how individuals, groups and races have attempted to dominate others under the pretention that they are the "supermen." The author aptly states, "The Caesars, who arrogated divine honor and authority to themselves, Nietzsche's 'superman', and likewise the diverse fascist and communist *Führers* of our century are only particular manifestations of the primordial "gigantism" of which Genesis speaks." The third stage is the building of the tower of Babel, symbol of the desire to conquer Heaven by means of forces acquired and developed on the Earth.

"At the root of Cain's fratricide is the revolt of the 'lower self' against the 'true self'—of the fallen 'likeness' against the intact 'image.' At the root of the generations of giants is the marriage of the 'lower self' with the entities of the fallen hierarchies—instead of the true self. And at the root of the building of the tower of Babel is the collective will of 'lower selves' to achieve the replacing of the 'true self' of the celestial hierarchies and God with a superstructure of universal significance fabricated through this will."

The consequences to these subsequent stages of the "Fall" impact us at a psychological, sociological and global level. The evil of a self-willed severance from one's own true higher self is but a psychological suicide. Perpetuated long enough, one will fall from the cycles of reincarnation and become no more than an elemental demon whose only purpose can be to play out evils upon the Earth. Such a soul will become a wanderer, endlessly seeking for what he has slain. The evil of severing the holy bond of the "I and Thou" relationship can lead only to an unholy alliance with the adversarial beings whose aim is to pit man against man, and to place each soul in a state of infinite isolation. Such a soul is bound to fall prey to madness. The evil of severing the natural and divinely ordained cooperation between nature and spirit makes the Earth an abyss, one that can become a space for only destruction. Such souls will be blasted by a thunderbolt casting them into humiliation and rendering each of them into a state of perpetual purgatory.

The Tower of Babel is destroyed by a heavenly power that is charged with light and heat. It comes from above and places what belongs below back into its proper placement. It destroys in order to create the harmony that needs to be reinstated between nature and spirit. The lightning rod or thunderbolt is a wonderful symbolic representation of the planet Uranus. Appearing suddenly and with a power beyond the earthly, the celestial fire strikes at all buildings that are presumptuous claims made by human beings assuming to be gods. Mistaking the Tower of Babel for being a Tree of Life is the cardinal sin that those infected by evil desires often make. The fruits of the Tree of Life can be experienced through the senses, but the Tree of Life itself cannot be apprehended by our 12 senses. To comprehend it one must develop inner sight, imaginative capacities. By aligning one's life with the Tree of Life that has its roots in the divine intention of Love, one can grow up into the promise of being a co-creator. Uranus bears this distinctive signature of development—the vision of the future of humanity. From this vision all historical change has come—revolutions, innovations, elevated states of consciousness, etc.

Uranus can be associated with the activity of the Spirits of Harmony, who seek to guide humanity into its rightful place both on the Earth and in the Heavens. It takes eighty-four years for it to orbit the Sun. In that time Jupiter makes 6 orbits around the Sun, hence the hexagonal pattern or, if you will, the Seal of Solomon is created. The Seal conveys the message of the Hermetic Axiom, "As above, so below."

Reflections on the historical study of the last hexagonal pattern of Jupiter conjunct Uranus reveals how central the theme of human evil has been from 1926 to the present. Uranus has certainly been evident in the events cited above. The question of human evil has been the predominant concern of the twentieth century. As we move through the twenty-first century, this question faces us with a measure of urgency never felt by humanity before this time.

The Emperor Arrives at the Tower of Destruction in the Region of the Hanged Man

As in 1926/1927 Jupiter and Uranus will conjoin in the sign of the Fishes in 2010. If we are to anticipate the significance of this celestial event on Earth, we can have no better preparation than to learn from history. This does not mean that the historical events of that time need repeat themselves, but it does imply that similar themes will be on the horizon. A review of the historical events at the outset of this article can serve as focal points for meditation. For instance, what have we to learn about the last Jupiter/Uranus conjunction? How does the uncontested merger between Morgan Stanley and Dean Witter for 10 billion dollars exemplify an inflated greed to dominate and to satisfy the terrestrial desires? What is the future of cloning meant to serve. Whom does it serve? Although these events stood in the foreground of the sign of the Goat and thereby were colored by the economic and scientific institutions, the human tendency to commit evil in the name of progress remains the consistent concern.

Before we can consider the particular coloring of the Jupiter/Uranus conjunctions of 2010, we must focus on what the esoteric dimension of the Fishes has to tell us.

Fishes: The Hanged Man, letter xii in *Meditations on the Tarot*

"Now, the domain of freedom—the spiritual life—is found placed between two gravitational fields with two different centers. The Gospel designates them as 'heaven' and 'this world'…and it designates those whose will follows or is submitted to the gravitation of 'this world' as the *children of this world*, and those whose will follows the gravitation of 'heaven' as the *children of light*." The Hanged Man is a child of light, who freely chose to orient his will toward the heavenly light. He identifies with and absorbs into himself all the heavenly lights, and thus has "zodiacalized" his will. The darkness of fear does not disturb him, for he is concentrated on the light of divine love.

Rudolf Steiner states in his *Human and Cosmic Thought* (1914) lecture cycle that the Fishes are connected to the worldview of Psychism. For one who maintains this worldview he or she rises from accepting the ensoulment of the world to accepting the Spirit or the Spirits of the world. The animation of these Spirits has been understood as an experience of magnanimity and generosity. This activity can simply be restated as an expression of the virtues of love. The vernal point, which marks the Astrological Ages, entered the Fishes in 214 C.E. This astrological age ushered in at the same time Mani was born. It was Mani who brought forth the mission of esoteric Christianity, the task to transform evil through the intensification of love!

How, might you ask, can the Hanged Man take this mission on? The answer is through his *Faith*. Not through a simple mundane belief, but through a "firm assurance of things hoped for" and "the conviction of things not seen." The Hanged Man acts on his Faith and obeys the call of the Spirit of Love to love regardless of the apparent conditions. This capacity transforms the will from a "*my* will"

into "*thy* will." In this experience the feeling of unity is gained and the will becomes an organ of perception allowing one to see through the eyes of the Spirit. This seeing becomes an aptitude for comprehending moral logic.

With moral logic, thinking is warmed and enlivened. Every object of thought is held in devotion and love. The idea becomes an ideal that is not only thought, but also perceived. In essence, moral logic is the power of imagination. In fact, the author of the *Meditations on the Tarot* refers to this twelfth letter as "a practical school of education for the imagination." Having developed the aptitude of moral logic by being bathed in the region of the Fishes, the Emperor is capable of understanding that not all events of the present have their cause in the past, but that some events occur because the cause is a need of the future. Hence, not all Towers of Destruction should be viewed in negative terms alone, but be seen as the glorious descent of the future into the present.

Living with the Possibilities of the New Jupiter-Uranus Cycle Commencing in the Fishes

There is an uncanny similarity between the cultural, political, and economic conditions preceding this next conjunction, just as there was before the first conjunction of 1926. People all over the world are feeling disenfranchised, powerless, and discontented. However, amid this global economic collapse there are signs of hope. In the United States of America it is centered on the promises of President Barack Obama. Despite the growing suspicion that he may merely be a set up for the emergence of the Antichrist, there continues to be a large contingent of hopefuls who remain optimistic. For some, this is justified on the basis of a similar oratory skill and power as his inspirer, Dr. Martin Luther King, Jr. For many others, their sense of hope arises out of a feeling that things could not get worse, yet this view has historically, time and time again, proven to be faulty. Things can always get worse, and if one listens to the many prophecies regarding the highly anticipated 2012 turning point, things are expected to get worse.

And so where can we place our trust? How can we find the hope that quickens a brighter future? I suggest it is only by being faithful to the *call* to create a better future that we can keep the flame of hope aglow. This does not mean to know all that would allow us to act perfectly, but to have the conviction of our actions and to act with conviction. The conjunction in the sign of the Fishes highlights the sense of *hearing*. We must actively listen to the Spirits on both sides of the threshold who are pleading with us to found schools of imagination in our communities, schools wherein a moral logic can be cultivated. We are at a critical juncture in human history. A new paradigm is being asked for and must be responded to.

Inasmuch as we need to know how to meet the future, we also need to do in the present what can become redemption of our past. Resourcing the archetypes of our past is an excellent way to bring healing into present situations. With regard to the Jupiter/Uranus conjunctions I will propose that the August 16, 35 C.E., conjunction in the Lion be regarded as our guiding archetype. Although historical accuracy of St. Paul's conversion on the road to Damascus is questionable, this date can be considered as probable. (The author recalls a discussion with Willi Sucher wherein this probability was agreed upon.) It was St. Paul, who after having experienced the mystical touch of the Christ and having spiritually heard and seen the Christ in the etheric, developed the first Christian theology. Legend has it that he taught the members of the Damascus Christian community for three years thereafter. St. Paul is an example of an initiate who attained the experience to speak with authority and to found a school. He is also a living testament to the cathartic experience of being struck by a heavenly power in order to be infused with a new faith. Both the Jupiter/Emperor and the Uranus/Tower of Destruction correlations describe his story quite well.

It has also be noted that in approximately 35 C.E. the Church in Jerusalem under the leadership of the Twelve Apostles, with its decisiveness in responding to the needs of the faithful and its openness in blessing diversity in the community, prepared the ground for missionary activity in the Hellenistic world. Their mission was a Gospel of Love. Let this be our mission as we spread the "Good News" to be found in the wealth of Esoteric Christianity. As this new cycle of Jupiter/Uranus conjunctions begins once again in the Fishes we can endeavor to make the esoteric mysteries of Christianity more accessible, not as a continuation of religion, but as the template for the turning point in evolution. In this context, we may re-enliven our sacraments with genuine acknowledgement of the cosmological significance of the deeds of Christ and we may celebrate our relationship to the Earth, knowing that Sophia is emerging as our guide in creating the new paradigm. Human beings are at the threshold of becoming the co-creators of their own existence. Each one of us is free to choose how we will go about executing this task. Together, as a community devoted to the Sophia–Christ, we can envision a new world and begin to cultivate the relationships needed to generate the intensification of love so radiant that the darkness of fear and the commission of evils are mitigated in their power to derail the rightful course of evolution. In this effort we must never underestimate the power of our contemplative studies, our prayers, our meditations, and our sacred celebrations. These activities become organs of perception for the "Spiritual Beings who full of grace behold our earnest heartfelt feelings, and in beholding, strengthen us from realms of light illuminating our lives in love."

References

Anonymous, (1967, 1985). *Meditations on the Tarot: A Journey into Christian Hermeticism* New York: Penguin.

Braud, W. & R. Anderson (1998). *Transpersonal Research Methods for the Social Sciences: Honoring Human Experience.* Thousand Oaks, CA: Sage Publications.

Scharmer, O. (2009). *Theory U: Leading from the Future as It Emerges.* San Francisco: Barrett-Koehler.

Steiner, Rudolf (1910, 1997). *An Outline of Esoteric Science.*

———, (1914, 1961). *Human and Cosmic Thought.* London: Rudolf Steiner Press.

WORLD PENTECOST

Robert Powell

This article is written to introduce the new *Journal for Star Wisdom* at this special time (2009 for 2010) leading up to the pivotal year 2012, the deeper significance of which is discussed here as the fulfillment of Rudolf Steiner's prophecy of the World Pentecost. The content of this article is an edited version of the transcript of my lecture on World Pentecost held on July 24, 2009 in Chapel Hill, North Carolina.[1] This article addresses from a different standpoint part of the content of a new book written by Kevin Dann and myself, *Christ & the Maya Calendar*.[2] A central theme of the book is the year 2012. This point in time is the end date of the Maya Long Count Calendar. This calendar is coming to an end at the winter solstice of the year 2012, specifically on December 21, 2012. Many books have been written about this date. Some authors are prophesying a variety of catastrophes. Others are saying that we are going to wake up on December 22, 2012, and find ourselves in a kind of paradise, with all the terrible things occurring here on the Earth finished ("over and done with"). These are two extremes, and obviously it is not so simple.

The Maya Long Count calendar began a long time ago, in the year 3114 B.C.E., specifically August 11, 3114 B.C.E. (Gregorian calendar date). Historians use a method of dating that excludes the year zero, referring to the year 3114 B.C.E. Astronomers have a slightly different method of dating. For astronomers, 3114 B.C.E. is the year -3113. Because historians go straight from 1 B.C.E. to 1 C.E., excluding the year zero, astronomers identify 1 B.C.E. as the year zero, 2 B.C.E. as the year -1, 3 B.C.E. as the year -2, etc., and this makes it a lot easier for computation with dates, by including the year zero. Given that the Maya Long Count calendar began in -3113 and finishes in 2012, we can add 2012 and -3113 and deduce that this calendar lasts for a total of 5,125 years.

The classical Maya culture flourished from between about 250 to about 900 C.E., a period of almost 700 years. During this time the Maya civilization flourished as an agriculturally intensive and city-centered culture. It was a period of large-scale construction and the recording of inscriptions on monuments, exemplifying a significant intellectual and artistic development, the most notable monuments being their stepped pyramids. There were a number of remarkable Maya cities in Mesoamerica, and it was a culture that included highly developed art and architecture, agriculture and astronomy. Then this culture collapsed in a relatively short space of time, whereby most of the cities were abandoned, although some Maya cities in the Yucatan continued to flourish for centuries more until the Yucatan was conquered by the Spanish in the sixteenth century. Although many ideas have been put forward to explain the collapse of the classical Maya civilization, to this day we do not know with any degree of certainty what really happened. All kinds of monuments were left behind. During the twentieth century these were decoded and the few surviving Maya texts were deciphered. From this breakthrough came the discovery that there were actually three calendars that the Maya used. The one that ends

---

1. In gratitude to Kelly Calegar, who organized and transcribed the lecture and organized two subsequent workshops in Chapel Hill, North Carolina.
2. Robert Powell & Kevin Dann, *Christ & the Maya Calendar: 2012 and the Coming of the Antichrist.*

in the year 2012 is called the Maya Long Count calendar. What is this calendar about?

Although the Maya retreated from their cities, there are at the present time still about seven million descendants of the Maya in southern Mexico, the Yucatan Peninsula, Guatemala, Belize, El Salvador, and western Honduras. From those who have done research among these descendants, there is some knowledge of the ideas and beliefs of the Maya. For example, it is surmised that the period of 5,125 years of the Long Count Calendar is what the Maya called the *Fourth Age* or *Age of the Fourth Sun*. The fourth age is followed by the fifth age, and anyone who has studied chronology can recognize that here there is a parallel with Hindu chronology.[3] In Hindu chronology, the ages are called *Yugas*. According to the book called *The Laws of Manu* we are still in the fourth age, or fourth Yuga, referred to as the *Kali Yuga*. Hindu chronology refers to a sequence of four Yugas, whose names are Krita Yuga, Treta Yuga, Dvapara Yuga, and Kali Yuga. Then, according to some Hindu sources, will follow the fifth Yuga, called Satya Yuga. *Yuga* means simply *age*.

This teaching of the Yugas became transmitted to Greece, where expressions were used that are more familiar to us. The Greek poet Hesiod, for instance, used the designations Golden Age, Silver Age, Bronze Age, and Iron Age. The Iron Age of the Greeks corresponds to the Hindu Dark Age or Kali Yuga. Against the background of Hindu chronology, we have a fairly clear idea of what is signified by the succession of ages or Yugas.

It is striking that in Hindu chronology the fourth age, Kali Yuga, began very close in time to the start of the fourth age in the Maya calendar. Kali Yuga, according to Hindu chronology, began at midnight on February 17/18 in the year 3102 B.C.E. (astronomers would say, in the year -3101). And this date differs by merely twelve years from the start of the Maya Long Count Calendar. Clearly there is a correspondence here. However, according to the dating for the Kali Yuga originally derived from the ancient Sanscrit text entitled *The Laws of Manu*, it is stated that the Kali Yuga lasts for 432,000 years. If we accept this dating, it would imply that at the present time we are less than 5,120 years into Kali Yuga, which would then last a further (approximately) 427,000 years.

Interestingly, there are Hindu teachers, including Sri Yukteswar, the teacher of Yogananda,[4] who indicated that one has to look at the dating of the Yugas differently—that they are not the purported great, lengthy periods of time. Another individual who also took up the theme of the dating of the Yugas was Rudolf Steiner, who mentioned on various occasions that Kali Yuga lasted for a period of five thousand years. My astrosophical research confirms this indication, and I was able to determine the end date of Kali Yuga to be September 10, 1899.[5] Between -3101 and 1899, five thousand years elapsed, this being the length of Kali Yuga, which is regarded as the fourth age.

Moreover, Rudolf Steiner gave a very precise meaning to the ending of the fourth age, Kali Yuga. He spoke of the New Age, the *Age of Light*, which then began in 1899. In Hindu chronology, according to some sources, the Age of Light is Satya Yuga, the fifth age that follows the fourth age, Kali Yuga. This fifth age or Satya Yuga, according to Rudolf Steiner, has to do with an event he refers to as the *second coming of Christ* which, however, is not the return of Christ in a physical body. Instead, Christ's return is in an *ethereal body*—a body of light. Through his reappearance in the world of the etheric, the invisible world of life forces, Christ has the ability to appear simultaneously to people in different places around the world. This is occurring now, during this Age of Light (Satya Yuga) that began in 1899.[6]

---

3. Ibid., chapter 6, for the parallel between the Hindu Yugas and the Maya calendar.

4. Yogananda came from India to the United States and founded the Self Realization fellowship in Southern California in 1920.

5. Robert Powell, *Chronicle of the Living Christ: Foundations of Cosmic Christianity* (SteinerBooks, 1996), p. 418. See also, Robert Powell, *The Christ Mystery: Reflections on the Second Coming* (Fair Oaks, CA: Rudolf Steiner College Press, 1999).

6. Rudolf Steiner, *The Reappearance of Christ in the Etheric* (SteinerBooks, 2003), lecture of January 25, 1910.

Following these indications, I have written a book about this called *The Christ Mystery*, and in this book I translated into English various accounts of people who have had experiences of Christ in his ethereal form.[7] The experiences described there generally occurred as a matter of grace, and on the whole they are very beautiful and profound life-changing experiences. In November 2008 I had the good fortune of meeting a young woman, Judith von Halle, who on Good Friday in the year 2004 received the stigmata, which are the visible wounds/signs of Christ.[8] She is Jewish, and it is very unusual for a Jewish woman to receive this grace of bearing the stigmata—perhaps it is even the first case of this. In addition, she is not Catholic; up until now, virtually all recorded cases of the stigmata have been within the Catholic Church. Moreover, Judith von Halle is an anthroposophist, who has studied the works of Rudolf Steiner. What is striking about her experience is that until she received the stigmata she enjoyed eating, but from the time she received the stigmata she found she was no longer able to eat any food. In fact, eating made her ill. Now her only intake is water, and this only occasionally.

When I met her in November 2008 she had not eaten for four and a half years, yet she was radiantly healthy! In terms of her consciousness, an incredible change came about when she received the stigmata. She came into communion with Christ. In particular, she came into communion with the resurrection body of Christ. Through this communion with the resurrection body of Christ, she receives all she needs to live.[9] She does not need anything else. She receives such abundance from the communion with Christ's resurrection body that she does not need any physical nourishment. She is a living testimony to Steiner's indication about the reappearance of Christ, and that through this new and living relationship with Christ, human beings will have the possibility of undergoing a dramatic change of consciousness. Judith von Halle has indeed gone through a remarkable change of consciousness since Easter of the year 2004.

It was a significant meeting, to meet someone who is in contact with the living Christ to such a degree that she has received the visible wounds of Christ, the stigmata. She is a remarkable testimony to the unfolding of the New Age which, in light of Rudolf Steiner's indications, is the age of Christ's second coming. Today, the expression *New Age* is well known; it is a widely used expression. However, most people do not realize that it was Rudolf Steiner who introduced this term and that it has a very explicit meaning having to do with the return of Christ in an ethereal form— his *second coming*. To summarize: the end of Kali Yuga, the Dark Age, in 1899 heralded the beginning of the New Age, the Age of Light, Satya Yuga, the age of Christ's second coming. However, there is still the question what this has to do with the year 2012? In order to grasp this connection, we need to first consider the Hindu understanding of Kali Yuga.

The Hindu understanding of the starting date of Kali Yuga is that it was also the death date of Krishna. In India there are a tremendous number of gods and goddesses who are revered in the Hindu religion. There are many different spiritual groups and movements. But all love Krishna! Krishna is the central figure in

---

7. Ibid, chapter 1.
8. Judith von Halle was born in Berlin in 1972. She attended school in Germany and the U.S. and studied architecture, graduating in 1998. She encountered Anthroposophy in 1997 and began working as a staff member at Rudolf Steiner House in Berlin, where she also lectured from 2001, while maintaining an architectural practice. In 2004, her life was transformed when she received the stigmata. Her first book was published in German in 2005, and she now works principally as a lecturer and author. She lives part-time in Berlin and in Dornach, Switzerland. Among her books in English are: *And If He Had Not Been Raised...: The Stations of Christ's Path to Spirit Man* (London: Temple Lodge, 2007), *Illness and Healing: The Mystery Language of the Gospels* (Temple Lodge, 2008), *The Lord's Prayer: The Living Word of God* (Temple Lodge, 2007), *Secrets of the Stations of the Cross and the Grail Blood: The Mystery of Transformation* (Temple Lodge, 2008).

9. Judith von Halle, *And If He Had Not Been Raised...*, p. 23: "The life force emanating from the Resurrection strengthens me inwardly so much that I can be outwardly nourished by it."

Hinduism. Rudolf Steiner spoke about Krishna, and what he indicated points to a relationship between Krishna and Jesus. Rudolf Steiner, when speaking of Jesus of Nazareth, spoke of a pure soul that had never gone through the event of the Fall, a pure soul that had come into incarnation on the Earth *for the first time* as Jesus. In other words, Jesus of Nazareth had never been incarnated on the Earth before and was therefore a pure being. However, Steiner also indicated that even though Jesus had not been incarnated on the Earth before, he had worked from higher realms to assist humankind on the path of spiritual evolution. In fact, according to Steiner, Jesus of Nazareth is the same being who in the Hindu religion is called Krishna—in other words, Krishna and Jesus are one and the same.[10]

If we read the *Bhagavad Gita* carefully, as the primary source for our understanding of Krishna and the most widely known Hindu sacred scripture, we come to recognize that Krishna had not been incarnated in a physical body but had overlighted an individual and had taught through that individual. Krishna was not actually incarnated but was overlighting Arjuna the charioteer. The teachings of Krishna were presented *through* Arjuna. When speaking of the "death" of Krishna at that point in time, at the start of Kali Yuga, what is really meant by this is that the "death" of Krishna was actually the event of Krishna withdrawing from Arjuna to return to higher realms. The remarkable level of consciousness that Arjuna had attained through being overlighted by Krishna was no longer. For Arjuna it meant darkness; he had been enveloped in the incredible light coming from Krishna, and then, when Krishna "died"—or rather, withdrew—Arjuna experienced darkness.

This experience was symptomatic for nearly all human beings who would experience this darkness sooner or later in the subsequent period of time, during the course of Kali Yuga. It was indicative of the future period of time in which humanity would experience the loss of light consciousness, which is why this time period is called the Dark Age, or Kali Yuga. In our time we find this darkness to be the normal state of consciousness. Generally we are not aware of our spiritual origin, that we are divine beings who have incarnated here upon the Earth. And usually we are not aware of our previous lives on the Earth, let alone our experience in spiritual realms in between incarnations on this planet. Thus, more often than not, we are unaware of who we are in a deeper sense or where we were before we came into existence here on Earth. From the standpoint of Krishna consciousness, which Arjuna received through being overlighted, we are living in darkness. And now, the Age of Light means the coming again of this *same being* who overlighted Arjuna and was then incarnated as Jesus of Nazareth. Through his second coming he is *again* awakening the light-filled consciousness that existed at the time of Krishna/Arjuna and that, later, various people received through Christ—St. John, the author of the book of Revelation, being a notable example of an individual who was overlighted by Jesus Christ.

We can find many outstanding examples of human beings who have attained this light consciousness even during the Dark Age. St. Paul, for example, had an experience of blinding light at the gates of Damascus through which he received an imprint of Jesus Christ, whom he then proclaimed on his travels to the different communities scattered around the Mediterranean. Other individuals, as well, attained this light-filled Christ consciousness that filled both Paul and John. These individuals were forerunners of the new experience of Christ that is opening up in our time. Through grace, they received Christ consciousness even during the Dark Age of Kali Yuga. Now, during the New Age, Satya Yuga, we are coming into a time when more and more human beings are attaining Christ consciousness that existed in a preliminary form as Krishna consciousness in ancient times and which is reappearing in our time in a new way through the encounter with Christ in his second coming.

---

10. Rudolf Steiner, *The Bhagavad Gita and the West: The Esoteric Significance of the Bhagavad Gita and Its Relation to the Epistles of Paul* (SteinerBooks, 2009).

Judith von Halle, whom I mentioned previously, is an example of someone who has come into this light-filled consciousness, from which she is able to communicate extraordinary things. Rudolf Steiner himself bore witness to the presence of Christ. He had a "Paul" or "Arjuna" experience in 1899, which he describes in his autobiography. *Out of this direct experience he then began his life's work as a spiritual teacher to proclaim the reality of the event of Christ's return in a new form, an ethereal form, in our time.* What Steiner stressed, however, is that we come into Christ consciousness, this light-filled consciousness of spiritual awareness, if we actively seek it, because Christ leaves us completely free, and if we do not ask, we do not receive, unless by virtue of grace. Generally speaking—although there are, as described earlier, also Christ encounters through grace—we come into Christ consciousness above all through actively seeking Christ. This is a very important consideration. The question is: What does all this have to do with the year 2012?

In *Christ & the Maya Calendar,* I indicated that we are able to come to a true understanding of the significance of the transition in 1899 from the Dark Age to the New Age of Light if we comprehend that since 1899 Christ is working in Earth evolution in a new way—yet, nevertheless, at the same time the impulses of the Dark Age continue on into the present time. In other words, since 1899 we are living in a period of a great epic struggle between the forces of light, led by Christ, and forces of darkness, which are opposing the light of Christ. In the Christian tradition the *Letters of John* refer to the *Antichrist* as the force opposing Christ. From the subtitle of *Christ & the Maya Calendar*—"*2012 and the Coming of the Antichrist*"—it is evident that this theme is a central focus in the book, the theme of the apocalyptic struggle between the forces of light and the forces of darkness since 1899 and continuing into our time.

Let us now consider the difference between the end date of the Kali Yuga according to Rudolf Steiner, which is the year 1899, and the end date of the Maya calendar, which is the year 2012. What is this difference about? My understanding is that the Maya astronomers were aware, like the Hindu chronologists, that humanity entered into a dark age which would end around the present time. As discussed above, looking at the starting points of both the Maya calendar (in 3114 B.C.E.) and Kali Yuga (in 3102 B.C.E.), there is only a twelve year difference between these two starting dates. However, what the Maya astronomers seemed to have grasped is that there would be a period of conflict between the forces of light and darkness before the *real* New Age would begin. That would explain why the Maya astronomers came to the year 2012 as the start of the New Age instead of the year 1899.

At this point in time we are rapidly approaching the year 2012. Summarizing the above: Rudolf Steiner spoke of 1899 as the start of the New Age, which can also be thought of as the Age of Christ's second coming. However, for those people who originally devised the Maya Calendar, it seems that they intuited that the *real* start of the New Age would not be until the year 2012, since they may have recognized the possibility that humanity must first pass through a little more than a century of experiencing the conflict between the forces of light and those of darkness—in the period from 1899 to 2012.

There is, moreover, a cosmological background to the 2012 date. In order to grasp this background, it requires that we first understand the structure of our galaxy. A map of the galaxy shows the center of the galaxy, called the "Galactic Center" (see image). In the Platonic tradition, what was conceived to be at the Galactic Center was called the "Supra-Celestial Sun," thought of as a Great Sun in amid the stars of our galaxy; whereby, of course, the ancients had a completely different relationship to the heavens than we have now through modern astronomy, and so their understanding of the galaxy was quite different from ours.

As a starting point, let us consider that all the stars in the heavens are Suns like our Sun. We can think of our Sun as our *local star.* Every single star, or Sun, is a miniature copy of the Supra-Celestial Sun—at least, this was the conception in the

An image of the Milky Way Galaxy

Platonic stream to which Neo-Platonists such as Proclus (412–485) belonged. I shall refer to it simply as the *Central Sun*, a term that conveniently expresses the fact that it is located at the center of the galaxy. The Central Sun *is* the Supra-Celestial Sun at the center of the galaxy, i.e., at the Galactic Center. However, it is to be noted that this is somewhat different from the understanding of modern astronomy. The current astronomical concept of the Galactic Center is that there is a "super-massive black hole" there, whereby it has to be borne in mind that this is purely a theoretical concept which is, moreover, an inadequate concept—one that does not grasp that in the central region of the galaxy, at the Galactic Center, there is the point of transition from creation to pure spirit, or *vice versa* from pure spirit to creation.

Everything has come into existence from the Central Sun. All the stars in our galaxy have been born, directly or indirectly, from this great center which, if we were able to enter into this realm, we would find is a realm of pure spirit.[11]

In the book *Christ & the Maya Calendar* there is an appendix about the Central Sun, revealing that it is not at all a super-massive black hole. It is a great center which can be thought of as the Divine Heart of our galaxy, supporting everything in the galaxy, just as the heart maintains everything in the human organism. Ultimately it is the power of Divine Love that streams from this Divine Heart, the Central Sun. In the words of Dante it is a matter of "the love that moves the Sun and the other stars" (*The Divine Comedy: Paradise* 33:144–145). All the stars (our Sun is one of about 100 billion stars in the Milky Way galaxy) are orbiting around the Central Sun in a clockwise direction. Our Sun takes approximately 227 million years to go once around the Central Sun. On its passage around the Central Sun, it travels through different regions of the galaxy. This is a key concept for understanding what the Dark Age is and how it arose.

Imagine walking in nature on a beautiful, sunny day and then an enormous black cloud comes and hides the Sun, so that the atmosphere grows cold and dark. In experiencing this, one knows that the Sun is going to re-appear and so normally one would not be overly concerned. By way of analogy, it may be surmised that it was something like this which Maya and Hindu chronologists perceived long ago in relation to the passage of our Sun around the Central Sun. Of course, they could not formulate it in this way, because at that time there was not a clear conception of the movement of our Sun around the Galactic Center. For us now, knowing of this movement by way of modern astronomy, the question is: What is emanating from the Central Sun which holds everything together (100 billion or more stars) in their orbits around this great center?

The answer lies in considering the Central Sun as the Ultimate Source of existence from which is streaming Divine Love, Light, and Life[12]—issuing forth from the Central Sun at the heart of our

---

11. The expression "all the stars" has to be modified. Certainly it is true to say that all first generation stars have been born directly from the Galactic Center. However, there are second generation stars which have been born from first generation stars. For these second generation stars, therefore, it is appropriate to say that "by virtue of line of descent" they have been born from the Central Sun—in other words, indirectly (rather than directly).

12. Here, *Divine Love, Light, and Life* has been abbreviated as *"Divine Love"* in the following text.

galaxy and sustaining all 100 billion stars in their orbits. This means that every star in the galaxy, including our Sun, receives from the Central Sun. In turn, from our Sun it is "stepped down" to a level of vibration appropriate for us here on the Earth. Thus, Divine Love—stepped down to an appropriate level—pours through our solar system, emanating from our Sun. Literally, our existence is maintained not only from the Sun, but also, in a larger sense, from the Ultimate Source, the Central Sun.

The Sun moves in a clockwise direction around the Central Sun and the Earth moves in a counter clockwise direction around the Sun. Visualizing the yearly passage of the Earth around the Sun, there is a time each year when the Earth is between our Sun and the Central Sun. At this moment there is an alignment: *Sun–Earth–Central Sun*. Then, visualizing the Earth's passage continuing around the Sun, a new alignment occurs six months later in which, from the Earth, the Sun is seen in conjunction with the Central Sun. At this moment during the cycle of the year there is then a line, or alignment: *Earth–Sun–Central Sun*. At the present time in the twenty-first century, this alignment happens every year around December 18/19. Visualizing the Earth continuing to progress around the Sun, it returns again a further six months later to its position between the Sun and the Central Sun: *Sun–Earth–Central Sun*. This cosmic alignment happens six months later, because the Earth takes one year to go around the Sun, and between the two forms of alignment the Earth makes half a circuit around the Sun during which half a year elapses. At the present time, the cosmic alignment of the Earth between the Sun and the Central Sun happens every year around June 18/19 (six months after December 18/19). It was extraordinary to discover that this galactic alignment (*Sun–Earth–Central Sun*) took place at the historical event of Pentecost. When I discovered this, I realized that it is an important key revealing that Christianity is a cosmic religion. The event of Pentecost was a cosmic event, a galactic alignment of the Earth with the Central Sun at the heart of our galaxy.

It is important to note that in our time the alignment of the Earth between the Central Sun and our Sun takes place June 18/19 each year. However, because of the phenomenon known as the *precession of the equinoxes*, this date changes in the course of the centuries. When we go back to the time of Christ, because of the shift that occurs on account of the precession of the equinoxes, this alignment was on a different date (on May 24, 33 C.E.), which was the historical date of Pentecost. In *Chronicle of the Living Christ* I have written how this date and many other dates in the life of Christ were determined with a very high degree of accuracy.

What took place at that historical event of Pentecost? If we take seriously the words of Christ, "I and the Father are one" (John 10:30), the implication is that Christ was one with the whole galaxy, that his being extended all the way up to the Galactic Center, the Divine Heart at the center of our galaxy. This consideration is supported by the statement made by Rudolf Steiner that every step that Christ took was in harmony with the whole universe:

> In Palestine during the time that Jesus of Nazareth walked on Earth as Jesus Christ—during the three years of His life, from His thirtieth to His thirty-third year—the entire Being of the cosmic Christ was acting uninterruptedly upon Him, and was working into Him. The Christ stood always under the influence of the entire cosmos; He made no step without this working of the cosmic forces into and in Him.... It was always in accordance with the collective Being of the whole universe with whom the Earth is in harmony, that all which Jesus Christ did took place.[13]

Thus, "I and the Father are one" could be formulated in modern language as "I and the collective Being of the whole universe are one." At the time of Rudolf Steiner, during the first quarter of the twentieth century, "the universe" meant "the galaxy." There was no conception at that time,

---

13. Rudolf Steiner, *Spiritual Guidance of the Individual and Humanity* (Anthroposophic Press, 1992), p. 28.

generally speaking, that there were other galaxies beyond our galaxy. Speaking of "the whole universe," Rudolf Steiner's words meant to his audience of that time "the whole Milky Way galaxy." In other words, Christ was connected with the whole Milky Way galaxy with every step he took and, correspondingly, he was inwardly united with the Central Sun, the Divine Heart at the center of our galaxy.

Let us now consider Dante's great vision from his extraordinary poem *The Divine Comedy*. In the last half of *The Divine Comedy*, the part entitled *Paradise*, Dante describes being inwardly transported to the highest realm of existence, which he refers to as the *Empyrean*. In contemplating the image on this page—a depiction of Dante's experience of the Empyrean by Gustav Doré—are we not reminded of the image of our galaxy on page 58?

This portrayal by Doré is of Dante's vision of the snow-white rose in the Empyrean. In the language of the book of Revelation, what is here in the center of this celestial white rose is the *Throne of God*. Around the Throne of God are the angelic beings of the spiritual hierarchies, participating in the work of creation. The whole, in the words of Dante, is shaped in the form of a snow-white rose, which is also an image for Divine Sophia. In the mystical tradition, to which Daniel Andreev's *Rose of the World* is a recent contribution, Sophia is conceived of as being the celestial rose.[14] Sophia embodies the Wisdom ("plan") of creation. Sophia embraces the whole of our galaxy. Like Christ, she is an "offspring" of the Creator, a *God-born* being (rather than a created being like the angelic beings of the spiritual hierarchies). She embodies the plan of creation. Further, in the book of Revelation, Sophia is referred to as the *Bride of the Lamb*. The Lamb is the expression used in the book of Revelation for Christ. Sophia is the Divine Feminine counterpart of Christ. It thus emerges that Christ is a being who—like his

Dante and Beatrice beholding the Empyrean in the form of a snow-white rose. The word Empyrean *derives from the Ancient Greek word* Pyr, *for fire, which reminds us of Daniel Andreev's expression "Astrofire" for the Galactic Center. (Gustave Doré's illustration for Dante's* Divine Comedy: Paradiso.*)*

Divine Feminine counterpart, Sophia—is connected with the whole Milky Way galaxy. Long ago Christ chose to incarnate upon the Earth in the human being Jesus of Nazareth, a process that extended over aeons of time.[15]

From his vantage point in higher realms, the being we call Christ was able to see that humanity was entering a period of darkness, the dark age of Kali Yuga. He came in the middle of this Dark Age in order to bring the light of the Central Sun into the darkness. In the words from the prologue to the Gospel of John: "The light shines in the darkness, and the darkness overcometh it not" (John 1:5).

Christ incarnated to prepare a group of human beings, the twelve disciples, to be able to receive *directly* the Divine Love emanating from the

---

14. Daniel Andreev, *The Rose of the World* (Lindisfarne Books, 1997). See also, Robert Powell & Kevin Dann, *Christ & the Maya Calendar,* chapter 9 and appendix 1.

15. Robert Powell, "Sophia and the Rose of the World," http://sophiafoundation.org/articles.

Central Sun. Exactly this was the event of Pentecost. The work of Christ was to prepare this group of human beings to receive the outpouring of Divine Love from the Central Sun. In the Christian tradition this is depicted as tongues of fire coming down on the heads of the disciples. Through this event the disciples became enlightened and transformed. Christ consciousness was born within them. They received the Holy Spirit, and they were then able to go out and teach and heal in the name of Christ. They became apostles.

The Holy Spirit is nothing other than the continual outpouring of Divine Love from the Central Sun—the pouring out of the fire of Divine Love that underlies all existence and which has brought all things into being. Christ came from the Central Sun and prepared a group of human beings on Earth to be able to receive at Pentecost the outpouring of Divine Love *directly* from the Central Sun, through which they came into Christ consciousness. Let us recall, as indicated above, that Pentecost on May 24, 33 C.E., was a cosmic event at which the alignment *Sun—Earth—Central Sun* took place.

According to Rudolf Steiner, the event of Pentecost, which took place nearly two thousand years ago, is to become a world event. He spoke of this as the coming *World Pentecost*. What does he mean by this? The World Pentecost is an event comparable to Pentecost two thousand years ago. However, it will be a *world event*, not just an event that impacts a relatively small group of people in a particular geographical location. At that time in 33 C.E., it was a matter of many thousands of people, initially the twelve disciples who became apostles, who then went out onto the streets of Jerusalem, to the pool of Bethesda, and baptized three thousand people that day (and thousands more subsequently). In contrast, the World Pentecost will be an event of the outpouring of Divine Love *for the whole of humanity*. Will humanity be sufficiently prepared to receive this? And when is the World Pentecost going to happen? And, further, what might this foretell concerning our primary question regarding the significance of the year 2012?

Let us contemplate once again the movement of our Sun around the Central Sun. From the beginning of Kali Yuga or the Maya calendar, around 5,120 years ago, our Sun entered a part of the galaxy where previously there had been a constellation that had been destroyed long ago. Our Sun thus came into a region of cosmic debris that acted as a shield of cosmic dust, so that our Sun—and consequently the entire solar system—no longer received the full outpouring of the great wave of Divine Love from the Central Sun.

The spiritual beings undergoing their evolution upon our Sun are at such a high level of spirituality that they are still able to focus upon and receive the outpouring of Divine Love from the Central Sun, but this is not the case for most human beings on the Earth, with the exception of a few highly evolved spiritual masters. The Hindu and Maya astronomer/chronologists evidently intuited that this shielding effect impeding the inflow of the great wave of Divine Love from the Central Sun would last for only a limited period of time, as in the analogy used earlier of being out on a walk and experiencing the Sun disappearing behind a cloud, knowing that the Sun will eventually reappear from behind the cloud.

The date that the New Age begins has been a matter of forecasting when the Sun would pass out of the shielding effect of cosmic dust of that long-ago destroyed constellation through which our Sun has been passing for some 5,120 years. Thus, it is a matter of forecasting when our Sun will pass out from this galactic region of cosmic dust and debris to begin to receive again the great wave of Divine Love that is continually proceeding from the Central Sun. The prophecy of the Maya astronomers, who were attuned to the galactic level of existence, is that this will occur around the end of 2012. This is not so far away. According to the astrosophical research presented in this article, we are rapidly approaching the event of a galactic alignment at the winter solstice in 2012 through which humanity as a whole will receive a great wave of Divine Love—and this is precisely the event prophesied by Rudolf Steiner as the *World Pentecost*. Whether this event will occur exactly when the galactic alignment occurs on December 21, 2012, or whether it takes place at some later point in time, it is important that we consciously prepare for it.

In using the expression *galactic alignment* in relation to the year 2012, it has to be clarified that this galactic alignment is not with the Central Sun as at the historical event of Pentecost. Rather, it has to do with the Sun at the winter solstice crossing the Galactic Equator during the thirty-six-year period from 1980 to 2016, as discussed in *Christ & the Maya Calendar*, where the expression "2012 Window" is used to denote this thirty-six-year period. In an earlier article in this issue of the *Journal for Star Wisdom*, "Sun on the Galactic Center" by David Tresemer, it is pointed out that the galactic alignment of the winter solstice Sun with the Galactic Center will not take place until about the year 2230, which raises the question whether *this* will be the time of the World Pentecost rather than 2012? In the voluminous literature concerning the date of the end of the Maya calendar, 2012 is well known as falling within the period 1980 to 2016 of the galactic alignment of the winter solstice Sun with the Galactic Equator. The new perspective offered in this article is that—if this date intuited by the Maya truly does denote the *real* start of the New Age—2012 marks the end of the (approximately) 5,120-year period of the Sun's passage through the local galactic region of cosmic dust and debris obscuring our solar system from the Central Sun and that the exit of our Sun from this dust-filled local galactic region signifies the (re-)opening to the great wave of Divine Love proceeding from the Central Sun *and that this is the World Pentecost.*

Obviously, it is important that as many people as possible know about this approaching event. For we can only receive the benefits of the great wave of Divine Love if we know about it and prepare for it; otherwise it is possible that we might experience it as a kind of scourging. How may this be understood?

There is a grand and magnificent painting by Michelangelo in the Sistine Chapel in Rome, *The Last Judgment*. There in the middle of this picture one sees Christ together with the Virgin Mary, surrounded by the apostles. One also sees on one side souls descending, fleeing away from Christ. These are referred to as *the souls of the damned*. On the other side one sees souls ascending; these souls, who are being drawn toward Christ, are called *the souls of the blessed*. This great work of art portrays the two possible ways of encountering the approaching great wave of Divine Love. In other words, the coming World Pentecost can be experienced either as a tremendous blessing or as a scourging. It will be experienced as a scourging if the presence of Divine Love calls forth shame for all of the negative things one has ever done, calling forth shame to such a degree that one is overwhelmed and one's inner response is to flee the World Conscience, who is Christ. Potentially, therefore, shame can cause one to become overwhelmed to such a degree that it results in the impulse to flee. Therefore, in order to prepare for the World Pentecost, to be prepared to receive the powerful incoming wave of Divine Love, one needs to come to terms with one's *shadow side*, so that one is not overwhelmed by one's *lower nature* when it is exposed to the light of the World Conscience (Christ). A further important point in contemplating Michelangelo's great work of art is that Christ does not at all appear in a judgmental mode at the center of the painting. He appears in a blessing way. Nevertheless, judgment takes place *simply by virtue of Christ's presence*. The souls of the damned flee because their conscience shrinks in the face of the World Conscience (Christ), whereas the souls of the blessed, having attained a certain degree of expiation through raising the content of the subconscious into consciousness and thus purifying their lower nature, are attracted irresistibly toward the World Conscience.

Expressed in a positive way, we have to raise our level of vibration in order to come into and receive the approaching wave of Divine Love. Let us remember that this is an event that is happening on a global scale. Throughout the whole world human beings have to come to terms with the shadow, the lower side of human nature, and at least *begin* to work upon transforming the negative into something positive; hence the importance of knowing the deeper level of significance of the year 2012. This also helps us to understand why some people write of 2012 as a kind of "stepping into paradise," because in a certain respect—at least, potentially—this is true. It also helps us understand why others write of tremendous catastrophes associated with the end date of the Maya calendar in 2012, which could also be true if humanity does not prepare to receive the great wave of Divine Love, preparation for which entails undergoing purification. Purification can be undertaken voluntarily. On the other hand, catastrophe brings with it the necessity of new orientation and, correspondingly, purification.

To summarize: the work of Christ in returning in an ethereal form in the twentieth century has been—and continues to be—to prepare *humanity as a whole* to receive and come into harmony with and unite with the approaching great wave of Divine Love from the Central Sun—the event described by Rudolf Steiner as *World Pentecost*, a galactic alignment, just as Pentecost in 33 C.E. was an alignment with the Central Sun at the heart of our galaxy. Rudolf Steiner's life was dedicated to preparing humanity for the awakening of Christ consciousness in order that as many human beings as possible are able to experience the World Pentecost positively. As Christ was descending from above in ethereal form to enter into the Earth's etheric aura in 1933, Rudolf Steiner was striving on an ascending path to meet with Christ descending from the cosmos.[16] In Rudolf Steiner's biography, toward the end of his life, a very significant event took place through which Christ's path of descent met with Rudolf Steiner's ascending path so that he was able to receive directly from the Etheric Christ. Through this encounter, which took place at Christmas 1923, Christ imparted to Rudolf Steiner a *direct transmission (infusion)* though which he was imbued with a cosmic impulse from the Etheric Christ. The nature of that impulse is best characterized by the words *Divine Love*. As a result of this encounter, through Rudolf Steiner the Etheric Christ gave to humanity a meditation—the Foundation Stone Meditation—in which is encapsulated that which is called the *Foundation Stone of Love*, and through this meditation it is possible to enter into the impulse of Divine Love which is an expression of the *direct presence* of the Etheric Christ in our time. This came through Rudolf Steiner *for the whole of humanity* and is something of extraordinary significance! Working with the Foundation Stone of Love helps one to enter into the right level of vibration to be able to receive the great wave of Divine Love that is coming at the World Pentecost.[17]

There are many other aspects relating to the present time that are discussed in the book *Christ & the Maya Calendar*. One important aspect concerns the forces of darkness opposing the coming of Christ. Because of the approaching World Pentecost, the forces of darkness know that they do not have much time to accomplish their agenda, which is to take over the world, including humanity and the whole of nature. There are all kinds of phenomena in the present world that are working upon the consciousness of human beings in a negative way. Whereas Christ respects individual human freedom, these opposing forces *do not,* and they work not only upon adults, who are at least capable of freedom of choice through exercising their free will (based upon a conscious understanding of what is entailed in making a choice),

---

16. The year 1899 denotes the dawn of the New Age, the beginning of the return of Christ into the Earth's etheric aura, a process which took thirty-three and one-third years to complete, on January 8, 1933, thirty-three and one-third years being the length of Christ's life. As described later in this article, some twenty-four years into this period (on December 25, 1923), a most significant occurrence within this process took place, corresponding to the *baptism* in relation to the Etheric Christ. This baptismal event at Christmas 1923 is evident when it is cognized that Rudolf Steiner stood in relation to the Etheric Christ, preparing the way for him, in a way analogous to that of John the Baptist who prepared the way for the coming of Christ into a physical body at the baptism in the River Jordan.

17. Lacquanna Paul & Robert Powell, *The Foundation Stone Meditation in the Sacred Dance of Eurythmy* (Sophia Foundation of North America, 2007).

but also upon children and young people in all kinds of ways.

In particular, the opposing forces work through certain aspects of modern technology. There are all kinds of ways in which a young person's consciousness is captured by modern technology. It is not unusual to find thirteen-year olds who return home from school and go to their bedrooms, which are equipped with their own television sets and computers, not to mention omnipresent mobile phones, and in the privacy of the bedroom enter a virtual world largely cut off from the rest of the family. Moreover, increasingly sophisticated technologies are being developed to seduce the consciousness of young people, who in former times would play in nature or with friends, and who would often have something of an inner religious life, including prayer and even meditation. It used to be natural for a child between the age of seven and fourteen to come into some form of religious consciousness—turning toward the angels or toward God. Nowadays, there is hardly a possibility of turning toward the angels, because the mobile phone is in use or because of some other technological distraction, preventing the interior dialogue that forms the foundation for suprasensory experience. How can young people receive communications from their guardian angel when they are constantly bombarded by technology? *This is an enormous challenge in our time.* This is not to say we should not use technology, because it is undoubtedly very useful on a practical level. However, we have to be aware of the negative impact of technology, and how *this negative impact is affecting precisely the part of us we call the life body or the etheric body through which we are able to connect with Christ!*

As a remedy to this attempt by the forces of darkness to penetrate and harden our etheric bodies, endeavoring to cut us off from Christ and attempting to prevent us from being open and receptive to the gift of Divine Love, we need to strengthen our etheric body and open ourselves to the meeting with Christ, whose being *is* Divine Love and who is seeking, above all, *to unite with human beings*. However, it is important that we turn to him *in freedom*, and open ourselves to him whose being is *unfathomable mercy*. It is Rudolf Steiner's great gift to humanity to have brought into existence a new form of sacred movement, eurythmy, which strengthens the etheric body and prepares us for union with the being of Christ in his ethereal form at the present time, as the bearer of Divine Love and unfathomable mercy and compassion. Eurythmy is by no means the only way, yet it is one of the ways offering a path leading to what is needed as a preparation for the approaching great wave of Divine Love.

Whether or not the onset of the great wave of Divine Love will be around December 21, 2012 remains to be seen. Apart from the Maya calendar, there are other prophecies that point to this time period as a time of transition.[18] In the last analysis, however, it is difficult to pinpoint with any degree of accuracy the exact time when our solar system will exit the region of cosmic dust and debris in this local part of the galaxy which our Sun—on its path around the Central Sun—has been traversing now for some 5,120 years. However, that the World Pentecost will come, of this we can be sure. And it is essentially and intrinsically an *inner event* for which inner preparation is required.

In light of the foregoing, it emerges that Christ's incarnation some two thousand years ago is now being replicated, but on a different level. Two thousand years ago the events surrounding Christ's coming unfolded on the physical level in the region of Palestine, whereas now they are taking place on a global level, impacting the whole world. And now the time-scale is different, extending over a much longer period of time than the three and a half years of Christ's ministry. Rudolf Steiner's Christ experience in 1899, denoting the commencement of his mission to proclaim the coming of the Etheric Christ, can be likened to the beginning of John the Baptist's mission in 29 C.E. The flow of the baptismal waters of Rudolf Steiner's proclamation to his followers culminated in their participation in the profound baptismal event of the Christmas Foundation Meeting—the

---

18. Robert Powell & Kevin Dann, *Christ & the Maya Calendar*, chapter 10.

giving of the Foundation Stone Meditation on December 25, 1923. Even the time at which the Foundation Stone Meditation was first spoken (10 a.m.) coincides with the time (10 a.m.) of the baptism of Jesus in the River Jordan on September 23, 29 C.E.[19] As Rudolf Steiner indicated, he heard the words of the Foundation Stone Meditation from the World Logos (Christ). Just as the Logos descended to unite with the physical vessel provided by Jesus of Nazareth at the baptism in the Jordan, so the Etheric Christ descended to unite with the vessel created by the assembled people at the Christmas Foundation Meeting and spoke to those gathered there through the words of the Foundation Stone Meditation spoken by Rudolf Steiner.

Through bringing down the Foundation Stone of Love from cosmic heights—in the shape of a dodecahedron (this being the form, visible in the etheric realm, of the "Grail stone")—the Etheric Christ began his work of preparing humanity for the World Pentecost, just as two thousand years ago Christ during the three and a half years of his ministry prepared his twelve disciples for the event of Pentecost at the galactic alignment on May 24, 33 C.E. What has not been described in this article, and which will be the subject of a subsequent article, is where the Crucifixion and the Resurrection of the Etheric Christ fit into this discussion. This would lead too far afield, to go into right now. Instead the focus in this article is upon the Etheric Christ's Baptism on December 25, 1923, paralleling the event of the baptism of Jesus in the River Jordan on September 23, 29 C.E., on the one hand, and upon the World Pentecost event—if the Maya prediction is correct, due to commence with the galactic alignment on December 21, 2012—paralleling the historical Pentecost event at the galactic alignment on May 24, 33 C.E. As expressed in the closing words of the Foundation Stone Meditation, words through which the human being turns to the Etheric Christ for his light in one's mind, his love in one's heart, and his goodness in one's will:

> *Divine light,*
> *Christ Sun,*
> *warm through*
> *our hearts,*
> *illumine*
> *our heads*
> *so that what*
> *we would create*
> *from our hearts*
> *and guide from our heads,*
> *in sure willing,*
> *may be good.*

This is the essence of what we need to prepare for the approaching World Pentecost.

---

19. Robert Powell, *Chronicle of the Living Christ: Foundations of Cosmic Christianity*, pp. 37–38.

> *A star is above my head.*
> *Christ speaks from the star:*
> *"Let your soul be borne*
> *Through my strong force.*
> *I am with you.*
> *I am in you.*
> *I am for you.*
> *I am your I."*
> —RUDOLF STEINER

COMMENTARIES AND EPHEMERIDES: JANUARY–DECEMBER 2010

INTRODUCTION TO COMMENTARIES FOR 2010

January through August: by Claudia McLaren Lainson and David Tresemer; September through December: by William Bento; and planetary locations by Sally Nurney. "ASPECTS" indicate the rarer hard aspects (conjunction, opposition, square). For one-degree orbs, aspects for Sun, Venus, and Mars are typically one to three days. For other aspects, the duration is given. References to *Chron.* refer to *Chronicle of the Living Christ* by Robert Powell, and those to *CSC* refer to *Christian Star Calendar* from years past.

To help light-hearted beings enter a deeper embodied connection with these celestial events, we welcome stories, experiences, and feedback to info@StarWisdom.org.

SYMBOLS USED IN CHARTS

	PLANETS		**ZODIACAL SIGNS**		**ASPECTS**
⊕	Earth	♈	Aries (Ram)	☌	Conjunction 0°
☉	Sun	♉	Taurus (Bull)	✱	Sextile 60°
☽	Moon	♊	Gemini (Twins)	□	Square 90°
☿	Mercury	♋	Cancer (Crab)	△	Trine 120°
♀	Venus	♌	Leo (Lion)	☍	Opposition 180°
♂	Mars	♍	Virgo (Virgin)		
♃	Jupiter	♎	Libra (Scales)		
♄	Saturn	♏	Scorpio (Scorpion)		
♅	Uranus	♐	Sagittarius (Archer)		
♆	Neptune	♑	Capricorn (Goat)		
♇	Pluto	♒	Aquarius (Waterman)		
		♓	Pisces (Fishes)		

OTHER

☊	Ascending (North) Node	☉̇	Sun Eclipse
☋	Descending (South) Node	☽̇	Moon Eclipse
P	Perihelion/Perigee	ⁱ☌	Inferior Conjunction
A	Aphelion/Apogee	ˢ☌	Superior Conjunction
ᴺ☐	Maximum Latitude	⚷	Chiron
ˢ☐	Minimum Latitude		

Time[1]

The information relating to daily geocentric and heliocentric planetary positions in the sidereal zodiac is tabulated in the form of an ephemeris for each month, where the planetary positions are given at 0 hours universal time (UT) each day. Beneath the geocentric and heliocentric ephemeris for each month, the information relating to planetary aspects is given in the form of an aspectarian, listing the most important aspects—geocentric and heliocentric/hermetic—between the planets for the month in question. The day and the time of occurrence of the aspect on that day are indicated, all times being given in universal time, which is identical to Greenwich mean time. For example, 0 hours universal time is midnight Greenwich time. This time system applies in Britain; however, when summer time is in use, one hour has to be added to all times.

In other countries, the time has to be adjusted according to whether it is ahead of or behind Britain. For example, in Germany, where the time is one hour ahead of British time, one hour has to be added and, when summer time is in use in Germany, two hours have to be added to all times. On the other hand, in California, where the time is eight hours behind that of London, eight hours have to be subtracted and, for daylight saving time in California, seven hours have to be subtracted from all times.[1] This subtraction will often change the date of an astronomical occurrence, shifting it back one day. On this account, since most of the readers of this calendar live on the American Continent, astronomical occurrences during the early hours of day x are listed as occurring on days x-1/x. For example, an eclipse occurring at 03:00 UT on the 12th is listed as occurring on the 11/12th since in America it takes place on the 11th.

---

1. See *General Introduction to the Christian Star Calendar: A Key to Understanding*, new edition (Palo Alto, CA: Sophia Foundation of North America, 2003) for an in-depth clarification of the features of the calendar in the *Journal for Star Wisdom*, including indications as to how to work with it. Using the calendar in the USA, do the following subtraction from all time indications according to time zone: Pacific time subtract 8 hours (7 hours when daylight saving time is in use); mountain time subtract 7 hours (6 hours when daylight saving time is in use); central time subtract 6 hours (5 hours when daylight saving time is in use); eastern time subtract 5 hours (4 hours when daylight saving time is in use).

JANUARY

We begin our year with the **Sun** in the Archer (Sagittarius), and an inferior conjunction with **Mercury** (retrograde until the 16th) on the 4th. **Mercury** will not be seen until sometime after the 15th, when it will be visible low in the east in the predawn hours. **Venus** is also hidden in the brightness of the Sun's shine this entire month. Not until the end of March will she emerge into view in the western sky at sunset (as the "evening star"). **Jupiter** will be visible at the beginning of the month (next to "invisible" **Neptune**) in the first degrees of Aquarius, to the southwest as the **Sun** sets. On the 18th, expect beauty as the tiniest waxing crescent **Moon** conjoins **Jupiter** in the Waterbearer (Aquarius). As the month unfolds, **Jupiter** will disappear into the Sun's light. The **Sun** moves into the constellation of the Sea Goat (Capricorn) on the 16th.

Mars begins the year retrograde, traveling through the Crab (Cancer) until stationing direct in early March. **Saturn** in Virgo stations Retrograde on the 14th (until going direct 5/31). **Neptune** enters Aquarius on the 10th.

★ ★ ★

1   Sun at 16° Sagittarius: Birth of the Nathan Jesus. The Nathan Jesus sacrificed his physical body that Christ could be born into the Earth on the hill of Golgotha. This being represents the pure, pre-Fall substance of the divine image of humanity. (See *Chron.*, chapter 2) This first day of the year is a good day to focus our attention on all the goodness in the world.

3   Sun at 17° Sagittarius: Conception of the Virgin Mary

14–15   New Moon at 29° Sagittarius: When the Sun was at this place, Jesus summoned Simon for the first time, giving him the new name of Cephas or Peter, The Rock. This was the beginning of the discipleship of this significant individual. One might listen for a higher calling in this New Moon day. Today Pluto crosses 8° 55 Sagittarius. Note that Pluto goes back and forth for the entire year over this important point in the heavens that is the exact location of Pluto at the third temptation of Jesus Christ, wherein he was challenged to turn stones into bread. This is the temptation to ensnare humanity in the netherworld of virtual reality in opposition to the heavenly world spoken into existence by the Word. What bears within it the Word is the true nourishment of humanity. This temptation is very much connected to the economic realm and the destruction of seeds. The fact that this temptation is occurring for the eighth time and is occurring within the historical time of humanity's collective confrontation with this temptation, 1988 to 2018, (according to *The Apocalypse Code* by Robert Powell, *CSC* 2009) gives us the special task of unmasking what things of this world have behind them a ruling will that has not been kindled in our Father's House. This occurs exactly at three dates (mid-January, early July, and mid-November), but never wavers far during the whole year.

21   Sun at 6° Capricorn: When the Sun was at this place Mary Magdalene was initiated into the seven mysteries at her final conversion (Matt. 12:43, *Chron.* 267). This is an imagination for transforming darkness into light. This is one of the stories in "Signature of Jupiter" from this edition of *Journal of Star Wisdom* (through the links found in that article) and shows both Sun and Jupiter influences.

23   Sun at 8°: The event of the wedding of Cana (December 28, 29 C.E.; *Chron.* 213). Christ infused the water with the fire of Divine Love, transforming memory from

SIDEREAL GEOCENTRIC LONGITUDES : JANUARY 2010 Gregorian at 0 hours UT

DAY		☉	☽	☊	☿	♀	♂	♃	♄	♅	♆	♇
1	FR	15 ♐ 34	18 ♊ 22	26 ♐ 12R	24 ♐ 7R	12 ♐ 58	23 ♋ 56R	1 ♒ 29	9 ♍ 38	28 ♒ 13	29 ♑ 42	8 ♐ 26
2	SA	16 35	3 ♋ 27	26 12D	23 2	14 14	23 47	1 41	9 39	28 14	29 44	8 28
3	SU	17 37	18 29	26 13	21 49	15 29	23 36	1 53	9 40	28 16	29 46	8 30
4	MO	18 38	3 ♌ 22	26 13	20 31	16 45	23 25	2 6	9 41	28 17	29 48	8 32
5	TU	19 39	17 58	26 14	19 10	18 0	23 13	2 18	9 42	28 19	29 50	8 34
6	WE	20 40	2 ♍ 13	26 14	17 49	19 16	23 0	2 30	9 43	28 21	29 51	8 36
7	TH	21 41	16 6	26 14	16 31	20 31	22 46	2 43	9 44	28 22	29 53	8 39
8	FR	22 42	29 36	26 14R	15 17	21 47	22 32	2 56	9 45	28 24	29 55	8 41
9	SA	23 43	12 ♎ 45	26 14	14 10	23 2	22 16	3 8	9 45	28 26	29 57	8 43
10	SU	24 45	25 36	26 14	13 12	24 18	22 0	3 21	9 46	28 28	29 59	8 45
11	MO	25 46	8 ♏ 10	26 14	12 23	25 33	21 44	3 34	9 46	28 30	0 ♒ 1	8 47
12	TU	26 47	20 30	26 14D	11 43	26 49	21 26	3 47	9 46	28 32	0 3	8 49
13	WE	27 48	2 ♐ 40	26 14	11 13	28 4	21 8	4 0	9 46	28 34	0 5	8 51
14	TH	28 49	14 41	26 14	10 53	29 20	20 50	4 13	9 46R	28 36	0 7	8 53
15	FR	29 50	26 36	26 14R	10 43	0 ♑ 35	20 30	4 26	9 46	28 38	0 9	8 55
16	SA	0 ♑ 51	8 ♑ 26	26 14	10 41D	1 51	20 10	4 39	9 46	28 40	0 11	8 57
17	SU	1 53	20 14	26 13	10 47	3 6	19 50	4 53	9 46	28 42	0 13	8 59
18	MO	2 54	2 ♒ 2	26 13	11 2	4 21	19 29	5 6	9 45	28 45	0 15	9 1
19	TU	3 55	13 52	26 12	11 23	5 37	19 7	5 19	9 45	28 47	0 17	9 3
20	WE	4 56	25 47	26 10	11 50	6 52	18 45	5 33	9 44	28 49	0 19	9 5
21	TH	5 57	7 ♓ 51	26 9	12 24	8 8	18 23	5 46	9 43	28 52	0 21	9 7
22	FR	6 58	20 7	26 8	13 3	9 23	18 0	6 0	9 43	28 54	0 24	9 9
23	SA	7 59	2 ♈ 39	26 8	13 46	10 39	17 37	6 13	9 42	28 56	0 26	9 11
24	SU	9 0	15 32	26 8D	14 34	11 54	17 14	6 27	9 40	28 59	0 28	9 13
25	MO	10 1	28 48	26 8	15 26	13 9	16 50	6 41	9 39	29 1	0 30	9 15
26	TU	11 2	12 ♉ 30	26 9	16 21	14 25	16 27	6 54	9 38	29 4	0 32	9 17
27	WE	12 3	26 39	26 11	17 19	15 40	16 3	7 8	9 37	29 6	0 34	9 19
28	TH	13 4	11 ♊ 14	26 12	18 21	16 55	15 39	7 22	9 35	29 9	0 37	9 21
29	FR	14 5	26 11	26 12R	19 25	18 11	15 15	7 36	9 34	29 12	0 39	9 23
30	SA	15 6	11 ♋ 22	26 11	20 31	19 26	14 51	7 50	9 32	29 14	0 41	9 25
31	SU	16 7	26 38	26 10	21 40	20 41	14 27	8 4	9 30	29 17	0 43	9 27

INGRESSES :

1	☽ → ♋ 18:31	20	☽ → ♓ 8:24		
3	☽ → ♌ 18:32	22	☽ → ♈ 18:57		
5	☽ → ♍ 20:12	25	☽ → ♉ 2: 8		
8	☽ → ♎ 0:42	27	☽ → ♊ 5:33		
10	☽ → ♏ 8:21	29	☽ → ♋ 6: 3		
	♆ → ♒ 11: 7	31	☽ → ♌ 5:17		
12	☽ → ♐ 18:42				
14	♀ → ♑ 12:51				
15	☉ → ♑ 3:48				
	☽ → ♑ 6:53				
17	☽ → ♒ 19:51				

ASPECTS & ECLIPSES :

1	☽ ☍ ☿ 8:33	11	☉ ☌ ☊ 11: 0		☽ ☌ ♆ 20:22		☉ ☍ ☽ 6:16
	☽ ☌ ☋ 12:28		♀ ☌ ☊ 12:55	18	☽ ☌ ♃ 6:20		☽ ☌ P 9:11
	☽ ☌ P 20:34		☉ s☌ ♀ 21: 4	20	☽ ☌ ♅ 6: 4		☽ ☍ ♀ 13:48
3	☽ ☌ ♂ 8: 6	13	☽ ☌ ♇ 12:21	21	☽ ☍ ♄ 3:40	31	☽ ☍ ♆ 6:26
	☽ ☍ ♆ 18:11		☽ ☌ ☿ 16:33	23	☉ □ ☽ 10:52		☽ ☍ ♃ 18:18
	☽ ☍ ♃ 21:54	14	☽ ☌ ☊ 23:15	27	♀ ☍ ♂ 5:28		♄ □ ♇ 22:29
4	☉ i☌ ☿ 19: 5	15	☉ ● A 7: 6		☽ ☍ ♇ 20:55		
5	☿ ☌ ♀ 10:38		☉ ☌ ☽ 7:10	28	☽ ☍ ☿ 12:20		
	☽ ☍ ♅ 17:23		☽ ☌ ♀ 9: 1	29	☽ ☌ ☋ 0: 1		
6	☽ ☌ ♄ 12:53	16	☽ ☍ ♂ 23:11		☉ ☍ ♂ 19:42		
7	☉ □ ☽ 10:38	17	☽ ☌ A 1:55	30	☽ ☌ ♂ 5:19		

SIDEREAL HELIOCENTRIC LONGITUDES : JANUARY 2010 Gregorian at 0 hours UT

DAY		Sid. Time	☿	♀	⊕	♂	♃	♄	♅	♆	♇	Vernal Point
1	FR	6:42: 9	25 ♉ 42	9 ♐ 27	15 ♊ 34	1 ♋ 54	9 ♒ 36	3 ♍ 42	0 ♓ 53	1 ♒ 1	8 ♐ 12	5 ♓ 7'14"
2	SA	6:46: 6	2 ♊ 1	11 2	16 36	2 22	9 41	3 44	0 54	1 1	8 13	5 ♓ 7'14"
3	SU	6:50: 2	8 18	12 37	17 37	2 49	9 46	3 46	0 54	1 2	8 13	5 ♓ 7'14"
4	MO	6:53:59	14 32	14 12	18 38	3 16	9 52	3 48	0 55	1 2	8 13	5 ♓ 7'13"
5	TU	6:57:55	20 42	15 47	19 39	3 44	9 57	3 50	0 56	1 2	8 14	5 ♓ 7'13"
6	WE	7: 1:52	26 45	17 22	20 40	4 11	10 3	3 52	0 56	1 3	8 14	5 ♓ 7'13"
7	TH	7: 5:48	2 ♋ 42	18 57	21 41	4 38	10 8	3 54	0 57	1 3	8 14	5 ♓ 7'13"
8	FR	7: 9:45	8 31	20 32	22 42	5 6	10 13	3 56	0 57	1 3	8 15	5 ♓ 7'13"
9	SA	7:13:41	14 11	22 6	23 44	5 33	10 19	3 58	0 58	1 4	8 15	5 ♓ 7'13"
10	SU	7:17:38	19 42	23 41	24 45	6 0	10 24	4 0	0 59	1 4	8 15	5 ♓ 7'13"
11	MO	7:21:35	25 3	25 16	25 46	6 27	10 30	4 2	0 59	1 4	8 16	5 ♓ 7'13"
12	TU	7:25:31	0 ♌ 15	26 51	26 47	6 54	10 35	4 4	1 0	1 5	8 16	5 ♓ 7'12"
13	WE	7:29:28	5 18	28 26	27 48	7 22	10 40	4 6	1 1	1 5	8 17	5 ♓ 7'12"
14	TH	7:33:24	10 10	0 ♑ 1	28 49	7 49	10 46	4 8	1 1	1 6	8 17	5 ♓ 7'12"
15	FR	7:37:21	14 54	1 36	29 50	8 16	10 51	4 10	1 2	1 6	8 17	5 ♓ 7'12"
16	SA	7:41:17	19 28	3 10	0 ♋ 52	8 43	10 56	4 12	1 3	1 6	8 18	5 ♓ 7'12"
17	SU	7:45:14	23 53	4 45	1 53	9 10	11 2	4 14	1 3	1 7	8 18	5 ♓ 7'12"
18	MO	7:49:10	28 10	6 20	2 54	9 37	11 7	4 16	1 4	1 7	8 18	5 ♓ 7'12"
19	TU	7:53: 7	2 ♍ 19	7 55	3 55	10 4	11 13	4 18	1 5	1 7	8 19	5 ♓ 7'11"
20	WE	7:57: 4	6 20	9 30	4 56	10 31	11 18	4 20	1 5	1 8	8 19	5 ♓ 7'11"
21	TH	8: 1: 0	10 15	11 5	5 57	10 58	11 23	4 22	1 6	1 8	8 19	5 ♓ 7'11"
22	FR	8: 4:57	14 2	12 40	6 58	11 25	11 29	4 24	1 6	1 8	8 20	5 ♓ 7'11"
23	SA	8: 8:53	17 43	14 14	7 59	11 52	11 34	4 26	1 7	1 9	8 20	5 ♓ 7'11"
24	SU	8:12:50	21 19	15 49	9 0	12 19	11 40	4 28	1 8	1 9	8 20	5 ♓ 7'11"
25	MO	8:16:46	24 49	17 24	10 1	12 45	11 45	4 30	1 8	1 9	8 21	5 ♓ 7'11"
26	TU	8:20:43	28 13	18 59	11 2	13 12	11 50	4 32	1 9	1 10	8 21	5 ♓ 7'10"
27	WE	8:24:39	1 ♎ 34	20 34	12 3	13 39	11 56	4 34	1 10	1 10	8 21	5 ♓ 7'10"
28	TH	8:28:36	4 49	22 9	13 4	14 6	12 1	4 36	1 10	1 11	8 22	5 ♓ 7'10"
29	FR	8:32:33	8 1	23 44	14 5	14 33	12 7	4 38	1 11	1 11	8 22	5 ♓ 7'10"
30	SA	8:36:29	11 9	25 19	15 6	15 0	12 12	4 40	1 12	1 11	8 22	5 ♓ 7'10"
31	SU	8:40:26	14 14	26 54	16 7	15 26	12 17	4 42	1 12	1 12	8 23	5 ♓ 7'10"

INGRESSES :

1	☿ → ♊ 16:20
6	☿ → ♋ 13: 2
11	☿ → ♌ 22:48
13	♀ → ♑ 23:48
15	⊕ → ♋ 3:46
18	☿ → ♍ 10:30
26	☿ → ♎ 12:43

ASPECTS (HELIOCENTRIC +MOON(TYCHONIC)) :

1	♀ ✶ ♃ 2:15		☿ ☌ ⊕ 19: 5		☿ △ ♇ 14:36		☿ ☌ ♄ 11:51	27	☽ ☍ ♇ 19:18
	☿ □ ♅ 19:44	5	♂ ✶ ♄ 5:38	14	☿ ☍ ♃ 3: 1		☿ ✶ ⊕ 12:38	29	☿ ✶ ♇ 2:39
	☿ △ ♆ 20:13		☽ ☍ ♅ 21:48		♀ ✶ ♅ 15:26	20	☽ ☌ ♅ 10:35		⊕ ☌ ♂ 19:30
	☽ ☌ ♂ 22:13	6	☽ ☌ ♄ 2:48	15	☽ ☌ ♀ 11:40		☿ □ ♇ 12: 4	30	☽ ☌ ♂ 5:51
2	☿ □ ♄ 6:33		☿ △ ♅ 16:52	16	☽ ☍ ♂ 0:35		☽ ☍ ♄ 17: 5		☿ △ ♃ 8:21
	☿ ☍ ♇ 23:40	7	☿ ✶ ♄ 4:55		⊕ △ ♅ 4:24		♀ ☍ ♂ 21:35	31	☽ ☍ ♀ 0:26
3	☿ △ ♃ 5:43		☿ ☌ ♂ 8:37		♀ △ ♄ 15:55	21	☿ ✶ ♂ 5: 6		☽ ☍ ♆ 7:10
	⊕ ☌ P 14:34	10	☿ N ☊ 17:16	17	☽ ☌ ♆ 22: 8		☽ ☍ ☿ 6:51		☿ □ ♂ 11: 8
	☽ ☍ ♆ 20:12	11	♀ ☍ ⊕ 21: 4	18	☿ ☍ ♅ 16:43		☿ △ ♀ 8:55		☿ □ ⊕ 22:24
	☿ ☍ ♀ 22:15	12	☿ ☍ ♆ 3:53		☽ ☌ ♃ 18:34	24	♀ ☌ A 15:13		
4	☽ ☍ ♃ 10:41	13	☽ ☌ ♇ 11:10	19	⊕ ✶ ♄ 9:27	26	☿ △ ♆ 21:10		

the horizontal to the vertical and thereby weaving together spiritual communities born of the Holy Spirit rather than hereditary forces in the blood. This was the beginning of an awakening into relationships on a completely new level. This event is further empowered by the Full Moon at this location on July 25.

29–30 Full Moon, Sun at 15° Capricorn, Moon at 15° Cancer: The Sun was here at the death of John the Baptist, when the Queen, Herodias, tried to silence him, after a night of revelry in the castle at Machaerus. A powerful lesson stands in this event: "If one does not keep alert, the powers of evil will always find a way to gain entrance. They seek continually for the weakest point, the point of attack. But if one remains alert and takes care, the powers of evil are unable to enter" (Robert Powell, *Christian Hermetic Astrology*, pg 82). John's sacrifice helped to work against forces of evil and his spiritual presence over-lighting the disciples offered a protective power inspiring them through their mission. This Moon calls us to touch into the presence of spiritual help surrounding us.

ASPECT: Sun (15° Capricorn) opposed Mars (15° Cancer), thus Mars conjunct the Moon. The words we speak defile or ennoble our true self. In Jesus' life, the aspect Sun opposed Mars occurred: 1) on November 24, 30 C.E., when a madman was shouting in the temple; then Jesus said, "Silence!," and the man spoke no more, 2) on November 23, 30 C.E., when the press of the crowd was so great that Jesus could not deliver his words, 3) on June 5, 32 C.E., when messengers came to deliver an appeal to Jesus that he urgently attend the dying Lazarus, and 4) on January 14, 33 C.E., when Jesus instructed the youths who had accompanied him in the desert for some months to be completely silent about what had happened. What opposes or empowers our speaking and what seeks silence?

O Spirit of God…
Fill the hearts that seek Thee,
Seek Thee in deep longing,
Deep longing for health
For health and strong courage,
Strong courage that flows within our limbs,
Flows as a precious divine gift,
Divine gift from Thee,
O Spirit of God.

—RUDOLF STEINER

FEBRUARY

Mars is visible in the eastern sky after sunset, beginning in the "beehive" of Cancer (about 12°) and moving retrograde. **Mercury** can be seen in predawn light, but fades from view by midmonth. **Jupiter** stands before the Royal Star of Fomalhaut (9° Aquarius), the Watcher to the South from the 4th to 8th. The **Sun** moves into Aquarius on the 13th and will catch up with **Jupiter** mid Aquarius on the 28th.

Uranus (with the **Moon** as companion) ingresses into the Fishes (Pisces) on the 14th.

★ ★ ★

2   Sun at 18° Capricorn. Saturn stood at 18° Cancer, directly opposite the Sun today, during the night in Gethsemane where Christ sweated tears of blood. Satan was attacking the very self of Christ with the intention to create doubt. With the Sun in Capricorn we can face doubt with courage. Courage sees through doubt to the redemptive power shining in the awakening of conscience that it seeks to draw forth.

8–9 ASPECT: Venus conjunct Neptune (at 1° Aquarius). This is one of the markers of the end of the forty-day temptations, when angels ministered to Jesus (at 22° Capricorn). Another signature of a Venus conjunct Neptune was the Baptism in the Jordan (conception of Christ) where Venus and Neptune were in hermetic (viewed from the Sun) conjunction and three months later at the Wedding of Cana (See January 23) where Venus and Neptune were together in Capricorn from the earthly perspective (viewed from the Earth/geocentric). The spiritual deed of the baptism hermetically proclaimed what was geocentrically realized at the start of his ministry in Cana: Communion between inspirations from spirit realms coming into communities born of love on Earth.

13–14 New Moon at 1° Waterbearer (Aquarius). The Sun stood here when Jesus healed the paralyzed man (John 5:1–9) who had sat by the healing pool of Bethesda for thirty-eight years (January 19, 31 C.E.; *Chron.* 273). Near the man was the pool that, when its surface was stirred by springs welling up from below, had the capacity to heal the one who entered it first. The man had tried for thirty-eight years to be helped into the pool but, as he had been driven by passions in his past incarnation, ignoring both angels and fellow human beings, so now was he ignored by the angel in the pool and those around him. Jesus entered by a rear door to this place, and healed this particular man in a room full of those awaiting healing. Why him? We may ask for healing if we are willing to receive the healing waters of this Moon.

ASPECT: On this day Sun conjunct Neptune (1° Aquarius), an image of the self receiving spiritual inspirations or falling into 'dead' habits dragged from the past that whisper illusions.

25 Sun at 10½° Aquarius: Feeding of the 5000 and the Walking on Water (John 6:1–21), aligned with the super-mega star Deneb. After teaching the Beatitudes and the Lord's Prayer, Christ miraculously feeds 5,000 with five loaves of bread and two fish. The heart of Christ opens in communion to the beings within the twelve constellations of the zodiac encircling space. and his disciples bear witness to his spiritual Kingship. In the Walking on Water, which followed later that evening, we see the night experience of this day as Christ approaches the disciples, walking on water, and bestows the moral impression into their etheric

SIDEREAL GEOCENTRIC LONGITUDES : FEBRUARY 2010 Gregorian at 0 hours UT

DAY	☉	☽	☊	☿	♀	♂	♃	♄	♅	♆	♇
1 MO	17 ♑ 8	11 ♌ 49	26 ♐ 8R	22 ♐ 50	21 ♑ 57	14 ♋ 3R	8 ♒ 18	9 ♍ 28R	29 ♒ 20	0 ♒ 45	9 ♐ 28
2 TU	18 9	26 46	26 5	24 2	23 12	13 39	8 32	9 26	29 22	0 48	9 30
3 WE	19 9	11 ♍ 20	26 2	25 17	24 27	13 15	8 46	9 24	29 25	0 50	9 32
4 TH	20 10	25 27	25 59	26 32	25 42	12 52	9 0	9 22	29 28	0 52	9 34
5 FR	21 11	9 ♎ 6	25 57	27 50	26 58	12 29	9 14	9 20	29 31	0 54	9 36
6 SA	22 12	22 18	25 57	29 8	28 13	12 6	9 28	9 17	29 34	0 57	9 37
7 SU	23 13	5 ♏ 6	25 57D	0 ♑ 28	29 28	11 44	9 42	9 15	29 37	0 59	9 39
8 MO	24 13	17 33	25 59	1 49	0 ♒ 43	11 22	9 57	9 12	29 40	1 1	9 41
9 TU	25 14	29 45	26 0	3 12	1 59	11 0	10 11	9 10	29 43	1 3	9 42
10 WE	26 15	11 ♐ 45	26 2	4 35	3 14	10 39	10 25	9 7	29 45	1 6	9 44
11 TH	27 16	23 37	26 3	6 0	4 29	10 18	10 39	9 4	29 48	1 8	9 46
12 FR	28 16	5 ♑ 25	26 2R	7 26	5 44	9 58	10 54	9 1	29 52	1 10	9 47
13 SA	29 17	17 13	26 0	8 52	6 59	9 38	11 8	8 58	29 55	1 13	9 49
14 SU	0 ♒ 18	29 1	25 56	10 20	8 15	9 19	11 22	8 55	29 58	1 15	9 50
15 MO	1 18	10 ♒ 53	25 51	11 49	9 30	9 1	11 37	8 52	0 ♓ 1	1 17	9 52
16 TU	2 19	22 49	25 44	13 18	10 45	8 43	11 51	8 49	0 4	1 19	9 53
17 WE	3 20	4 ♓ 52	25 37	14 49	12 0	8 26	12 6	8 45	0 7	1 22	9 55
18 TH	4 20	17 4	25 30	16 20	13 15	8 10	12 20	8 42	0 10	1 24	9 56
19 FR	5 21	29 26	25 24	17 53	14 30	7 54	12 34	8 38	0 13	1 26	9 58
20 SA	6 21	12 ♈ 1	25 19	19 26	15 45	7 40	12 49	8 35	0 16	1 28	9 59
21 SU	7 22	24 52	25 17	21 0	17 0	7 25	13 3	8 31	0 20	1 31	10 0
22 MO	8 22	8 ♉ 1	25 16	22 36	18 15	7 12	13 18	8 27	0 23	1 33	10 2
23 TU	9 23	21 32	25 16D	24 12	19 30	7 0	13 32	8 24	0 26	1 35	10 3
24 WE	10 23	5 ♊ 26	25 18	25 49	20 45	6 48	13 47	8 20	0 29	1 38	10 4
25 TH	11 23	19 44	25 19	27 27	22 0	6 37	14 1	8 16	0 33	1 40	10 6
26 FR	12 24	4 ♋ 25	25 18R	29 6	23 15	6 27	14 16	8 12	0 36	1 42	10 7
27 SA	13 24	19 24	25 16	0 ♒ 46	24 30	6 17	14 30	8 8	0 39	1 44	10 8
28 SU	14 24	4 ♌ 34	25 11	2 27	25 45	6 8	14 45	8 4	0 43	1 47	10 9

INGRESSES :

2	☽ → ♍	5:16	19	☽ → ♈	1: 5
4	☽ → ♎	7:54	21	☽ → ♉	9:27
6	☽ → ♏	14:21	23	☽ → ♊	14:42
	☿ → ♑	15:35	25	☽ → ♋	16:49
7	♀ → ♒	10: 8	26	☿ → ♒	12:55
9	☽ → ♐	0:30	27	☽ → ♌	16:46
11	☽ → ♑	12:57			
13	☉ → ♒	16:57			
14	☽ → ♒	1:59			
	♅ → ♓	18:25			
16	☽ → ♓	14:19			

ASPECTS & ECLIPSES :

2	☽ ☍ ♅	4:15	14	☉ ☌ ☽	2:50	26	☽ ☌ ♂	3:13
	☽ ☌ ♄	20:47		☽ ☌ ♆	4:32	27	☿ ☌ ♆	14: 6
3	☿ ☌ ☊	13:47		☽ ☌ ♀	20:53		☽ ☍ ♆	19:34
5	☉ □ ☽	23:47		☉ ☌ ♆	23:25		☽ ☍ ☿	20:14
8	♀ ☌ ♆	5:48	15	☽ ☌ ♃	1:30		☽ ☌ P	21:45
9	☽ ☌ ♇	19:56	16	☽ ☌ ♅	14:31	28	☉ ☌ ♃	10:43
11	☽ ☌ ☊	4:56	17	♀ ☌ ♃	2:13		☽ ☍ ♃	16:19
12	☽ ☌ ☿	4:38		☽ ☍ ♄	7:38		☉ ☍ ☽	16:37
	☽ ☍ ♂	9: 0	22	☉ □ ☽	0:41			
13	☽ ☌ A	2:11	24	☽ ☍ ♇	7:52			
	☿ ☍ ♂	10:24	25	☽ ☌ ☋	9:10			

SIDEREAL HELIOCENTRIC LONGITUDES : FEBRUARY 2010 Gregorian at 0 hours UT

DAY	Sid. Time	☿	♀	⊕	♂	♃	♄	♅	♆	♇	Vernal Point
1 MO	8:44:22	17 ♎ 16	28 ♑ 29	17 ♋ 8	15 ♋ 53	12 ♒ 23	4 ♍ 44	1 ♓ 13	1 ♒ 12	8 ♐ 23	5 ♓ 7'10"
2 TU	8:48:19	20 15	0 ♒ 4	18 9	16 20	12 28	4 47	1 14	1 12	8 23	5 ♓ 7'10"
3 WE	8:52:15	23 11	1 39	19 9	16 46	12 34	4 49	1 14	1 13	8 24	5 ♓ 7' 9"
4 TH	8:56:12	26 5	3 14	20 10	17 13	12 39	4 51	1 15	1 13	8 24	5 ♓ 7' 9"
5 FR	9: 0: 8	28 58	4 49	21 11	17 40	12 44	4 53	1 15	1 13	8 24	5 ♓ 7' 9"
6 SA	9: 4: 5	1 ♏ 48	6 24	22 12	18 6	12 50	4 55	1 16	1 14	8 25	5 ♓ 7' 9"
7 SU	9: 8: 2	4 37	7 59	23 13	18 33	12 55	4 57	1 17	1 14	8 25	5 ♓ 7' 9"
8 MO	9:11:58	7 25	9 34	24 14	19 0	13 1	4 59	1 17	1 15	8 25	5 ♓ 7' 9"
9 TU	9:15:55	10 12	11 9	25 14	19 26	13 6	5 1	1 18	1 15	8 26	5 ♓ 7' 9"
10 WE	9:19:51	12 58	12 44	26 15	19 53	13 11	5 3	1 19	1 15	8 26	5 ♓ 7' 8"
11 TH	9:23:48	15 43	14 19	27 16	20 19	13 17	5 5	1 19	1 16	8 26	5 ♓ 7' 8"
12 FR	9:27:44	18 28	15 54	28 17	20 46	13 22	5 7	1 20	1 16	8 27	5 ♓ 7' 8"
13 SA	9:31:41	21 12	17 30	29 17	21 13	13 28	5 9	1 21	1 16	8 27	5 ♓ 7' 8"
14 SU	9:35:37	23 57	19 5	0 ♌ 18	21 39	13 33	5 11	1 21	1 17	8 28	5 ♓ 7' 8"
15 MO	9:39:34	26 42	20 40	1 19	22 6	13 38	5 13	1 22	1 17	8 28	5 ♓ 7' 8"
16 TU	9:43:31	29 27	22 15	2 19	22 32	13 44	5 15	1 23	1 17	8 28	5 ♓ 7' 8"
17 WE	9:47:27	2 ♐ 13	23 50	3 20	22 59	13 49	5 17	1 23	1 18	8 29	5 ♓ 7' 7"
18 TH	9:51:24	5 0	25 26	4 20	23 25	13 55	5 19	1 24	1 18	8 29	5 ♓ 7' 7"
19 FR	9:55:20	7 47	27 1	5 21	23 51	14 0	5 21	1 24	1 19	8 29	5 ♓ 7' 7"
20 SA	9:59:17	10 36	28 36	6 21	24 18	14 6	5 23	1 25	1 19	8 30	5 ♓ 7' 7"
21 SU	10: 3:13	13 27	0 ♓ 12	7 22	24 44	14 11	5 25	1 26	1 19	8 30	5 ♓ 7' 7"
22 MO	10: 7:10	16 19	1 47	8 22	25 11	14 16	5 27	1 26	1 20	8 30	5 ♓ 7' 7"
23 TU	10:11: 6	19 13	3 22	9 23	25 37	14 22	5 29	1 27	1 20	8 31	5 ♓ 7' 7"
24 WE	10:15: 3	22 9	4 58	10 23	26 4	14 27	5 31	1 28	1 20	8 31	5 ♓ 7' 6"
25 TH	10:19: 0	25 8	6 33	11 23	26 30	14 33	5 33	1 28	1 21	8 31	5 ♓ 7' 6"
26 FR	10:22:56	28 9	8 9	12 24	26 56	14 38	5 35	1 29	1 21	8 32	5 ♓ 7' 6"
27 SA	10:26:53	1 ♑ 13	9 44	13 24	27 23	14 43	5 37	1 30	1 21	8 32	5 ♓ 7' 6"
28 SU	10:30:49	4 20	11 20	14 24	27 49	14 49	5 39	1 30	1 22	8 32	5 ♓ 7' 6"

INGRESSES :

1	♀ → ♒	23: 4
5	☿ → ♏	8:45
13	⊕ → ♌	16:55
16	☿ → ♐	4:45
20	♀ → ♓	21: 4
26	☿ → ♑	14:33

ASPECTS (HELIOCENTRIC +MOON(TYCHONIC)) :

1	☽ ☍ ♃	0:53		☿ □ ♀	19:25	16	☿ ⚹ ♆	16: 0	24	☽ ☍ ♇	5:13
2	☽ ☍ ♅	7:17	10	☿ □ ♃	2: 5		☿ □ ♅	16:46		♀ ☍ ♄	8:33
	☽ ☌ ♄	13: 8		♀ ☌ ♃	7:19		☽ ☌ ♅	17: 4	25	☽ ☍ ☿	11: 9
	♀ ☌ ♆	17:25	13	☿ △ ♂	0: 2	17	☽ ☍ ♄	0:48	26	♀ □ ♇	5:48
3	☿ ☌ ☋	3:10		☽ ☍ ♂	8:27		☿ △ ⊕	15: 6	27	☿ ⚹ ♅	2:10
5	☿ □ ♆	19: 8		☿ ☌ A	13:21	18	☿ □ ♄	2:47		☽ ☌ ♂	13: 0
	☿ △ ♅	19:27	14	☽ ☌ ♆	4:35	19	☿ ☌ ♇	5:57		☽ ☍ ♆	18:55
6	☽ ☌ ☿	22:50		⊕ ☍ ♆	23:25	21	♂ ⚻ ☊	0:51	28	☿ △ ♄	10: 8
7	☿ ⚹ ♄	2:48	15	☽ ☌ ♃	5:36		☿ ⚹ ♃	6:22		⊕ ☍ ♃	10:43
	♀ ⚹ ♇	6:40		♀ ⚼ ☊	18:31		♀ ☌ ♅	18:47		☽ ☍ ♃	16:15
9	☽ ☌ ♇	17:21		☽ ☌ ♀	22:41	22	⊕ △ ♇	3:11			

bodies of the kingly dignity he would soon bestow on all humanity. A picture of destiny communities (disciples in the boat) upheld through the power of Christ who calms storms and stills troubled waters born of our separateness. Christ speaks the words: "It is I, be not afraid." This we can remember when winds of change and waves of uncertainty threaten our equilibrium (*Chron.* 275).

27 Sun at 14° Aquarius: Jesus teaches on the same theme as the Sermon on the Mount: Beatitudes and the Lord's Prayer (Matt. 5:3–12; Matt. 6:9–13). The Beatitudes are the antidote to the temptations now facing humanity and address the ninefold human being. Each one of the Beatitudes is a teaching of infinite depths, revealing a cosmic psychology appropriate in our time.

28 Full Moon, Sun at 15° Waterbearer (Aquarius) and Moon at 15° Lion (Leo), exactly square to the axis of the heavens between 15° Taurus (the Royal Star Aldebaran) and 15° Scorpio (the Royal Star Antares). Together these make a grand cross.

ASPECT on this day—Sun conjunct Jupiter (15° Aquarius). (See the "Signature of Jupiter" paper in this *Journal*). The Sun was conjunct Jupiter at the conception of the Solomon Mary, the one whom we call Mother Mary, who was born before all the others (Jesus, Nathan Mary, John the Baptist), and died after all of them. In this aspect, the spirit spark from heaven conceives the Mother of All. At the conception of this Blessed Virgin Mary, her future union with Wisdom (Jupiter) Sophia at Pentecost is emblazoned in the stars. A more modern example: The first sighting of Mother Mary at Fatima in Portugal on May 13, 1917 (Sun at 28 Aries).

> *My heart radiates.*
> *Above my head radiates a star.*
> *Heart and star radiate together.*
> *I feel soul warmth*
> *In radiance of the stars*
> *In warmth of heart.*
>
> —RUDOLF STEINER

MARCH

Mars continues to be visible, slightly higher to the southeast at sunset, stationing direct in the Crab on the 11th. Neither **Venus**, trailing the **Sun** nor **Mercury** racing before, are visible until the end of the month, as **Venus**, the "evening star," becomes visible in the low west after sunset. **Mercury** is conjunct the **Sun** in a superior conjunction on the 14th. **Jupiter** (Aquarius) begins to be visible in predawn hours after the 15th. The **Sun** joins with **Uranus** on the 17th and **Saturn** on the 22nd. The **Sun** moves into Pisces on the 15th.

✶ ✶ ✶

3–4 ASPECT: Venus conjunct Uranus (1° Pisces). This was one of the aspects at the raising of Lazarus from the dead (July 26, 32 C.E., Venus at 18° Leo). Thus the being of love, Christ, breathes into Lazarus the light of healing force that fills him with the presence of Christ. Lazarus becomes the first Christian initiate. Uranus brings future visions into time and Venus lovingly listens. Also on this day, we find other examples of unexpected change. On November 9, 1989 (Venus at 9° Sagittarius), residents of West Berlin heard an inner call (imaginations written into the collective consciousness of humanity—Uranus) to go out of their houses with candles (to bring the light of the future into the darkness) and serve the uniting mission of love (Venus), finding there many others with candles, who then all went to the Berlin Wall—where they were not shot as expected, and they boldly began to demolish the wall with sledge hammers (Uranus). (We discuss this event in another context on May 23 and August 16.) Where can we bring down walls that divide and make room for new imaginations of brother/sisterhood?

8 Sun 24½° Aquarius: Healing of the Syrophoenician woman and her daughter (Matt. 15:21, *Chron.* 279). Healing possession and finding the will to be healed.

13 Sun 28° Aquarius: Jupiter was at 28° Aquarius during the three temptations of Christ in the wilderness and on the 40th day, when angels came to minister to him. Jupiter represents the in-streaming of cosmic thoughts and Aquarius pours out the living waters of life coming to meet us from the future age of Aquarius (2375 C.E.). This water is the healing source of meditative strength that imbues the etheric with forces of cognition. This cognition helps us see beyond the temptations of our time to the spiritual guidance leading us forward.

15 New Moon at 1° Fishes (Pisces)—When the Sun was at this place on February 18, 31 C.E., Jesus went to the house once occupied by the widow and her son who, at the point of starving, were visited by Elijah who promised to magically keep their flour and oil pots ever full. In this house, the boy died and Elijah revived him by lying on the boy's body three times, eye to eye, heart to heart, and breathing into him. As our earthly "I" is initiated into greater communion with our spirit self, our soul will be nourished from unending urns of spiritual manna and our higher "I" will gradually resurrect our lower self from its enslavement to maya/illusion. At this New Moon we may ask: What new forces of the higher self am I willing to receive into my innermost being though the cost is loss for my earthly self?

17 ASPECT: Sun conjunct Uranus (2° Pisces). In this same sign (Pisces) and in this same aspect, the parents of Solomon Jesus took

SIDEREAL GEOCENTRIC LONGITUDES : MARCH 2010 Gregorian at 0 hours UT

DAY	☉	☽	☊	☿	♀	♂	♃	♄	⛢	♆	♇
1 MO	15 ♒ 24	19 ♌ 46	25 ♐ 4R	4 ♒ 9	26 ♒ 59	6 ♋ 1R	14 ♒ 59	8 ♍ 0R	0 ♓ 46	1 ♒ 49	10 ♐ 10
2 TU	16 25	4 ♍ 48	24 56	5 53	28 14	5 54	15 14	7 55	0 49	1 51	10 12
3 WE	17 25	19 32	24 48	7 37	29 29	5 47	15 28	7 51	0 53	1 53	10 13
4 TH	18 25	3 ♎ 51	24 40	9 22	0 ♓ 44	5 42	15 43	7 47	0 56	1 55	10 14
5 FR	19 25	17 40	24 34	11 8	1 59	5 37	15 57	7 43	0 59	1 58	10 15
6 SA	20 25	1 ♏ 0	24 30	12 56	3 13	5 33	16 12	7 38	1 3	2 0	10 16
7 SU	21 25	13 53	24 28	14 44	4 28	5 30	16 26	7 34	1 6	2 2	10 17
8 MO	22 25	26 22	24 28D	16 34	5 43	5 28	16 41	7 29	1 10	2 4	10 18
9 TU	23 25	8 ♐ 32	24 29	18 24	6 57	5 26	16 55	7 25	1 13	2 6	10 19
10 WE	24 25	20 30	24 29	20 16	8 12	5 25	17 9	7 20	1 16	2 8	10 20
11 TH	25 25	2 ♑ 19	24 29R	22 9	9 27	5 25D	17 24	7 16	1 20	2 11	10 21
12 FR	26 25	14 6	24 27	24 3	10 41	5 25	17 38	7 11	1 23	2 13	10 21
13 SA	27 25	25 53	24 22	25 58	11 56	5 27	17 53	7 7	1 27	2 15	10 22
14 SU	28 25	7 ♒ 44	24 15	27 54	13 10	5 29	18 7	7 2	1 30	2 17	10 23
15 MO	29 25	19 42	24 5	29 50	14 25	5 31	18 21	6 57	1 33	2 19	10 24
16 TU	0 ♓ 25	1 ♓ 48	23 53	1 ♓ 48	15 39	5 35	18 36	6 53	1 37	2 21	10 24
17 WE	1 24	14 4	23 41	3 47	16 54	5 39	18 50	6 48	1 40	2 23	10 25
18 TH	2 24	26 29	23 28	5 46	18 8	5 44	19 4	6 43	1 44	2 25	10 26
19 FR	3 24	9 ♈ 5	23 17	7 46	19 23	5 49	19 19	6 39	1 47	2 27	10 26
20 SA	4 24	21 53	23 8	9 46	20 37	5 55	19 33	6 34	1 51	2 29	10 27
21 SU	5 23	4 ♉ 52	23 2	11 46	21 51	6 2	19 47	6 29	1 54	2 31	10 27
22 MO	6 23	18 5	22 59	13 47	23 6	6 10	20 2	6 24	1 57	2 33	10 28
23 TU	7 22	1 ♊ 34	22 58	15 47	24 20	6 18	20 16	6 20	2 1	2 35	10 28
24 WE	8 22	15 19	22 58D	17 46	25 34	6 26	20 30	6 15	2 4	2 37	10 29
25 TH	9 21	29 23	22 58R	19 45	26 48	6 35	20 44	6 10	2 8	2 39	10 29
26 FR	10 21	13 ♋ 45	22 56	21 42	28 3	6 45	20 58	6 5	2 11	2 41	10 30
27 SA	11 20	28 23	22 52	23 38	29 17	6 56	21 12	6 1	2 14	2 43	10 30
28 SU	12 19	13 ♌ 12	22 46	25 31	0 ♈ 31	7 6	21 26	5 56	2 18	2 45	10 30
29 MO	13 19	28 6	22 36	27 23	1 45	7 18	21 40	5 51	2 21	2 47	10 31
30 TU	14 18	12 ♍ 55	22 25	29 11	2 59	7 30	21 54	5 47	2 25	2 48	10 31
31 WE	15 17	27 32	22 14	0 ♈ 56	4 13	7 42	22 8	5 42	2 28	2 50	10 31

INGRESSES :

1 ☽ → ♍	16:17	20 ☽ → ♉	15: 3
3 ♀ → ♓	9:55	22 ☽ → ♊	21:14
☽ → ♎	17:28	25 ☽ → ♋	1: 2
5 ☽ → ♏	22: 9	27 ☽ → ♌	2:38
8 ☽ → ♐	7: 6	♀ → ♈	14: 1
10 ☽ → ♑	19:16	29 ☽ → ♍	3: 4
13 ☽ → ♒	8:21	30 ☿ → ♈	11: 1
15 ☿ → ♓	1:57	31 ☽ → ♎	4: 5
☉ → ♓	14: 7		
☽ → ♓	20:26		
18 ☽ → ♈	6:43		

ASPECTS & ECLIPSES :

1 ☽ ☍ ♀	12:31	12 ☽ ☌ A	10:23	18 ☿ ☍ ♄	11: 3	29 ☽ ☍ ⛢	6:53
☽ ☍ ⛢	17:34	13 ☽ ☌ ♆	12:56	20 ☿ □ ♆	8:13	☽ ☌ ♄	12:28
2 ☽ ☌ ♄	5: 0	14 ☉ S☌ ☿	13:15	22 ☉ ☍ ♄	0:36	30 ☉ ☍ ☽	2:24
4 ♀ ☌ ⛢	4: 4	☽ ☌ ♃	21:15	23 ☉ □ ☽	10:59	31 ☽ ☍ ☿	6:26
7 ☉ □ ☽	15:40	15 ☉ ☌ ☽	21: 0	☽ ☍ ♆	15:36	☽ ☍ ♀	12:12
8 ☿ ☌ ♃	1:44	☿ ☌ ⛢	21:37	24 ☽ ☌ ☋	13: 6		
9 ☽ ☌ ♇	3:32	☽ ☌ ⛢	23:37	25 ☽ ☌ ♂	12:13		
♀ ☍ ♄	8:20	☽ ☌ ☿	23:59	26 ☉ □ ♇	3:40		
10 ☽ ☌ ☊	8: 5	16 ☽ ☍ ♄	9:54	27 ☽ ☍ ♆	7: 3		
11 ☽ ☍ ♂	6:17	17 ☽ ☌ ♀	6: 6	28 ☽ ☌ P	5:10		
♀ □ ♇	17:31	☉ ☌ ⛢	6:46	☽ ☍ ♃	13:28		

SIDEREAL HELIOCENTRIC LONGITUDES : MARCH 2010 Gregorian at 0 hours UT

DAY	Sid. Time	☿	♀	⊕	♂	♃	♄	⛢	♆	♇	Vernal Point
1 MO	10:34:46	7 ♑ 31	12 ♓ 55	15 ♌ 25	28 ♋ 15	14 ♒ 54	5 ♍ 41	1 ♓ 31	1 ♒ 22	8 ♐ 33	5♓ 7' 6"
2 TU	10:38:42	10 45	14 31	16 25	28 42	15 0	5 43	1 32	1 22	8 33	5♓ 7' 6"
3 WE	10:42:39	14 3	16 6	17 25	29 8	15 5	5 45	1 32	1 23	8 33	5♓ 7' 6"
4 TH	10:46:35	17 26	17 42	18 25	29 34	15 10	5 47	1 33	1 23	8 34	5♓ 7' 5"
5 FR	10:50:32	20 53	19 17	19 25	0 ♌ 1	15 16	5 49	1 33	1 24	8 34	5♓ 7' 5"
6 SA	10:54:29	24 26	20 53	20 25	0 27	15 21	5 51	1 34	1 24	8 34	5♓ 7' 5"
7 SU	10:58:25	28 3	22 29	21 25	0 53	15 27	5 53	1 35	1 24	8 35	5♓ 7' 5"
8 MO	11: 2:22	1 ♒ 47	24 4	22 25	1 20	15 32	5 55	1 35	1 25	8 35	5♓ 7' 5"
9 TU	11: 6:18	5 36	25 40	23 25	1 46	15 38	5 57	1 36	1 25	8 35	5♓ 7' 5"
10 WE	11:10:15	9 32	27 16	24 25	2 12	15 43	5 59	1 37	1 25	8 36	5♓ 7' 5"
11 TH	11:14:11	13 35	28 52	25 25	2 38	15 48	6 1	1 37	1 26	8 36	5♓ 7' 4"
12 FR	11:18: 8	17 45	0 ♈ 27	26 25	3 5	15 54	6 3	1 38	1 26	8 36	5♓ 7' 4"
13 SA	11:22: 4	22 2	2 3	27 25	3 31	15 59	6 5	1 39	1 26	8 37	5♓ 7' 4"
14 SU	11:26: 1	26 28	3 39	28 25	3 57	16 5	6 7	1 39	1 27	8 37	5♓ 7' 4"
15 MO	11:29:58	1 ♓ 2	5 15	29 25	4 23	16 10	6 10	1 40	1 27	8 37	5♓ 7' 4"
16 TU	11:33:54	5 44	6 51	0 ♍ 25	4 50	16 15	6 12	1 41	1 28	8 38	5♓ 7' 4"
17 WE	11:37:51	10 35	8 27	1 24	5 16	16 21	6 14	1 41	1 28	8 38	5♓ 7' 4"
18 TH	11:41:47	15 35	10 3	2 24	5 42	16 26	6 16	1 42	1 28	8 39	5♓ 7' 3"
19 FR	11:45:44	20 44	11 39	3 24	6 8	16 32	6 18	1 42	1 29	8 39	5♓ 7' 3"
20 SA	11:49:40	26 2	13 15	4 24	6 35	16 37	6 20	1 43	1 29	8 39	5♓ 7' 3"
21 SU	11:53:37	1 ♈ 30	14 51	5 23	7 1	16 43	6 22	1 44	1 29	8 40	5♓ 7' 3"
22 MO	11:57:33	7 6	16 27	6 23	7 27	16 48	6 24	1 44	1 30	8 40	5♓ 7' 3"
23 TU	12: 1:30	12 50	18 3	7 22	7 53	16 53	6 26	1 45	1 30	8 40	5♓ 7' 3"
24 WE	12: 5:27	18 43	19 39	8 22	8 19	16 59	6 28	1 46	1 30	8 41	5♓ 7' 3"
25 TH	12: 9:23	24 43	21 15	9 21	8 46	17 4	6 30	1 46	1 31	8 41	5♓ 7' 2"
26 FR	12:13:20	0 ♉ 49	22 51	10 21	9 12	17 10	6 32	1 47	1 31	8 41	5♓ 7' 2"
27 SA	12:17:16	7 0	24 28	11 20	9 38	17 15	6 34	1 48	1 31	8 42	5♓ 7' 2"
28 SU	12:21:13	13 15	26 4	12 20	10 4	17 21	6 36	1 48	1 32	8 42	5♓ 7' 2"
29 MO	12:25: 9	19 33	27 40	13 19	10 30	17 26	6 38	1 49	1 32	8 42	5♓ 7' 2"
30 TU	12:29: 6	25 53	29 16	14 18	10 57	17 31	6 40	1 50	1 33	8 43	5♓ 7' 2"
31 WE	12:33: 2	2 ♊ 12	0 ♉ 53	15 17	11 23	17 37	6 42	1 50	1 33	8 43	5♓ 7' 2"

INGRESSES :

4 ♂ → ♌	23:22
7 ☿ → ♒	12:36
11 ♀ → ♈	17: 7
14 ☿ → ♓	18:39
15 ⊕ → ♍	14: 5
20 ☿ → ♈	17:29
25 ☿ → ♉	20:49
30 ♀ → ♉	10:53
☿ → ♊	15:39

ASPECTS (HELIOCENTRIC +MOON(TYCHONIC)) :

1 ☽ ☍ ⛢	18:43	12 ♀ ✶ ♆	14:44	☿ □ ♇	14:27	24 ☿ ☌ ♀	5:10	28 ☽ ☍ ♃	6:43
2 ☽ ☌ ♄	1:28	13 ☽ ☌ ♆	11:16	17 ♀ △ ♇	2:51	⊕ □ ♆	7:35	☿ □ ♃	15:48
☽ ☍ ♀	17:39	☽ ☍ ♂	16: 3	⊕ ☍ ⛢	6:46	☿ ☌ ☊	19:28	29 ☽ ☍ ⛢	6: 0
4 ☿ ✶ ♀	3:28	14 ♀ △ ♂	6:12	19 ☽ ☌ ♀	5:31	♂ △ ♆	19:41	☿ ☌ P	12: 3
5 ☿ □S ☊	18:14	☿ ☍ ⊕	13:15	20 ☿ ✶ ♆	23:58	26 ☿ □ ♆	2:45	☽ ☌ ♄	13:49
7 ☿ ☍ ♂	20:43	☽ ☌ ♃	16:52	22 ⊕ ☌ ♄	0:20	☿ ✶ ⛢	3:47	30 ☿ △ ♆	21:32
☿ ☌ ♆	21:38	15 ☿ ☌ ⛢	3:18	☿ △ ♂	1:36	☿ △ ♄	22:18	☿ □ ⛢	22:38
8 ♂ ☍ ♆	4:41	☽ ☌ ⛢	23:44	♀ ✶ ♃	5:36	27 ☽ ☍ ♆	5: 6	♂ ☌ A	23:15
9 ☽ ☌ ♇	0: 6	16 ☿ ☍ ♄	2:19	☿ △ ♇	6:37	☿ □ ♂	10:53	31 ♀ □ ♆	10: 4
☿ ✶ ♇	18:18	☽ ☍ ♄	8:38	23 ☽ ☍ ♇	12:27	☽ ☌ ♂	18:47	♀ ✶ ⛢	14:25
11 ☿ ☌ ♃	13:10	☽ ☌ ☿	12:43	☿ ✶ ♃	16:51	☿ △ ⊕	19:47	☿ □ ♄	17:15

him to Egypt, fleeing from a jealous king (on March 2, 5 BCE).

22   ASPECT: Sun (6° Pisces) opposed to Saturn (6° Virgo), a meeting between the light of the essential self and cosmic truth. This aspect marked the end of the forty-day "temptations" (when the Sun lay at 10° Sagittarius)—see also February 8, May 14, and June 26, giving strength to this year as one of celebration (Sun) after trial (Saturn). Saturn shines strongest when opposite the Sun. The divine love from the kingdom of the Father pours into the Sun self uniting the heights and the depths. More about Saturn can be found in the "Signature of Saturn" series paper on Saturn (from CSC 2009 and at www.StarWisdom.org).

29   Full Moon—Sun at 14° Pisces, Moon at 14° Virgo. When the Sun was in this place, the Solomon Jesus—the reincarnation of the great teacher Zarathustra—was born (March 5, 6 B.C.E.). The Moon was full on that occasion as well, making this Full Moon of 2010 an exact replica and memory of the rebirth of the wisest teacher on Earth, holder of the great wisdom of the ages. The three kings in the lineage of Zarathustra recognized this event in the stars, and set off immediately across the desert to meet him. One year later, when the Sun was also at this place, on March 2, 5 B.C.E., the parents of the Solomon Jesus took him swiftly toward Egypt. (An aspect of the flight was mentioned at the 17th of this month.) This is a day that proclaims the love accompanying this great birth (and all births) and its protection.

To the starry heavens above
I direct my gaze
Starlight penetrates into my heart
The heart's power strengthens my eyes
My eyes strengthen the inner light of my soul
Peace streams into my soul
    (based on a verse by Rudolf Steiner)

APRIL

Jupiter continues to be visible (in Aquarius) in predawn for the month, with the slim waning **Moon** joining it on the 11th, rising about 2 hours before sunrise. After sunset this month, both **Mars** and **Saturn** are seen, with **Mars** high in the south in the Crab, **Saturn** in the low eastern horizon in the Virgin. On the 25th, the waxing half **Moon** will join **Saturn**.

The **Sun** moves into Aries on the 14th. **Venus** continues to shine in the western evening sky. **Mercury** is there as well, but stations retrograde on the 19th, so begins to disappear into the Sun's light around the 12th, with an inferior conjunction with the **Sun** on the 28th.

Pluto stations (before going retrograde) on the 8th (until moving direct in mid-September).

✷ ✷ ✷

6   Neptune at 3° Aquarius starting today and continuing through July 29, 2010. Neptune was at 3° Aquarius from March 24, 33 through Pentecost (24/May/33). As Neptune entered 3° Aquarius, Jesus spoke his Woe to the Pharisees (Matt. 23:2–39), powerful words for our time and a throwing down of the gauntlet in his time. These are words that ring with urgency in our time as a reminder to awaken from the degree of compromise into which we have fallen (*Chron.* 345).

9   Sun at 25° Pisces: Feeding of the 4,000 (Matt. 15:29–39; *Chron.* 248). At the feeding of the 4000 we see the *temporal* aspect of our communion with the Sun Being. Seven represents the sevenfold nature of our being and the quest to live "Not I but Christ in me" through each of the 7 chakras. The archetype of this sevenfold union is revealed in the Transfiguration on Mt. Tabor.

14   New Moon—Sun and Moon at 29° Pisces as they were at the triumphant entry into Jerusalem. At this triumphant entry into Jerusalem, the new Sun consciousness born by Christ eclipsed the moon-like consciousness of the times. Today, our brain-bound thinking can just as easily eclipse the light-filled life of the Sun and entomb us in dead thoughts. Where is our dependency on our intellect eclipsing the light of our greater self and world revelations newly coming into time?

23   ASPECT—Venus (3° Taurus) square Neptune (3° Aquarius). When Venus was at this place on March 19, 31 C.E., Jesus asked of his students, "Whom do you say I am?" Peter saw the majesty of Jesus, proclaimed his divinity and was given the keys. Peter receiving the keys to the kingdom of heaven was his appointment to draw from the Kingdom of the Father the power to hold in check the forces of the underworld arising through the gates of Hell/Moon chakra. Here is the angst (square) of new inspiration (Neptune) expanding the personal limitations of self (Venus).

25   Sun 10° Aries: the Visitation. The Nathan Mary visited her cousin Elizabeth, who was pregnant with John the Baptist. During that meeting, all four of them were filled with Holy Awe as the Old Adam, John the Baptist, he who experienced the Fall, was quickened in the womb by the presence of the New Adam, the Jesus Being, he who would redeem humanity from the consequences of the Fall by incarnating the substance of spirit that would give humanity the capacity to heal themselves and choose, in freedom, to again become Children of God. Where in my meetings with others may I find the light of spiritual communion?

SIDEREAL GEOCENTRIC LONGITUDES : APRIL 2010 Gregorian at 0 hours UT

DAY	☉	☽	☊	☿	♀	♂	♃	♄	♅	♆	♇
1 TH	16 ♓ 17	11 ♎ 49	22 ♐ 2R	2 ♈ 38	5 ♈ 27	7 ♋ 55	22 ♒ 22	5 ♍ 38R	2 ♓ 31	2 ♒ 52	10 ♐ 31
2 FR	17 16	25 40	21 53	4 16	6 41	8 9	22 36	5 33	2 35	2 54	10 32
3 SA	18 15	9 ♏ 3	21 46	5 49	7 55	8 23	22 50	5 28	2 38	2 55	10 32
4 SU	19 14	22 0	21 41	7 17	9 9	8 37	23 3	5 24	2 41	2 57	10 32
5 MO	20 13	4 ♐ 33	21 39	8 41	10 22	8 52	23 17	5 19	2 45	2 59	10 32
6 TU	21 12	16 47	21 39	9 59	11 36	9 8	23 31	5 15	2 48	3 1	10 32
7 WE	22 11	28 46	21 39	11 12	12 50	9 24	23 44	5 10	2 51	3 2	10 32
8 TH	23 10	10 ♑ 37	21 38	12 18	14 4	9 40	23 58	5 6	2 55	3 4	10 32R
9 FR	24 9	22 25	21 35	13 19	15 17	9 57	24 11	5 2	2 58	3 5	10 32
10 SA	25 8	4 ♒ 14	21 30	14 14	16 31	10 14	24 25	4 57	3 1	3 7	10 32
11 SU	26 7	16 10	21 23	15 3	17 45	10 31	24 38	4 53	3 4	3 9	10 32
12 MO	27 6	28 14	21 13	15 45	18 58	10 49	24 52	4 49	3 7	3 10	10 32
13 TU	28 5	10 ♓ 31	21 0	16 21	20 12	11 8	25 5	4 45	3 11	3 12	10 31
14 WE	29 4	23 0	20 47	16 51	21 25	11 26	25 18	4 41	3 14	3 13	10 31
15 TH	0 ♈ 3	5 ♈ 42	20 33	17 14	22 39	11 46	25 32	4 37	3 17	3 15	10 31
16 FR	1 1	18 37	20 21	17 30	23 52	12 5	25 45	4 33	3 20	3 16	10 31
17 SA	2 0	1 ♉ 45	20 12	17 41	25 6	12 25	25 58	4 29	3 23	3 17	10 30
18 SU	2 59	15 3	20 5	17 45	26 19	12 45	26 11	4 25	3 26	3 19	10 30
19 MO	3 57	28 31	20 1	17 43R	27 32	13 6	26 24	4 21	3 29	3 20	10 30
20 TU	4 56	12 ♊ 10	20 0	17 35	28 46	13 27	26 37	4 17	3 33	3 21	10 29
21 WE	5 55	25 59	20 0D	17 22	29 59	13 48	26 50	4 14	3 36	3 23	10 29
22 TH	6 53	9 ♋ 59	20 0R	17 3	1 ♉ 12	14 10	27 2	4 10	3 39	3 24	10 29
23 FR	7 52	24 9	19 59	16 40	2 25	14 31	27 15	4 7	3 42	3 25	10 28
24 SA	8 50	8 ♌ 29	19 56	16 12	3 38	14 54	27 28	4 3	3 44	3 26	10 28
25 SU	9 49	22 54	19 50	15 41	4 52	15 16	27 40	4 0	3 47	3 28	10 27
26 MO	10 47	7 ♍ 22	19 42	15 7	6 5	15 39	27 53	3 56	3 50	3 29	10 26
27 TU	11 45	21 47	19 32	14 30	7 18	16 2	28 5	3 53	3 53	3 30	10 26
28 WE	12 44	6 ♎ 1	19 22	13 52	8 30	16 25	28 17	3 50	3 56	3 31	10 25
29 TH	13 42	20 1	19 12	13 12	9 43	16 49	28 30	3 47	3 59	3 32	10 25
30 FR	14 40	3 ♏ 40	19 3	12 33	10 56	17 13	28 42	3 44	4 2	3 33	10 24

INGRESSES :

2 ☽ → ♏ 7:41
4 ☽ → ♐ 15:13
7 ☽ → ♑ 2:28
9 ☽ → ♒ 15:24
12 ☽ → ♓ 3:28
14 ☽ → ♈ 13:16
☉ → ♈ 22:57
16 ☽ → ♉ 20:49
19 ☽ → ♊ 2:36
21 ♀ → ♉ 0:20
☽ → ♋ 6:54
23 ☽ → ♌ 9:49
25 ☽ → ♍ 11:46
27 ☽ → ♎ 13:48
29 ☽ → ♏ 17:29

ASPECTS & ECLIPSES :

3 ♀ □ ♂ 11:23
5 ☿ □ ♂ 4:16
☽ ☌ ♇ 11:40
6 ☉ □ ☽ 9:35
☽ ☌ ☊ 9:41
7 ☽ ☍ ♂ 22: 1
9 ☽ ☌ A 3: 1
☽ ☌ ♆ 21:43
11 ☽ ☌ ♃ 17:12
12 ☽ ☌ ♅ 9:38
☽ ☍ ♄ 12:50
14 ☉ ☌ ☽ 12:28
15 ☽ ☌ ☿ 21:54
16 ☽ ☌ ♀ 10:38
19 ☽ ☍ ♇ 21: 3
20 ☽ ☌ ☋ 13:37
21 ☉ □ ☽ 18:18
22 ☽ ☌ ♂ 7:17
23 ☽ ☍ ♆ 15:34
♀ □ ♆ 19:58
24 ☽ ☌ P 21:12
25 ☽ ☍ ♃ 8: 1
☿ □ ♂ 10:40
☽ ☍ ♅ 18: 7
☽ ☌ ♄ 18:19
26 ♄ ☍ ♅ 23:40
28 ☉ ☍ ☽ 12:17
☽ ☍ ☿ 12:47
☉ ☌ ☿ 16:42
30 ☽ ☍ ♀ 14:21

SIDEREAL HELIOCENTRIC LONGITUDES : APRIL 2010 Gregorian at 0 hours UT

DAY	Sid. Time	☿	♀	⊕	♂	♃	♄	♅	♆	♇	Vernal Point
1 TH	12:36:59	8 ♊ 29	2 ♉ 29	16 ♍ 17	11 ♌ 49	17 ♒ 42	6 ♍ 44	1 ♓ 51	1 ♒ 33	8 ♐ 43	5 ♓ 7' 2"
2 FR	12:40:56	14 43	4 5	17 16	12 15	17 48	6 46	1 51	1 34	8 44	5 ♓ 7' 1"
3 SA	12:44:52	20 52	5 42	18 15	12 41	17 53	6 48	1 52	1 34	8 44	5 ♓ 7' 1"
4 SU	12:48:49	26 56	7 18	19 14	13 8	17 59	6 50	1 53	1 34	8 44	5 ♓ 7' 1"
5 MO	12:52:45	2 ♋ 52	8 55	20 13	13 34	18 4	6 52	1 53	1 35	8 45	5 ♓ 7' 1"
6 TU	12:56:42	8 41	10 31	21 12	14 0	18 9	6 54	1 54	1 35	8 45	5 ♓ 7' 1"
7 WE	13: 0:38	14 21	12 8	22 11	14 26	18 15	6 56	1 55	1 35	8 45	5 ♓ 7' 1"
8 TH	13: 4:35	19 52	13 44	23 10	14 52	18 20	6 58	1 55	1 36	8 46	5 ♓ 7' 1"
9 FR	13: 8:31	25 13	15 21	24 9	15 19	18 26	7 0	1 56	1 36	8 46	5 ♓ 7' 0"
10 SA	13:12:28	0 ♌ 25	16 57	25 8	15 45	18 31	7 2	1 57	1 37	8 46	5 ♓ 7' 0"
11 SU	13:16:25	5 27	18 34	26 7	16 11	18 37	7 4	1 57	1 37	8 47	5 ♓ 7' 0"
12 MO	13:20:21	10 19	20 11	27 6	16 37	18 42	7 6	1 58	1 37	8 47	5 ♓ 7' 0"
13 TU	13:24:18	15 2	21 47	28 5	17 3	18 47	7 8	1 59	1 38	8 47	5 ♓ 7' 0"
14 WE	13:28:14	19 36	23 24	29 4	17 30	18 53	7 10	1 59	1 38	8 48	5 ♓ 7' 0"
15 TH	13:32:11	24 1	25 1	0 ♎ 3	17 56	18 58	7 12	2 0	1 38	8 48	5 ♓ 7' 0"
16 FR	13:36: 7	28 18	26 38	1 1	18 22	19 4	7 14	2 0	1 39	8 48	5 ♓ 6'59"
17 SA	13:40: 4	2 ♍ 27	28 15	2 0	18 48	19 9	7 16	2 1	1 39	8 49	5 ♓ 6'59"
18 SU	13:44: 0	6 28	29 51	2 59	19 15	19 15	7 18	2 2	1 39	8 49	5 ♓ 6'59"
19 MO	13:47:57	10 22	1 ♊ 28	3 57	19 41	19 20	7 20	2 2	1 40	8 49	5 ♓ 6'59"
20 TU	13:51:54	14 9	3 5	4 56	20 7	19 25	7 22	2 3	1 40	8 50	5 ♓ 6'59"
21 WE	13:55:50	17 50	4 42	5 55	20 33	19 31	7 24	2 4	1 41	8 50	5 ♓ 6'59"
22 TH	13:59:47	21 26	6 19	6 53	21 0	19 36	7 26	2 4	1 41	8 51	5 ♓ 6'59"
23 FR	14: 3:43	24 55	7 56	7 52	21 26	19 42	7 28	2 5	1 41	8 51	5 ♓ 6'58"
24 SA	14: 7:40	28 20	9 33	8 50	21 52	19 47	7 30	2 6	1 42	8 51	5 ♓ 6'58"
25 SU	14:11:36	1 ♎ 40	11 10	9 49	22 18	19 53	7 32	2 6	1 42	8 52	5 ♓ 6'58"
26 MO	14:15:33	4 56	12 47	10 47	22 45	19 58	7 34	2 7	1 42	8 52	5 ♓ 6'58"
27 TU	14:19:29	8 7	14 24	11 45	23 11	20 4	7 36	2 7	1 43	8 52	5 ♓ 6'58"
28 WE	14:23:26	11 15	16 2	12 44	23 37	20 9	7 38	2 8	1 43	8 53	5 ♓ 6'58"
29 TH	14:27:23	14 20	17 39	13 42	24 4	20 14	7 40	2 9	1 43	8 53	5 ♓ 6'58"
30 FR	14:31:19	17 22	19 16	14 40	24 30	20 20	7 42	2 9	1 44	8 53	5 ♓ 6'58"

INGRESSES :

4 ☿ → ♋ 12:20
9 ☿ → ♌ 22: 4
14 ⊕ → ♎ 22:55
16 ☿ → ♍ 9:45
18 ♀ → ♊ 2: 8
24 ☿ → ♎ 11:55

ASPECTS (HELIOCENTRIC +MOON(TYCHONIC)) :

1 ☿ ☍ ♇ 0:55
☿ ⚹ ♂ 13:46
2 ☿ □ ⊕ 11:47
☿ △ ♃ 12: 8
☽ ☍ ♀ 17: 4
3 ♀ △ ♄ 16:48
4 ☿ △ ♅ 19:59
5 ☽ ☌ ♇ 8:10
☿ ⚹ ♄ 16:32
6 ☿ ⚹ ♀ 10:46
8 ☿ ☌ ☊ 16:32
☿ ⚹ ⊕ 18: 6
♀ □ ♂ 23:14
9 ☽ ☍ ☿ 10:14
☽ ☌ ♆ 18:40
10 ☿ ☍ ♆ 5:39
11 ☽ ☍ ♂ 0: 2
♀ □ ♃ 0:39
☽ ☌ ♃ 4:55
☿ △ ♇ 16:21
12 ☽ ☌ ♅ 7:20
☽ ☍ ♄ 17:25
13 ♀ ☌ ☊ 1:28
☿ ☌ ♂ 11:38
☿ ☍ ♃ 20: 4
15 ☿ □ ♀ 8:48
16 ⊕ △ ♆ 15:20
☿ ☍ ♅ 21:28
17 ♂ ☍ ♃ 23:59
18 ☿ ☌ ♄ 5: 7
☿ □ ♇ 14:24
19 ♀ △ ♆ 2:51
☽ ☌ ♀ 5:54
♀ □ ♅ 8:29
☽ ☍ ♇ 18: 9
22 ♀ □ ♄ 16:57
♀ △ ⊕ 21:18
23 ☽ ☍ ♆ 12:39
♀ ☍ ♇ 13:35
24 ⊕ ⚹ ♇ 0:24
☽ ☍ ♃ 18:56
☽ ☌ ♂ 22:58
25 ☿ △ ♆ 0:13
☽ ☍ ♅ 15:16
26 ☽ ☌ ♄ 0:20
27 ☿ ⚹ ♇ 5:41
28 ☽ ☌ ☿ 11:26
☿ ☌ ⊕ 16:42
30 ♀ △ ♃ 16:43

26 ASPECT—Saturn (4° Virgo) opposed Uranus (4° Pisces), one-degree orb from April 18 to May 9, a relatively rare aspect. We discuss this aspect in greater detail at July 26, where it returns for the last time. With this aspect, Padre Pio received the five wounds of the stigmata on September 20, 1918 (Saturn at 29° Cancer, Uranus at 1° Aquarius). The stigmata can be understood as the opening of future organs of the will. Also in this aspect, the young soldier Adolf Hitler was poisoned by mustard gas on the battlefields of World War I (on October 15, 1918, Saturn at 1° Leo and Uranus at 0° Aquarius), slipping into a coma. When he recovered, his friends observed that he was another person, with expanded power and reduced morality. Thus, there are other ways in which new organs can be generated.

28 Full Moon—Sun at 13° Aries, Moon at 13° Libra. The Sun and Moon were in these same positions from the Last Supper to the nailing of Christ upon the cross. This Full Moon remembers the Mystery of Golgotha (April 3, 33 C.E.). Each step of the way must be contemplated as the greatest mystery of Earth evolution. Each step then taken gives Christ, in his etheric return, the means through which he may touch us inwardly. During this Full Moon, ask to know the essence of this profound event in world history and its significance for our time.

29 Sun 14° Aries: Transfiguration (April 3/4, 31 C.E.) and Crucifixion (exactly two years later: April 3, 33 C.E.). To comprehend the Crucifixion in terms of the Transfiguration (and vice versa) helps one understand the cosmic significance of both. The death of Jesus on the cross is the birth of the Christ into the Earth. This birth marks the descent into Hell; a time when the Spiritual world held its breath, wondering if the Son of God would achieve his goal. In our time we too must descend, in the presence of Christ, into our subconscious to reclaim our lost light that the new light can find us in this time of the second coming. Raphael's painting of the Transfiguration was incomplete at his death. His disciples finished the lower (dark) half of the painting based on Raphael's sketches. This lower half shows the picture of the boy possessed. We, as disciples of John, are called to finish this masterpiece within our own soul, for there is no ascent without a descent; the journey to the Father is mirrored in the descent to the Mother.

MAY

Mercury continues to keep close to the **Sun**, invisible to the eye and stationing direct on the 12th. **Venus**, however, is radiant in the western twilight sky and is in front of Aldebaran (Royal Star of Persia, Watcher to the East) on the 4th. **Jupiter** enters Pisces on the 6th. The **Sun** enters Taurus on the 15th.

Mars (moving from Cancer into Leo on the 28th) and **Saturn** (in Virgo) continue to fill the night sky. The **Moon** joins them, waxing around half **Moon** on the 20th (**Mars**) and the 22nd (**Saturn**). **Jupiter** is directly opposed **Saturn** on the 23rd, and **Saturn** stations direct on the 31st.

✫ ✫ ✫

1   Sun at 15 ½° Aries: Resurrection of Christ. This central region of the constellation of Aries was the location of the Sun during the deepest mysteries of Jesus Christ, referred to in scriptures as the Son of Man: The Transfiguration (14° Aries), the Crucifixion (14° Aries), and today's remembrance: the Resurrection. Thus, this central heart region of Aries remembers the Mystery of Golgotha, which was a Sun Mystery, and this decan is ruled by the Sun. The starry script that supports this region of the heavens is Cassiopeia, "The Enthroned Woman," who stretches her starry body out as the protectress of this region. She is a symbol for Sophia, "the woman clothed with the Sun" described in chapter 12 of the book of Revelation. The mystery of Christ and Sophia, the Lamb and his Bride, in their interweaving throughout time is here envisioned.

ASPECT: Saturn opposed Uranus. For a one-degree orb, from the 18th of April, until the 9th of May, Saturn opposes Uranus, in its fourth of five returns. See this pass described on April 26 and the last pass described on July 26.

10 Sun 25° Aries: The appearance of the Risen One to the seven disciples at the northeast end of the Sea of Galilee (John 21:1–23). Here Peter is bid three times to "Feed my Sheep." Peter is given the task to be the spiritual leader of the Church of Peter, to ensure that the sacraments, above all Holy Communion, continue to be celebrated for all time. Peter asks what will become of John and the Risen One answers: "If it is my will that he remain until I come, what is that to you?" Implicit here is the task of the Church of John to wait until the second coming of Christ in the etheric realms. The Church of John is centered in the heart and those who chose to join this Church are summoned by the call of the Grail. This is communion with the Tree of Life and the petition, "Give us this day our daily bread" as the spiritual counterpart to communion by way of the Holy Sacrament. This is a mystery involving Shambhala, the realm of the Mother. The Moon on this day, as today, was in Pisces.

14 New Moon: Sun and Moon at 28° Aries. When the Sun was directly across (at 29° Libra), Jesus began the forty-day fast known as the Temptations in the Wilderness, whose ending we celebrate on June 26 of this year. A New Moon always asks us to find the primal light and warmth of the Sun within our own will. Receiving light casts dark shadows. Passing through temptation prepares us to receive the light. We may ask: Is my "I" in right relationship to my spiritual aims?

19 ASPECT: Sun square Neptune. Sun was square Neptune when Mother Mary received her first communion on April 23, 33 C.E., with Sun at 2° Taurus 24 and

SIDEREAL GEOCENTRIC LONGITUDES : MAY 2010 Gregorian at 0 hours UT

DAY	☉	☽	☊	☿	♀	♂	♃	♄	♅	♆	♇
1 SA	15 ♈ 39	16 ♏ 57	18 ♐ 56R	11 ♈ 53R	12 ♉ 9	17 ♋ 37	28 ♒ 54	3 ♍ 41R	4 ♓ 4	3 ♒ 34	10 ♐ 23R
2 SU	16 37	29 51	18 52	11 15	13 22	18 2	29 6	3 38	4 7	3 35	10 23
3 MO	17 35	12 ♐ 24	18 51	10 39	14 35	18 26	29 18	3 35	4 10	3 36	10 22
4 TU	18 33	24 40	18 51D	10 5	15 47	18 51	29 30	3 33	4 13	3 37	10 21
5 WE	19 31	6 ♑ 41	18 51	9 34	17 0	19 16	29 42	3 30	4 15	3 38	10 20
6 TH	20 29	18 34	18 52R	9 6	18 12	19 42	29 53	3 28	4 18	3 39	10 19
7 FR	21 28	0 ♒ 24	18 51	8 42	19 25	20 7	0 ♓ 5	3 25	4 20	3 39	10 19
8 SA	22 26	12 16	18 49	8 22	20 37	20 33	0 16	3 23	4 23	3 40	10 18
9 SU	23 24	24 15	18 44	8 6	21 50	20 59	0 28	3 21	4 26	3 41	10 17
10 MO	24 22	6 ♓ 24	18 38	7 55	23 2	21 26	0 39	3 19	4 28	3 42	10 16
11 TU	25 20	18 48	18 30	7 49	24 15	21 52	0 50	3 17	4 30	3 42	10 15
12 WE	26 18	1 ♈ 29	18 21	7 47D	25 27	22 19	1 2	3 15	4 33	3 43	10 14
13 TH	27 16	14 26	18 12	7 49	26 39	22 46	1 13	3 13	4 35	3 44	10 13
14 FR	28 14	27 41	18 4	7 56	27 51	23 13	1 24	3 11	4 38	3 44	10 12
15 SA	29 11	11 ♉ 10	17 57	8 8	29 4	23 41	1 34	3 9	4 40	3 45	10 11
16 SU	0 ♉ 9	24 52	17 53	8 25	0 ♊ 16	24 8	1 45	3 8	4 42	3 45	10 10
17 MO	1 7	8 ♊ 45	17 50	8 45	1 28	24 36	1 56	3 6	4 45	3 46	10 9
18 TU	2 5	22 45	17 50D	9 11	2 40	25 4	2 6	3 5	4 47	3 46	10 8
19 WE	3 3	6 ♋ 50	17 51	9 40	3 52	25 32	2 17	3 4	4 49	3 47	10 6
20 TH	4 1	20 58	17 52	10 13	5 4	26 1	2 27	3 3	4 51	3 47	10 5
21 FR	4 58	5 ♌ 8	17 53R	10 51	6 16	26 29	2 37	3 2	4 53	3 47	10 4
22 SA	5 56	19 19	17 52	11 32	7 27	26 58	2 47	3 1	4 55	3 48	10 3
23 SU	6 54	3 ♍ 28	17 50	12 17	8 39	27 27	2 57	3 0	4 57	3 48	10 2
24 MO	7 51	17 32	17 46	13 5	9 51	27 56	3 7	2 59	4 59	3 48	10 0
25 TU	8 49	1 ♎ 30	17 40	13 57	11 2	28 25	3 17	2 59	5 1	3 49	9 59
26 WE	9 47	15 17	17 34	14 53	12 14	28 54	3 27	2 58	5 3	3 49	9 58
27 TH	10 44	28 51	17 28	15 51	13 25	29 24	3 36	2 58	5 5	3 49	9 57
28 FR	11 42	12 ♏ 9	17 24	16 53	14 37	29 54	3 46	2 57	5 7	3 49	9 55
29 SA	12 39	25 10	17 20	17 58	15 48	0 ♌ 24	3 55	2 57	5 8	3 49	9 54
30 SU	13 37	7 ♐ 53	17 18	19 6	16 59	0 54	4 4	2 57	5 10	3 49	9 53
31 MO	14 34	20 20	17 18D	20 18	18 11	1 24	4 13	2 57D	5 12	3 49	9 51

INGRESSES :

2	☽ → ♐	0:16	20	☽ → ♌	15:17
4	☽ → ♑	10:36	22	☽ → ♍	18: 7
6	♃ → ♓	13:52	24	☽ → ♎	21:24
	☽ → ♒	23:10	27	☽ → ♏	2: 3
9	☽ → ♓	11:24	28	♂ → ♌	5: 4
11	☽ → ♈	21:13	29	☽ → ♐	9: 3
14	☽ → ♉	4: 9	31	☽ → ♑	18:58
15	♀ → ♊	18:45			
	☉ → ♉	20: 7			
16	☽ → ♊	8:54			
18	☽ → ♋	12:22			

ASPECTS & ECLIPSES :

2	☽ ☌ ♇	20: 3	14	☉ ☌ ☽	1: 3		☉ □ ☽	23:41	☽ ☍ ♀	19:21
3	☽ ☌ ☊	12:32	16	☽ ☌ ♀	10:14	22	☽ ☍ ♃	23: 8		
4	☉ □ ♂	13: 7	17	☽ ☍ ♇	2:24		☽ ☌ ♄	23:12		
6	☽ ☍ ♂	2:21		♀ □ ♃	10:55	23	☽ ☍ ♅	2:32		
	☉ □ ☽	4:14		☽ ☌ ☋	15:36		♃ ☍ ♄	5:36		
	☽ ☌ A	22:16	18	♀ □ ♄	8:17	24	♀ ☍ ♇	3:10		
7	☽ ☌ ♆	6:36	19	☉ □ ♆	18:21	25	☽ ☍ ☿	23:14		
9	☽ ☌ ♃	12:31		♀ □ ♅	19:38	27	☉ ☍ ☽	23: 6		
	☽ ☍ ♄	17:56	20	☽ ☌ P	8:36	30	☽ ☌ ♇	3:47		
	☽ ☌ ♅	20:11		☽ ☌ ♂	8:50		♀ ☍ ☊	6:19		
12	☽ ☌ ☿	11:44		☽ ☍ ♆	21:42		☽ ☌ ☊	18: 6		

SIDEREAL HELIOCENTRIC LONGITUDES : MAY 2010 Gregorian at 0 hours UT

DAY	Sid. Time	☿	♀	⊕	♂	♃	♄	♅	♆	♇	Vernal Point
1 SA	14:35:16	20 ♎ 21	20 ♊ 53	15 ♎ 39	24 ♌ 56	20 ♒ 25	7 ♍ 44	2 ♓ 10	1 ♒ 44	8 ♐ 54	5 ♓ 6'57"
2 SU	14:39:12	23 17	22 30	16 37	25 23	20 31	7 46	2 11	1 44	8 54	5 ♓ 6'57"
3 MO	14:43: 9	26 11	24 8	17 35	25 49	20 36	7 48	2 11	1 45	8 54	5 ♓ 6'57"
4 TU	14:47: 5	29 3	25 45	18 33	26 15	20 42	7 50	2 12	1 45	8 55	5 ♓ 6'57"
5 WE	14:51: 2	1 ♏ 54	27 22	19 31	26 42	20 47	7 52	2 13	1 46	8 55	5 ♓ 6'57"
6 TH	14:54:58	4 43	29 0	20 29	27 8	20 52	7 54	2 13	1 46	8 55	5 ♓ 6'57"
7 FR	14:58:55	7 31	0 ♋ 37	21 28	27 35	20 58	7 56	2 14	1 46	8 56	5 ♓ 6'57"
8 SA	15: 2:52	10 17	2 14	22 26	28 1	21 3	7 58	2 15	1 47	8 56	5 ♓ 6'56"
9 SU	15: 6:48	13 3	3 52	23 24	28 27	21 9	8 0	2 15	1 47	8 56	5 ♓ 6'56"
10 MO	15:10:45	15 48	5 29	24 22	28 54	21 14	8 3	2 16	1 47	8 57	5 ♓ 6'56"
11 TU	15:14:41	18 33	7 6	25 20	29 20	21 20	8 5	2 16	1 48	8 57	5 ♓ 6'56"
12 WE	15:18:38	21 18	8 44	26 18	29 47	21 25	8 7	2 17	1 48	8 57	5 ♓ 6'56"
13 TH	15:22:34	24 3	10 21	27 16	0 ♍ 13	21 31	8 9	2 18	1 48	8 58	5 ♓ 6'56"
14 FR	15:26:31	26 48	11 59	28 14	0 40	21 36	8 11	2 18	1 49	8 58	5 ♓ 6'56"
15 SA	15:30:27	29 33	13 36	29 12	1 6	21 41	8 13	2 19	1 49	8 58	5 ♓ 6'55"
16 SU	15:34:24	2 ♐ 19	15 14	0 ♏ 9	1 33	21 47	8 15	2 20	1 50	8 59	5 ♓ 6'55"
17 MO	15:38:21	5 5	16 51	1 7	1 59	21 52	8 17	2 20	1 50	8 59	5 ♓ 6'55"
18 TU	15:42:17	7 53	18 29	2 5	2 26	21 58	8 19	2 21	1 50	8 59	5 ♓ 6'55"
19 WE	15:46:14	10 42	20 6	3 3	2 52	22 3	8 21	2 22	1 51	9 0	5 ♓ 6'55"
20 TH	15:50:10	13 33	21 44	4 1	3 19	22 9	8 23	2 22	1 51	9 0	5 ♓ 6'55"
21 FR	15:54: 7	16 25	23 21	4 58	3 46	22 14	8 25	2 23	1 51	9 0	5 ♓ 6'55"
22 SA	15:58: 3	19 19	24 59	5 56	4 12	22 20	8 27	2 24	1 52	9 1	5 ♓ 6'55"
23 SU	16: 2: 0	22 15	26 37	6 54	4 39	22 25	8 29	2 24	1 52	9 1	5 ♓ 6'54"
24 MO	16: 5:56	25 14	28 14	7 52	5 5	22 31	8 31	2 25	1 52	9 1	5 ♓ 6'54"
25 TU	16: 9:53	28 15	29 52	8 49	5 32	22 36	8 33	2 25	1 53	9 2	5 ♓ 6'54"
26 WE	16:13:50	1 ♑ 19	1 ♌ 29	9 47	5 59	22 41	8 35	2 26	1 53	9 2	5 ♓ 6'54"
27 TH	16:17:46	4 26	3 7	10 44	6 25	22 47	8 37	2 27	1 53	9 3	5 ♓ 6'54"
28 FR	16:21:43	7 37	4 44	11 42	6 52	22 52	8 39	2 27	1 54	9 3	5 ♓ 6'54"
29 SA	16:25:39	10 52	6 22	12 39	7 19	22 58	8 41	2 28	1 54	9 3	5 ♓ 6'54"
30 SU	16:29:36	14 10	7 59	13 37	7 46	23 3	8 43	2 29	1 55	9 4	5 ♓ 6'53"
31 MO	16:33:32	17 33	9 37	14 35	8 12	23 9	8 45	2 29	1 55	9 4	5 ♓ 6'53"

INGRESSES :

4	☿ → ♏	7:56
6	♀ → ♋	14:54
12	♂ → ♍	11:57
15	☿ → ♐	3:56
	⊕ → ♏	20: 5
25	♀ → ♌	2: 4
	☿ → ♑	13:44

ASPECTS (HELIOCENTRIC +MOON(TYCHONIC)) :

1	☿ △ ♃	0:38		☿ ✶ ♄	3:45	16	☿ □ ♅	0: 8		☽ ☍ ♆	18:26	29	☿ ✶ ⊕	18:27
	☿ △ ♀	9:45	8	♀ △ ♅	0: 4		☽ ☍ ☿	16: 7	22	☽ ☍ ♃	5: 8	30	☽ ☌ ♇	2:14
2	☿ ☌ ☋	2:20		☽ ☌ ♃	17:46		♀ ☌ P	23:32		☽ ☍ ♅	22:12		♀ △ ♇	15:52
	☽ ☌ ♇	17:14	9	☽ ☍ ♂	8:40	17	☽ ☍ ♇	0:24	23	☿ ✶ ♃	1:23			
	☿ ✶ ♂	20:23		☽ ☌ ♅	15:51		⊕ □ ♆	17:47		☽ ☌ ♂	2: 4			
4	☽ ☍ ♀	2:29	10	☽ ☍ ♄	3:11		♂ ☍ ♅	19:29		☽ ☌ ♄	8:33			
	♀ ✶ ♂	10:20	11	♀ ✶ ♄	14:36	18	☿ □ ♄	3:39	24	⊕ ✶ ♄	16:54			
	☿ □ ♆	22:49	12	☿ □ ♃	1: 4		⊕ △ ♅	6:39	26	♀ ☍ ♆	5:55			
5	☿ △ ♅	2:39		☿ ☌ A	12:32		☿ ☌ ♇	9:26		☿ ✶ ♅	8:40			
6	⊕ △ ♃	10:28	15	☿ □ ♂	16: 6		⊕ ✶ ♂	15:55	27	☿ △ ♂	17:28			
7	☽ ☌ ♆	2:46		☿ ✶ ♆	19:46	20	☽ ☌ ♀	1:27	28	☿ △ ♄	7:44			

Neptune at 3° Aquarius 37. This aspect comes on the same day the Sun returns to that place where the Sun was during the event of that communion. Shortly after midnight the Blessed Virgin Mary receives the holy sacrament from Peter (three weeks after the Last Supper). During this communion Jesus appears to her. Later she retires to her room to pray and toward dawn the Lord appears to her again and gives her power over the church, a protective force, such that light flows from him into her. We can see in this event the preparation for the event of Pentecost coming in the weeks that follow. This communion by a woman is born of new inspirations (Neptune) coming into tension with long held ideas by the collective law keepers of the Synagogue.

23 Official Pentecost festival observed this day. Pentecost falls on the first Sunday after the 40 days of the Resurrection and the 10 days following the Ascension of Christ. (Note cosmic Pentecost Sun memory on June 18.) ASPECT: Jupiter opposed Saturn, 1° orb from May 18 to 29. See August 16 for a summary.

27 Full Moon: Sun at 11° Taurus 40 opposite Moon at 11° Scorpio 40. On this day in 30 C.E., an artist arrived, sent by King Abgarus of Edessa, to draw Jesus' likeness. As he could not, Jesus asked for the woven parchment, which he laid on his own face. When he pulled it away, it bore an exact portrait of Jesus. The artist returned with this to King Abgarus, from whom the King received a healing. The portrait came to be known as the *mandylion*, known widely in the Russian church. It and many reproductions were used at the head of cities and armies as a talisman of power. What is the nature of a Force that "…overcometh every subtle thing and doth penetrate every solid substance" (11th Arcanum, *Meditations on the Tarot*).

31 Sun conjunct Aldebaran. The great hinge of the heavens spans from Aldebaran to Antares, the Heart of the Scorpion, and thus above you at midnight. While the Sun rests at the Life Star, Aldebaran, Antares shines down at night—the Star of Death and Resurrection.

JUNE

This month begins with the **Sun** conjunct Aldebaran (Royal Star of the East) on the 1st and **Neptune** beginning to travel retrograde until November. The **Sun** moves into Gemini on the 16th.

The waning half **Moon** passes by **Jupiter** and **Uranus** in the Fishes on the 6th and **Jupiter** joins exactly with **Uranus** on the 8th. They will be visible on the easterly horizon in the hour or two after midnight, climbing in the south to disappear into the dawn light. **Saturn** will be high above slightly south east at sunset. **Mars**, too, is visible (the Lion—Leo) and in front of Regulus (Royal Star of Persia—5° of the Bull) on the 8th. **Venus** continues her reign as evening star, with the waxing crescent **Moon** joining her at 6° Cancer on the 15th.

★ ★ ★

4   ASPECT—Mars (3° Leo) opposed Neptune (3° Aquarius): We find this aspect at the death of the Solomon Jesus. The Solomon Jesus sacrificed himself to serve the coming of the Word Incarnate, Christ. Examples of how the word (Mars) works into worldviews and potential illusions: Darwin has his eureka experience in discovering the mechanism of natural selection, the core of Darwinian evolutionary theory (September 28, 1838, Mars at 16° Cancer, Neptune at 16° Capricorn). Howard Carter opens King Tutankhamun's tomb (November 29, 1922, Mars at 27° Capricorn, Neptune at 25° Cancer). With Neptune we hear the inaudible sound of spiritual inspirations or we fall into the magnetized feelings of subearthly counter inspirations. To whom did Darwin listen? What inspiration was heard from the tomb of Tutankhamun? This aspect is the aggrandizement of self in illusion, or spiritual chastity that keeps false inspiration at bay. To what do you listen?

8   ASPECT—Jupiter conjunct Uranus in Pisces—a threefold conjunction. William Bento calls this the major celestial event of 2010. See William Bento's paper on this aspect in this *Journal for Star Wisdom*.

9   Sun 23° Taurus: The Ascension of Christ. Early in the morning of this day Jesus presented the Blessed Virgin Mary to the apostles and disciples as their advocate and as the center of the community. Here we see another stage in preparation for the coming event of Pentecost (see May 19). As the Sun climbed higher in the sky he proceeded to the Mount of Olives and ascended to the top, all the while becoming more and more radiant with light until he became more radiant than the midday Sun and disappeared into this radiance. Two angels then appeared saying: "Men of Galilee, why do you stand looking up to heaven? This Jesus, who was taken up from you into heaven, will come again in the same way as you saw him go into heaven." The Angelic voice sounds in our time as the promise of Christ's return in the etheric.

12 New Moon: Sun and Moon at 26° Taurus 30. With the Sun in this position on May 17, 32 C.E., Jesus blessed a thousand children, instructing them, laying his hand on some heads, embracing others, giving a loving caress to some. The Moon is exalted in Taurus and remembers the karma of our lower nature. How can we find the balance to participate in such a transmission of blessing and wisdom?

18 Sun 2½° Gemini opposite the Galactic Center (2° Sagittarius): The Descent of the Holy Spirit at Pentecost. The Galactic Center, also known as the Central Sun, is the Divine Heart of the galaxy and the source

SIDEREAL GEOCENTRIC LONGITUDES : JUNE 2010 Gregorian at 0 hours UT

DAY	☉	☽	☊	☿	♀	♂	♃	♄	⛢	♆	♇
1 TU	15 ♉ 32	2 ♑ 32	17 ♐ 19	21 ♈ 32	19 ♊ 22	1 ♌ 54	4 ♓ 22	2 ♍ 57	5 ♓ 14	3 ♒ 49R	9 ♐ 50R
2 WE	16 29	14 33	17 21	22 48	20 33	2 24	4 31	2 57	5 15	3 49	9 49
3 TH	17 27	26 27	17 22	24 8	21 44	2 55	4 40	2 57	5 17	3 49	9 47
4 FR	18 24	8 ♒ 18	17 23	25 31	22 55	3 26	4 48	2 58	5 18	3 49	9 46
5 SA	19 22	20 11	17 24R	26 56	24 6	3 57	4 56	2 58	5 20	3 49	9 44
6 SU	20 19	2 ♓ 11	17 23	28 24	25 17	4 28	5 5	2 59	5 21	3 49	9 43
7 MO	21 17	14 22	17 21	29 55	26 28	4 59	5 13	2 59	5 22	3 49	9 42
8 TU	22 14	26 49	17 19	1 ♉ 28	27 38	5 30	5 21	3 0	5 24	3 48	9 40
9 WE	23 12	9 ♈ 35	17 15	3 4	28 49	6 2	5 29	3 1	5 25	3 48	9 39
10 TH	24 9	22 42	17 12	4 43	29 59	6 33	5 36	3 2	5 26	3 48	9 37
11 FR	25 6	6 ♉ 9	17 9	6 25	1 ♋ 10	7 5	5 44	3 3	5 28	3 48	9 36
12 SA	26 4	19 57	17 6	8 9	2 20	7 37	5 51	3 4	5 29	3 47	9 34
13 SU	27 1	4 ♊ 2	17 5	9 55	3 31	8 9	5 59	3 6	5 30	3 47	9 33
14 MO	27 58	18 20	17 5D	11 45	4 41	8 41	6 6	3 7	5 31	3 46	9 31
15 TU	28 56	2 ♋ 46	17 5	13 36	5 51	9 13	6 13	3 9	5 32	3 46	9 30
16 WE	29 53	17 15	17 6	15 31	7 1	9 45	6 19	3 10	5 33	3 46	9 28
17 TH	0 ♊ 50	1 ♌ 43	17 7	17 27	8 11	10 18	6 26	3 12	5 34	3 45	9 27
18 FR	1 48	16 5	17 8	19 26	9 21	10 50	6 33	3 14	5 35	3 45	9 25
19 SA	2 45	0 ♍ 18	17 8	21 27	10 31	11 23	6 39	3 16	5 36	3 44	9 24
20 SU	3 42	14 20	17 8R	23 31	11 41	11 56	6 45	3 18	5 36	3 43	9 22
21 MO	4 40	28 10	17 7	25 35	12 51	12 28	6 51	3 20	5 37	3 43	9 21
22 TU	5 37	11 ♎ 46	17 6	27 42	14 0	13 1	6 57	3 22	5 38	3 42	9 19
23 WE	6 34	25 9	17 5	29 50	15 10	13 35	7 3	3 24	5 38	3 41	9 18
24 TH	7 31	8 ♏ 18	17 3	1 ♊ 59	16 19	14 8	7 8	3 26	5 39	3 41	9 16
25 FR	8 28	21 12	17 3	4 10	17 28	14 41	7 14	3 29	5 39	3 40	9 15
26 SA	9 26	3 ♐ 53	17 2	6 20	18 38	15 14	7 19	3 32	5 40	3 39	9 13
27 SU	10 23	16 21	17 2D	8 32	19 47	15 48	7 24	3 34	5 40	3 38	9 11
28 MO	11 20	28 37	17 2	10 43	20 56	16 22	7 29	3 37	5 41	3 38	9 10
29 TU	12 17	10 ♑ 43	17 3	12 54	22 4	16 55	7 33	3 40	5 41	3 37	9 8
30 WE	13 14	22 40	17 3	15 4	23 13	17 29	7 38	3 43	5 41	3 36	9 7

INGRESSES :

3 ☽ → ♒ 7:10
5 ☽ → ♓ 19:39
7 ☿ → ♉ 1:22
8 ☽ → ♈ 6: 2
10 ♀ → ♋ 0:10
☽ → ♉ 13: 6
12 ☽ → ♊ 17:10
14 ☽ → ♋ 19:24
16 ☉ → ♊ 2:53
☽ → ♌ 21: 8
18 ☽ → ♍ 23:29
21 ☽ → ♎ 3:13
23 ☿ → ♊ 1:49
☽ → ♏ 8:48
25 ☽ → ♐ 16:35
28 ☽ → ♑ 2:43
30 ☽ → ♒ 14:47

ASPECTS & ECLIPSES :

3 ☽ ☍ ♂ 13:41
☽ ☌ ♆ 14:55
☽ ☌ A 17: 7
4 ♂ ☍ ♆ 18: 6
☉ □ ☽ 22:12
6 ☽ ☍ ♄ 1:35
☽ ☌ ♃ 5:48
☽ ☌ ⛢ 6:17
8 ♃ ☌ ⛢ 11: 9
9 ☿ □ ♆ 10:42
11 ☽ ☌ ☿ 0:30
☿ □ ♂ 13:26
12 ☉ ☌ ☽ 11:13
13 ☽ ☍ ♇ 9:16
☽ ☌ ☋ 21:53
15 ☽ ☌ ♀ 5:33
☽ ☌ P 15:19
17 ☽ ☍ ♆ 3:23
☽ ☌ ♂ 14:52
19 ☉ □ ☽ 4:28
☽ ☌ ♄ 5: 3
☽ ☍ ⛢ 9: 1
☽ ☍ ♃ 10:54
☉ □ ♄ 13:16
22 ☉ □ ⛢ 0:24
23 ☉ □ ♃ 13:19
24 ☿ □ ♄ 16:22
25 ☿ □ ⛢ 16:34
☉ ☍ ♇ 18:49
26 ☽ ☍ ☿ 5:40
☽ ☌ ♇ 10:11
☿ □ ♃ 11: 7
☉ ☍ ☽ 11:29
☽ •• P 11:36
27 ☽ ☌ ☊ 1:19
☿ ☍ ♇ 7:12
28 ☉ S☋ ☿ 12: 6
30 ☽ ☍ ♀ 1:13
☿ ☍ ☊ 21:59
☽ ☌ ♆ 22: 2

SIDEREAL HELIOCENTRIC LONGITUDES : JUNE 2010 Gregorian at 0 hours UT

DAY	Sid. Time	☿	♀	⊕	♂	♃	♄	⛢	♆	♇	Vernal Point
1 TU	16:37:29	21 ♑ 0	11 ♌ 14	15 ♏ 32	8 ♍ 39	23 ♒ 14	8 ♍ 47	2 ♓ 30	1 ♒ 55	9 ♐ 4	5 ♓ 6'53"
2 WE	16:41:25	24 33	12 52	16 30	9 6	23 20	8 49	2 31	1 56	9 5	5 ♓ 6'53"
3 TH	16:45:22	28 11	14 29	17 27	9 33	23 25	8 51	2 31	1 56	9 5	5 ♓ 6'53"
4 FR	16:49:19	1 ♒ 54	16 7	18 24	10 0	23 30	8 53	2 32	1 56	9 5	5 ♓ 6'53"
5 SA	16:53:15	5 44	17 44	19 22	10 26	23 36	8 55	2 33	1 57	9 6	5 ♓ 6'53"
6 SU	16:57:12	9 40	19 22	20 19	10 53	23 41	8 57	2 33	1 57	9 6	5 ♓ 6'52"
7 MO	17: 1: 8	13 43	20 59	21 17	11 20	23 47	8 59	2 34	1 57	9 6	5 ♓ 6'52"
8 TU	17: 5: 5	17 53	22 36	22 14	11 47	23 52	9 1	2 34	1 58	9 7	5 ♓ 6'52"
9 WE	17: 9: 1	22 11	24 14	23 12	12 14	23 58	9 3	2 35	1 58	9 7	5 ♓ 6'52"
10 TH	17:12:58	26 37	25 51	24 9	12 41	24 3	9 5	2 36	1 59	9 7	5 ♓ 6'52"
11 FR	17:16:54	1 ♓ 11	27 28	25 6	13 8	24 9	9 7	2 36	1 59	9 8	5 ♓ 6'52"
12 SA	17:20:51	5 53	29 6	26 4	13 35	24 14	9 9	2 37	1 59	9 8	5 ♓ 6'52"
13 SU	17:24:48	10 44	0 ♍ 43	27 1	14 2	24 20	9 11	2 38	2 0	9 8	5 ♓ 6'51"
14 MO	17:28:44	15 45	2 20	27 58	14 29	24 25	9 13	2 38	2 0	9 9	5 ♓ 6'51"
15 TU	17:32:41	20 54	3 57	28 56	14 56	24 31	9 15	2 39	2 0	9 9	5 ♓ 6'51"
16 WE	17:36:37	26 13	5 35	29 53	15 23	24 36	9 17	2 40	2 1	9 9	5 ♓ 6'51"
17 TH	17:40:34	1 ♈ 40	7 12	0 ♐ 50	15 50	24 41	9 19	2 40	2 1	9 10	5 ♓ 6'51"
18 FR	17:44:30	7 16	8 49	1 48	16 18	24 47	9 21	2 41	2 1	9 10	5 ♓ 6'51"
19 SA	17:48:27	13 1	10 26	2 45	16 45	24 52	9 23	2 42	2 2	9 10	5 ♓ 6'51"
20 SU	17:52:23	18 54	12 3	3 42	17 12	24 58	9 25	2 42	2 2	9 11	5 ♓ 6'51"
21 MO	17:56:20	24 54	13 40	4 40	17 39	25 3	9 27	2 43	2 3	9 11	5 ♓ 6'50"
22 TU	18: 0:17	1 ♉ 0	15 17	5 37	18 6	25 9	9 29	2 43	2 3	9 11	5 ♓ 6'50"
23 WE	18: 4:13	7 11	16 54	6 34	18 34	25 14	9 31	2 44	2 3	9 12	5 ♓ 6'50"
24 TH	18: 8:10	13 27	18 31	7 31	19 1	25 20	9 33	2 45	2 4	9 12	5 ♓ 6'50"
25 FR	18:12: 6	19 45	20 7	8 28	19 28	25 25	9 35	2 45	2 4	9 12	5 ♓ 6'50"
26 SA	18:16: 3	26 4	21 44	9 26	19 56	25 31	9 37	2 46	2 4	9 13	5 ♓ 6'50"
27 SU	18:19:59	2 ♊ 23	23 21	10 23	20 23	25 36	9 39	2 47	2 5	9 13	5 ♓ 6'50"
28 MO	18:23:56	8 40	24 58	11 20	20 51	25 41	9 41	2 47	2 5	9 13	5 ♓ 6'49"
29 TU	18:27:52	14 54	26 34	12 17	21 18	25 47	9 43	2 48	2 5	9 14	5 ♓ 6'49"
30 WE	18:31:49	21 3	28 11	13 14	21 45	25 52	9 45	2 49	2 6	9 14	5 ♓ 6'49"

INGRESSES :

3 ☿ → ♒ 11:48
10 ☿ → ♓ 17:53
12 ♀ → ♍ 13:24
16 ⊕ → ♐ 2:52
☿ → ♈ 16:44
21 ☿ → ♉ 20: 6
26 ☿ → ♊ 14:56

ASPECTS (HELIOCENTRIC +MOON(TYCHONIC)) :

1 ♂ ☌ ♄ 7:22
☿ S☋ ☊ 17:25
♂ □ ♇ 22:43
3 ☽ ☌ ☿ 5: 4
☽ ☌ ♆ 11: 6
4 ☿ ☌ ♆ 0:13
☽ ☍ ♀ 18:17
5 ☽ ☌ ♃ 6:54
☿ ⚹ ♇ 20:33
6 ☽ ☌ ⛢ 0:44
☽ ☍ ♄ 13:24
☽ ☍ ♂ 17:50
7 ♀ □ ⊕ 10:43
♀ N☋ ☊ 13:23
8 ♀ ☍ ♃ 19:50
9 ☿ □ ⊕ 7: 4
☿ ☌ ♃ 9:56
☿ ☍ ♀ 17:36
⊕ □ ♃ 21:19
11 ☿ ☌ ⛢ 7:23
♄ □ ♇ 10:48
12 ☿ □ ♇ 16: 9
☿ ☍ ♄ 16:19
13 ☽ ☍ ♇ 8:36
☿ ☍ ♂ 17:27
14 ♀ ☍ ⛢ 4:31
16 ☿ △ ⊕ 19:39
17 ☽ ☍ ♆ 0:30
☿ ⚹ ♆ 1:31
18 ♀ □ ♇ 5:16
⊕ ⚹ ♆ 5:45
☿ △ ♇ 7:59
♀ ☌ ♄ 8: 7
☽ ☍ ♃ 14:45
⊕ □ ⛢ 22:31
19 ☽ ☍ ⛢ 4: 4
☽ ☌ ♄ 15:32
☽ ☌ ♀ 19:33
20 ☽ ☌ ♂ 5: 6
☿ ☌ ☊ 18:43
21 ☿ ⚹ ♃ 0:38
22 ☿ □ ♆ 4: 5
☿ ⚹ ⛢ 6:44
23 ☿ △ ♄ 9: 0
24 ♀ ☌ ♂ 10:30
☽ ☍ ☿ 18:36
☿ △ ♂ 22:53
25 ☿ △ ♀ 1:56
☿ ☌ P 11:21
⊕ ☌ ♇ 18:33
☿ □ ♃ 21:51
26 ⊕ □ ♄ 4:56
☽ ☌ ♇ 10:12
☿ △ ♆ 22:50
27 ☿ □ ⛢ 1:30
28 ☿ ☍ ♇ 2: 8
☿ □ ♄ 3:55
☿ ☍ ⊕ 12: 6
30 ☿ □ ♂ 3: 1
☽ ☌ ♆ 19: 2
☿ △ ♃ 19:23

of the Holy Spirit. Christ was born into the Earth at Pentecost and became the spirit of the Earth; since this first Pentecost the Christ spirit has lived with human souls on Earth. This was brought forth by the Blessed Virgin Mary, standing in the center of the disciples as the advocate of Christ (see May 19 and June 9). She united with Holy Sophia and the sparks of fire that issued forth from her Blessed soul were the manifestation of Christ's cosmic "I Am" carried by the Holy Spirit from the very heart of the galaxy. Pentecost was an awakening of the apostles from a dream-like state where they united with the principle of love on Earth. Today we celebrate this Sun remembrance by opening to our true heritage as Sons and Daughters of Light.

2   ASPECT: Sun square Saturn. See "The Signature of Saturn" stories in *CSC* 2009 (archived at www.StarWisdom.org) to get the sense of this empowerment of Saturn.

23 ASPECT: Sun square Jupiter. See "The Signature of Jupiter" stories in this *Journal for Star Wisdom*.

25 ASPECT: Sun opposed Pluto. See "The Signature of Pluto" in *CSC* 2008. Rudolf Steiner went through great trials in relation to this opposition. This is a very potent aspect. Here we face blessed union with Divine Love, or, the ensnared forces of sub-natural powers rising from the abyss.

26 Full Moon: Sun at 9° Gemini 53 and Moon at 9° Sagittarius 53, a partial lunar eclipse. When the Sun stood at 9° Sagittarius 58, angels came to minister to Jesus at the end of the trials of his forty days in the wilderness. The cave was decorated with twining vines of green, as heavenly foods were served by numerous spirits.

29 Sun at 12° Gemini: Birth of John the Baptist (June 4, 2 B.C.E.).

30 Sun 14° Gemini: Death of Solomon Jesus (Master Jesus—June 5, 12 C.E.).

JULY

Jupiter with his too-far-to-be-seen partner **Uranus** continues to be visible around midnight and earlier as the month progresses. Both of these wandering stars station retrograde: **Uranus** on the 6th (until December) and **Jupiter** on the 24th (until November). The **Moon** will join their late night sky on the 3rd as a waning gibbous **Moon**—look to the east 4 hours past sunset to watch these arise.

The **Sun** moves into the Crab on the 17th. **Mars** moves into Virgo on the 21st. **Saturn** and **Uranus** oppose one another on the 26th. **Mars** joins this opposition to **Uranus** on the 30th, conjunct **Saturn** on the 31st.

Earlier in the month the waxing crescent **Moon** will join **Venus** on the 14th to be seen in the west after sunset and will pass before **Mars** and **Saturn** (8° apart) on the 16th, all lined up in the southwestern sky after sunset.

✦ ✦ ✦

6   Sun 19½° Gemini aligned with Sirius, the brightest star in the heavens, the star of the Master Jesus and revered by the Egyptians as the star of Isis (pre-Christian manifestation of Sophia). A triangular relationship is formed between Sirius, our Sun and Shambhala, the golden realm at the heart of the Earth—the Earth's heart chakra. This suggests mighty influences sounding through the meridian connections of the Daughter in the Heights, the Mother in the Depths.

7   Second time Pluto crosses exactly where it was at the third Temptation in the Wilderness (8° Sagittarius 55). According to the Apocalypse Code of Robert Powell the time of this third temptation for humanity began in 1988 and ends in 2018. Humanity is now facing the temptation of materialism supported by unprecedented technologies of virtual reality. We are summoned to discern the living from the dead; the world of the serpent from the divine world. This is the eighth return of Pluto to this position. What makes this return special is that this return occurs during the actual historical period of the third temptation, 1988–2018 (see Jan. 14/15).

11 New Moon: Sun and Moon both at 24° of the Twins. A complete solar eclipse traces a path over the South Pacific Ocean, at its very end touching Patagonia in South America. The time of the peak is 19:33 UT, or 12:33 PM Pacific saving time. Every solar eclipse is a call to 'grail' for the Sun's life and light as vessels of love to fill the void created by the extraordinary darkness. Pluto today (8° 50 Sagittarius) is where it was at the first temptation of Christ in the wilderness.

18 Sun 1° Cancer, aligned with Procyon (redeemed or redeeming) in the Lesser Dog, where the Sun was when Jesus taught concerning the baptism by fire (Luke 12:49, *Chron.* 305).

25 Full Moon: Sun at 8° of the Crab (Cancer) and Moon at 8° of the Goat (Capricorn). When the Sun was at 8° of the Goat, Jesus turned water into wine at the wedding of Cana. This full Moon receives the Sun memory of the spiritualization of the old wine into new wine; blood imbued with the spirit of Christ is more powerful than any authority of heredity. (This event echoes January 23.) Do we have the courage to outgrow the limitations of our ego and open to the house of the Father; the house of our higher self?

26 ASPECT—Saturn opposed Uranus, one-degree orb extending from July 16 to August 5. This is the fifth and final opposition in this series of these slow-moving

SIDEREAL GEOCENTRIC LONGITUDES : JULY 2010 Gregorian at 0 hours UT

DAY	☉	☽	☊	☿	♀	♂	♃	♄	♅	♆	♇
1 TH	14 ♊ 12	4 ♒ 33	17 ♐ 3	17 ♊ 14	24 ♋ 22	18 ♌ 3	7 ♓ 42	3 ♍ 46	5 ♓ 42	3 ♒ 35R	9 ♐ 5R
2 FR	15 9	16 24	17 4	19 23	25 30	18 37	7 46	3 49	5 42	3 34	9 4
3 SA	16 6	28 17	17 4	21 31	26 39	19 11	7 50	3 52	5 42	3 33	9 2
4 SU	17 3	10 ♓ 16	17 4R	23 38	27 47	19 45	7 54	3 55	5 42	3 32	9 1
5 MO	18 0	22 26	17 4	25 43	28 55	20 20	7 58	3 59	5 42	3 31	8 59
6 TU	18 58	4 ♈ 52	17 4D	27 46	0 ♌ 3	20 54	8 1	4 2	5 42R	3 30	8 58
7 WE	19 55	17 37	17 4	29 48	1 11	21 29	8 5	4 6	5 42	3 29	8 56
8 TH	20 52	0 ♉ 45	17 4	1 ♋ 48	2 19	22 3	8 8	4 9	5 42	3 28	8 55
9 FR	21 49	14 17	17 4	3 47	3 27	22 38	8 10	4 13	5 42	3 27	8 53
10 SA	22 46	28 13	17 5	5 43	4 34	23 13	8 13	4 17	5 42	3 26	8 52
11 SU	23 44	12 ♊ 33	17 5	7 38	5 42	23 48	8 16	4 21	5 42	3 25	8 50
12 MO	24 41	27 10	17 5R	9 31	6 49	24 23	8 18	4 25	5 41	3 23	8 49
13 TU	25 38	12 ♋ 0	17 5	11 21	7 56	24 58	8 20	4 29	5 41	3 22	8 47
14 WE	26 35	26 55	17 4	13 10	9 3	25 33	8 22	4 33	5 41	3 21	8 46
15 TH	27 33	11 ♌ 46	17 3	14 57	10 10	26 8	8 24	4 37	5 40	3 20	8 44
16 FR	28 30	26 26	17 2	16 43	11 17	26 43	8 25	4 41	5 40	3 19	8 43
17 SA	29 27	10 ♍ 51	17 1	18 26	12 24	27 19	8 27	4 46	5 39	3 17	8 42
18 SU	0 ♋ 24	24 57	17 0	20 7	13 30	27 54	8 28	4 50	5 39	3 16	8 40
19 MO	1 22	8 ♎ 42	17 0D	21 47	14 36	28 30	8 29	4 55	5 38	3 15	8 39
20 TU	2 19	22 7	17 1	23 24	15 42	29 6	8 30	4 59	5 37	3 13	8 37
21 WE	3 16	5 ♏ 13	17 2	25 0	16 48	29 41	8 30	5 4	5 37	3 12	8 36
22 TH	4 13	18 3	17 3	26 33	17 54	0 ♍ 17	8 31	5 9	5 36	3 11	8 35
23 FR	5 11	0 ♐ 38	17 4	28 5	18 59	0 53	8 31	5 13	5 35	3 9	8 33
24 SA	6 8	13 1	17 5	29 35	20 5	1 29	8 31R	5 18	5 34	3 8	8 32
25 SU	7 5	25 14	17 5R	1 ♌ 3	21 10	2 5	8 31	5 23	5 33	3 6	8 31
26 MO	8 3	7 ♑ 18	17 4	2 29	22 15	2 42	8 30	5 28	5 32	3 5	8 29
27 TU	9 0	19 17	17 1	3 53	23 20	3 18	8 30	5 33	5 31	3 4	8 28
28 WE	9 57	1 ♒ 10	16 58	5 15	24 24	3 54	8 29	5 38	5 30	3 2	8 27
29 TH	10 55	13 1	16 54	6 34	25 28	4 31	8 28	5 44	5 29	3 1	8 26
30 FR	11 52	24 52	16 50	7 52	26 33	5 7	8 27	5 49	5 28	2 59	8 24
31 SA	12 49	6 ♓ 46	16 46	9 8	27 36	5 44	8 25	5 54	5 27	2 58	8 23

INGRESSES :

3	☽ → ♓ 3:27	20	☽ → ♏ 14:22		
5	☽ → ♈ 14:40	21	♂ → ♍ 12:23		
	♀ → ♌ 22:48	22	☽ → ♐ 22:46		
7	☿ → ♋ 2:21	24	☿ → ♌ 6:48		
	☽ → ♉ 22:39	25	☽ → ♑ 9:26		
10	☽ → ♊ 3: 0	27	☽ → ♒ 21:38		
12	☽ → ♋ 4:35	30	☽ → ♓ 10:22		
14	☽ → ♌ 4:58				
16	☽ → ♍ 5:53				
17	☉ → ♋ 13:45				
18	☽ → ♎ 8:44				

ASPECTS & ECLIPSES :

1	☽ ☌ A	10:40		☉ ☌ ☽	19:39	24	☽ ☌ ☊	7:57		☽ ☍ ♂	21:48
2	☽ ☍ ♂	4:43	12	☽ ☌ ☿	22:48	25	♃ □ ♇	0:11		☽ ☍ ♄	22:15
3	☽ ☍ ♄	11:16	13	☽ ☌ P	11:18	26	☉ ☍ ☽	1:35	31	☽ ☌ ♃	3:19
	☽ ☌ ♅	14:53	14	☽ ☍ ♆	10:22		☿ ☍ ♆	10: 7		♂ ☌ ♄	8: 6
	☽ ☌ ♃	19:15		☽ ☌ ♀	21:12		♄ ☍ ♅	16:47			
4	☉ ☍ ☊	0:11	16	☽ ☌ ♂	0:29	28	☽ ☌ ♆	3:45			
	☉ □ ☽	14:34		☽ ☌ ♄	13:44		☽ ☍ ☿	9:17			
9	♀ ☍ ♆	0: 0		☽ ☍ ♅	15:17	29	☽ ☌ A	0:15			
10	☽ ☍ ♇	17:51		☽ ☍ ♃	19:57	30	☽ ☍ ♀	3:43			
11	☽ ☌ ☋	7:29	18	☉ □ ☽	10: 9		♂ ☍ ♅	13:27			
	☉ ● T	19:33	23	☽ ☌ ♇	15:16		☽ ☌ ♅	21:21			

SIDEREAL HELIOCENTRIC LONGITUDES : JULY 2010 Gregorian at 0 hours UT

DAY	Sid. Time	☿	♀	⊕	♂	♃	♄	♅	♆	♇	Vernal Point
1 TH	18:35:46	27 ♊ 6	29 ♍ 48	14 ♐ 12	22 ♍ 13	25 ♒ 58	9 ♍ 47	2 ♓ 49	2 ♒ 6	9 ♐ 14	5 ♓ 6'49"
2 FR	18:39:42	3 ♋ 2	1 ♎ 24	15 9	22 40	26 3	9 49	2 50	2 6	9 15	5 ♓ 6'49"
3 SA	18:43:39	8 51	3 1	16 6	23 8	26 9	9 51	2 51	2 7	9 15	5 ♓ 6'49"
4 SU	18:47:35	14 30	4 37	17 3	23 36	26 14	9 53	2 51	2 7	9 16	5 ♓ 6'49"
5 MO	18:51:32	20 1	6 14	18 0	24 3	26 20	9 55	2 52	2 8	9 16	5 ♓ 6'48"
6 TU	18:55:28	25 22	7 50	18 58	24 31	26 25	9 57	2 52	2 8	9 16	5 ♓ 6'48"
7 WE	18:59:25	0 ♌ 33	9 26	19 55	24 59	26 31	9 59	2 53	2 8	9 17	5 ♓ 6'48"
8 TH	19: 3:21	5 35	11 3	20 52	25 26	26 36	10 1	2 54	2 9	9 17	5 ♓ 6'48"
9 FR	19: 7:18	10 27	12 39	21 49	25 54	26 42	10 3	2 54	2 9	9 17	5 ♓ 6'48"
10 SA	19:11:15	15 10	14 15	22 47	26 22	26 47	10 5	2 55	2 9	9 18	5 ♓ 6'48"
11 SU	19:15:11	19 44	15 51	23 44	26 50	26 53	10 7	2 56	2 10	9 18	5 ♓ 6'48"
12 MO	19:19: 8	24 8	17 27	24 41	27 17	26 58	10 9	2 56	2 10	9 18	5 ♓ 6'47"
13 TU	19:23: 4	28 25	19 3	25 38	27 45	27 3	10 11	2 57	2 10	9 19	5 ♓ 6'47"
14 WE	19:27: 1	2 ♍ 34	20 39	26 35	28 13	27 9	10 13	2 58	2 11	9 19	5 ♓ 6'47"
15 TH	19:30:57	6 35	22 15	27 33	28 41	27 14	10 15	2 58	2 11	9 19	5 ♓ 6'47"
16 FR	19:34:54	10 28	23 51	28 30	29 9	27 20	10 17	2 59	2 12	9 20	5 ♓ 6'47"
17 SA	19:38:50	14 16	25 27	29 27	29 37	27 25	10 19	3 0	2 12	9 20	5 ♓ 6'47"
18 SU	19:42:47	17 56	27 3	0 ♑ 24	0 ♎ 5	27 31	10 21	3 0	2 12	9 20	5 ♓ 6'47"
19 MO	19:46:44	21 32	28 38	1 22	0 33	27 36	10 23	3 1	2 13	9 21	5 ♓ 6'47"
20 TU	19:50:40	25 1	0 ♏ 14	2 19	1 1	27 42	10 25	3 1	2 13	9 21	5 ♓ 6'46"
21 WE	19:54:37	28 26	1 50	3 16	1 29	27 47	10 27	3 2	2 13	9 21	5 ♓ 6'46"
22 TH	19:58:33	1 ♎ 46	3 26	4 13	1 57	27 53	10 29	3 3	2 14	9 22	5 ♓ 6'46"
23 FR	20: 2:30	5 1	5 1	5 11	2 26	27 58	10 31	3 3	2 14	9 22	5 ♓ 6'46"
24 SA	20: 6:26	8 13	6 37	6 8	2 54	28 4	10 33	3 4	2 14	9 22	5 ♓ 6'46"
25 SU	20:10:23	11 21	8 12	7 5	3 22	28 9	10 35	3 5	2 15	9 23	5 ♓ 6'46"
26 MO	20:14:19	14 25	9 48	8 3	3 50	28 15	10 37	3 5	2 15	9 23	5 ♓ 6'46"
27 TU	20:18:16	17 27	11 23	9 0	4 19	28 20	10 39	3 6	2 15	9 23	5 ♓ 6'45"
28 WE	20:22:13	20 26	12 59	9 57	4 47	28 25	10 41	3 7	2 16	9 24	5 ♓ 6'45"
29 TH	20:26: 9	23 22	14 34	10 55	5 16	28 31	10 43	3 7	2 16	9 24	5 ♓ 6'45"
30 FR	20:30: 6	26 16	16 9	11 52	5 44	28 36	10 45	3 8	2 17	9 24	5 ♓ 6'45"
31 SA	20:34: 2	29 8	17 45	12 49	6 13	28 42	10 47	3 9	2 17	9 25	5 ♓ 6'45"

INGRESSES :

1	♀ → ♎ 3: 4
	☿ → ♋ 11:39
6	☿ → ♌ 21:24
13	☿ → ♍ 9: 5
17	⊕ → ♑ 13:44
	♂ → ♎ 19:43
19	♀ → ♏ 20:25
21	☿ → ♎ 11:15
31	☿ → ♏ 7:15

ASPECTS (HELIOCENTRIC +MOON(TYCHONIC)) :

1	☿ □ ♀	14:50	6	☽ ☍ ♀	6:27	15	☿ □ ♇	16:51	21	♀ □ ♆	5:53		⊕ △ ♄	19: 5
	☿ △ ♅	23: 9		♀ ⚹ ♇	21:34		☿ ☌ ♄	22:49		♀ △ ♅	18:14	29	☿ ☌ ☋	1:39
2	♀ △ ♆	10:33	7	☿ ☍ ♆	7:29	16	☽ ☍ ♃	1:29	22	☿ ☌ ♂	1:40	30	☽ ☌ ♃	7:36
	☽ ☌ ♃	19:40	8	☿ △ ♇	18:10		☽ ☍ ♅	10:50		☿ △ ♆	3:25		☽ ☌ ♅	16:42
3	☿ ⚹ ♄	4:15	9	☿ ⚹ ♀	16:48		☽ ☌ ♄	23: 6		♂ △ ♆	14: 1		☿ △ ♃	20:10
	☽ ☌ ♅	9:10	10	☽ ☍ ♇	18:36	17	☽ ☌ ☿	7:47	23	☿ □ ⊕	1:41	31	☽ ☍ ♄	8: 6
	☽ ☍ ♄	23:14	12	☿ △ ⊕	3:51		⊕ □ ♂	7:59		♀ ⚹ ⊕	6: 0			
5	☽ ☍ ♂	3:16		☿ ☍ ♃	16: 7	18	♀ △ ♃	7:27		☽ ☌ ♇	16:53			
	⊕ ☌ A	5:38	14	☿ ☍ ♅	2:22		☽ ☌ ♂	9:12	24	☿ ⚹ ♇	8:51			
	☿ ⚼ ☊	15:52		☽ ☍ ♆	8:29	20	☽ ☌ ♀	16:51	26	♀ ⚹ ♄	12:41			
	☿ ⚹ ♂	19:46		⊕ ⚹ ♃	15:29		⊕ ⚹ ♅	18: 0	28	☽ ☌ ♆	2:13			

planets. (The fourth spans from April into May, centered at April 26.) The first in this series began with the general elections in the USA on November 4, 2008, from which an unexpected president emerged. At its best, this transit expresses new imaginations finding forms on Earth aligned with spirit will. Upheavals are caused to the degree forms on Earth are unprepared to receive new imaginations. An example of the harmony of new imaginations coming into form is Padre Pio who received the stigmata—the wounds of Christ, wherein the hands, feet, and side of the body to the heart become opened as organs of new perception—when Saturn (29° Cancer 26°) opposed Uranus (0° Aquarius 58).

31 Sun 12½° Cancer, at Praesepe, the beehive. The beehive is at the center of the spiraling arms of Cancer, the heart of the Crab. It was through this gateway that the Greeks believed human souls entered earthly incarnation to gather the golden nectar of earthly experience to take back to the Queen of the cosmic realm, Sophia.

ASPECT: Saturn conjunct Mars at 5° Virgo. Mars was conjunct Saturn (in Taurus) when the Nathan Mary visited Elizabeth (the Visitation) who was six months pregnant with John, who became the Baptist, March 30, 2 B.C.E. (See April 25.) Saturn is the portal to the kingdom of the Father and Mars is the manifestation of spiritual will through moral speech and right action in the world. The child in Mary's immaculate womb was he who would incarnate the Divine Love of the Father as the Logos, as the "Word become Flesh." The child in Elizabeth's womb was he who would prepare the way for the incarnation of the Word. The Logos *is* the manifestation of the Father's will.

> *He said there was something called the Grail,*
>
> *whose name—how it is known—he had read clearly in the stars.*
>
> *A [heavenly] host left it upon the Earth,*
>
> *and then flew up above the stars on high.*
>
> —WOLFRAM VON ESCHENBACH, *Parsifal* 454, 21–25

AUGUST

Every August is marked by the Perseids Meteor showers and as a bright **Moon** can obscure the "shooting stars" the waxing crescent may get in the way, rising about midnight the night of the showers peak on the 12th.

The **Sun** moves into the Lion—Leo on the 17th. **Jupiter** opposes **Saturn** on the 16th.

If you are able to find level ground in the beginning of the month, you will also catch a show "starring" **Mercury**, **Venus**, **Mars** and **Saturn**: **Venus** joins **Saturn** in Virgo on the 8th, joining **Mars** (who caught up to **Saturn** on July 31). This group should be visible in the low western sky as the sun sets, with **Mercury** in Leo even closer to the **Sun** (and lower on the horizon). This grouping gets more interesting as the slim waxing crescent **Moon** emerges from the Sun's light to join **Mercury** on the 12th, and **Saturn**, **Venus** and **Mars** on the 13th. A gorgeous opportunity! **Mars** and **Venus** hold hands on the 20th, moving on through the zodiac. Slower **Saturn** will be lost in the Sun's radiance by the end of the month.

On the 27th, the waxing gibbous **Moon** will join **Jupiter** and **Uranus** in Pisces, rising about 2 hours after sunset.

★ ★ ★

4   ASPECT—Mars opposed Jupiter. Examples: The Emancipation Proclamation was issued by President Abraham Lincoln (January 1, 1863—Mars at 0° Aries, Jupiter at 2° Libra) freeing thousands of slaves. Later, in the same aspect, Martin Luther King Jr. gave his "I have a Dream" speech on the steps of the Lincoln memorial (August 28, 1963—Mars at 26° Virgo, Jupiter at 24° Pisces). How in this day can we care for the power of our words so that they align with wisdom to bring forth the greatest good for all communities of people?

9   New Moon: Sun and Moon both at 22° of the Crab. When the Sun was at this location, Lazarus died. From now until August 21 the Sun traces the path of Lazarus's journey through death. This degree is also the location of the Moon at the death of the Nathan Mary (24° Cancer). Today, her *death* Moon cradles Lazarus's *death* Sun. See her other connections to this month on the 13th, 24th and 30th, intertwining with the initiation of Lazarus.

13   Sun 25° of Cancer: Birth of the Nathan Mary. Mary's *birth* Sun today in Cancer gestures an ensouling into the depths of earthly matter and on the 30th her *death* Sun presents a picture of the "pierced heart" (Leo) that opens to know the thoughts of many hearts because it has so completely penetrated the mysteries of matter and the needs of humanity.

16   ASPECT—Jupiter opposed Saturn, 1° orb from August 11 to 22. This is the third return of this aspect (See May 23, 2010, for the second). Sophianic Wisdom stands before Cosmic Memory! What wisdom can be remembered in order to form Sophianic communities on Earth?

20   Sun 2° Leo: Conversation at Jacob's Well with the Samaritan woman. The zodiacal sign Leo corresponds to the human heart wherein the Christ impulse is implanted. The Sun in Leo is a sign in heaven for the awakening of the Christ impulse. This was the event for the Samaritan woman at this conversation with Christ; her heart awakened to the presence of Christ and the "living waters…a spring of water welling up to eternal life." This is a day to open our hearts to the mystery of Christ in me.

ASPECT: Sun opposite Neptune. There was an opposition between Sun and Neptune at the raising of Lazarus and at the death of

SIDEREAL GEOCENTRIC LONGITUDES : AUGUST 2010 Gregorian at 0 hours UT

DAY	☉	☽	☊	☿	♀	♂	♃	♄	♅	♆	♇
1 SU	13 ♋ 47	18 ♓ 45	16 ♐ 43R	10 ♌ 21	28 ♌ 40	6 ♍ 20	8 ♓ 24R	6 ♍ 0	5 ♓ 26R	2 ♒ 56R	8 ♐ 22R
2 MO	14 44	0 ♈ 55	16 41	11 32	29 44	6 57	8 22	6 5	5 25	2 55	8 21
3 TU	15 41	13 18	16 40	12 41	0 ♍ 47	7 34	8 20	6 11	5 23	2 53	8 20
4 WE	16 39	25 58	16 40D	13 47	1 50	8 11	8 18	6 16	5 22	2 51	8 19
5 TH	17 36	9 ♉ 1	16 41	14 51	2 52	8 48	8 16	6 22	5 21	2 50	8 17
6 FR	18 34	22 29	16 43	15 52	3 55	9 25	8 13	6 28	5 19	2 48	8 16
7 SA	19 31	6 ♊ 24	16 44	16 51	4 57	10 2	8 10	6 33	5 18	2 47	8 15
8 SU	20 29	20 45	16 44R	17 46	5 59	10 39	8 7	6 39	5 16	2 45	8 14
9 MO	21 26	5 ♋ 30	16 43	18 39	7 0	11 17	8 4	6 45	5 15	2 44	8 13
10 TU	22 24	20 33	16 40	19 28	8 2	11 54	8 1	6 51	5 13	2 42	8 12
11 WE	23 21	5 ♌ 45	16 36	20 15	9 3	12 31	7 57	6 57	5 12	2 40	8 11
12 TH	24 19	20 56	16 31	20 57	10 4	13 9	7 54	7 3	5 10	2 39	8 10
13 FR	25 17	5 ♍ 55	16 26	21 36	11 4	13 47	7 50	7 9	5 9	2 37	8 9
14 SA	26 14	20 36	16 21	22 11	12 4	14 24	7 46	7 15	5 7	2 35	8 8
15 SU	27 12	4 ♎ 52	16 18	22 42	13 4	15 2	7 42	7 22	5 5	2 34	8 8
16 MO	28 10	18 41	16 16	23 9	14 3	15 40	7 37	7 28	5 3	2 32	8 7
17 TU	29 7	2 ♏ 4	16 15D	23 31	15 2	16 18	7 33	7 34	5 2	2 31	8 6
18 WE	0 ♌ 5	15 4	16 16	23 49	16 1	16 56	7 28	7 41	5 0	2 29	8 5
19 TH	1 3	27 43	16 18	24 1	16 59	17 34	7 23	7 47	4 58	2 27	8 4
20 FR	2 0	10 ♐ 6	16 19	24 8	17 57	18 12	7 18	7 53	4 56	2 26	8 4
21 SA	2 58	22 17	16 19R	24 10R	18 54	18 50	7 13	8 0	4 54	2 24	8 3
22 SU	3 56	4 ♑ 19	16 17	24 6	19 51	19 28	7 7	8 6	4 52	2 22	8 2
23 MO	4 54	16 14	16 13	23 57	20 48	20 7	7 2	8 13	4 50	2 21	8 1
24 TU	5 51	28 7	16 7	23 41	21 44	20 45	6 56	8 20	4 48	2 19	8 1
25 WE	6 49	9 ♒ 58	15 58	23 20	22 39	21 24	6 50	8 26	4 46	2 17	8 0
26 TH	7 47	21 50	15 49	22 53	23 34	22 2	6 44	8 33	4 44	2 16	8 0
27 FR	8 45	3 ♓ 43	15 39	22 20	24 29	22 41	6 38	8 40	4 42	2 14	7 59
28 SA	9 43	15 40	15 29	21 42	25 23	23 20	6 32	8 46	4 40	2 13	7 58
29 SU	10 41	27 44	15 20	20 59	26 16	23 58	6 26	8 53	4 38	2 11	7 58
30 MO	11 39	9 ♈ 55	15 14	20 11	27 9	24 37	6 19	9 0	4 36	2 9	7 57
31 TU	12 37	22 18	15 9	19 20	28 2	25 16	6 13	9 7	4 34	2 8	7 57

INGRESSES :

1	☽ → ♈ 22:13	21	☽ → ♑ 15:22
2	♀ → ♍ 6:14	24	☽ → ♒ 3:48
4	☽ → ♉ 7:29	26	☽ → ♓ 16:30
6	☽ → ♊ 13: 3	29	☽ → ♈ 4:29
8	☽ → ♋ 15: 6	31	☽ → ♉ 14:40
10	☽ → ♌ 14:56		
12	☽ → ♍ 14:28		
14	☽ → ♎ 15:44		
16	☽ → ♏ 20:13		
17	☉ → ♌ 21:57		
19	☽ → ♐ 4:22		

ASPECTS & ECLIPSES :

3	☉ □ ☽	4:57		☽ ☌ P	17:54	20	☉ ☍ ♆	10:13	28	☽ ☍ ♂	16: 7
	♃ □ ♇	9:37		☽ ☍ ♆	19: 9		☽ ☌ ☊	12:11		☽ ☍ ♀	20:53
4	♂ ☍ ♃	4:19	12	☽ ☌ ☿	0: 2		♀ ☌ ♂	18:47			
	♂ □ ♇	4:51		☽ ☍ ♅	22:44	21	♄ □ ♇	9:41			
7	☽ ☍ ♇	3: 8	13	☽ ☌ ♄	2: 0	24	☽ ☌ ♆	8:29			
	♀ ☍ ♅	7:56		☽ ☍ ♃	3: 4		☉ ☍ ☽	17: 3			
	☽ ☌ ☋	17:21		☽ ☌ ♀	8:57	25	☽ ☌ A	6: 7			
8	♀ ☌ ♄	17:22		☽ ☌ ♂	13:20	26	☽ ☍ ☿	2: 3			
9	♀ ☍ ♃	23:39	16	☉ □ ☽	18:13	27	☽ ☌ ♅	1:58			
10	☉ ☌ ☽	3: 7		♃ ☍ ♄	20:44		☽ ☌ ♃	5:49			
	♀ □ ♇	4: 0	19	☽ ☌ ♇	20: 0		☽ ☍ ♄	10: 2			

SIDEREAL HELIOCENTRIC LONGITUDES : AUGUST 2010 Gregorian at 0 hours UT

DAY	Sid. Time	☿	♀	⊕	♂	♃	♄	♅	♆	♇	Vernal Point
1 SU	20:37:59	1 ♏ 59	19 ♏ 20	13 ♑ 47	6 ♎ 41	28 ♒ 47	10 ♍ 49	3 ♓ 9	2 ♒ 17	9 ♐ 25	5 ♓ 6'45"
2 MO	20:41:55	4 48	20 55	14 44	7 10	28 53	10 51	3 10	2 18	9 25	5 ♓ 6'45"
3 TU	20:45:52	7 35	22 30	15 41	7 38	28 58	10 53	3 10	2 18	9 26	5 ♓ 6'44"
4 WE	20:49:48	10 22	24 6	16 39	8 7	29 4	10 55	3 11	2 18	9 26	5 ♓ 6'44"
5 TH	20:53:45	13 8	25 41	17 36	8 36	29 9	10 57	3 12	2 19	9 26	5 ♓ 6'44"
6 FR	20:57:42	15 53	27 16	18 34	9 4	29 15	10 59	3 12	2 19	9 27	5 ♓ 6'44"
7 SA	21: 1:38	18 38	28 51	19 31	9 33	29 20	11 1	3 13	2 19	9 27	5 ♓ 6'44"
8 SU	21: 5:35	21 23	0 ♐ 26	20 29	10 2	29 26	11 3	3 14	2 20	9 27	5 ♓ 6'44"
9 MO	21: 9:31	24 8	2 1	21 26	10 31	29 31	11 5	3 14	2 20	9 28	5 ♓ 6'44"
10 TU	21:13:28	26 52	3 36	22 24	11 0	29 37	11 7	3 15	2 21	9 28	5 ♓ 6'43"
11 WE	21:17:24	29 38	5 11	23 21	11 28	29 42	11 9	3 16	2 21	9 28	5 ♓ 6'43"
12 TH	21:21:21	2 ♐ 24	6 46	24 19	11 57	29 48	11 11	3 16	2 21	9 29	5 ♓ 6'43"
13 FR	21:25:17	5 11	8 21	25 17	12 26	29 53	11 13	3 17	2 22	9 29	5 ♓ 6'43"
14 SA	21:29:14	7 58	9 56	26 14	12 56	29 59	11 15	3 18	2 22	9 30	5 ♓ 6'43"
15 SU	21:33:11	10 47	11 31	27 12	13 25	0 ♓ 4	11 17	3 18	2 22	9 30	5 ♓ 6'43"
16 MO	21:37: 7	13 38	13 6	28 10	13 54	0 9	11 19	3 19	2 23	9 30	5 ♓ 6'43"
17 TU	21:41: 4	16 30	14 41	29 7	14 23	0 15	11 21	3 19	2 23	9 31	5 ♓ 6'43"
18 WE	21:45: 0	19 24	16 16	0 ♒ 5	14 52	0 20	11 23	3 20	2 23	9 31	5 ♓ 6'42"
19 TH	21:48:57	22 21	17 51	1 3	15 21	0 26	11 25	3 21	2 24	9 31	5 ♓ 6'42"
20 FR	21:52:53	25 19	19 26	2 0	15 51	0 31	11 27	3 21	2 24	9 32	5 ♓ 6'42"
21 SA	21:56:50	28 21	21 1	2 58	16 20	0 37	11 29	3 22	2 25	9 32	5 ♓ 6'42"
22 SU	22: 0:46	1 ♑ 25	22 36	3 56	16 49	0 42	11 31	3 23	2 25	9 32	5 ♓ 6'42"
23 MO	22: 4:43	4 32	24 10	4 54	17 19	0 48	11 33	3 23	2 25	9 33	5 ♓ 6'42"
24 TU	22: 8:40	7 43	25 45	5 51	17 48	0 53	11 35	3 24	2 26	9 33	5 ♓ 6'42"
25 WE	22:12:36	10 58	27 20	6 49	18 18	0 59	11 37	3 25	2 26	9 33	5 ♓ 6'41"
26 TH	22:16:33	14 16	28 55	7 47	18 47	1 4	11 39	3 25	2 26	9 34	5 ♓ 6'41"
27 FR	22:20:29	17 39	0 ♑ 30	8 45	19 17	1 10	11 41	3 26	2 27	9 34	5 ♓ 6'41"
28 SA	22:24:26	21 7	2 5	9 43	19 47	1 15	11 43	3 27	2 27	9 34	5 ♓ 6'41"
29 SU	22:28:22	24 40	3 40	10 41	20 16	1 21	11 45	3 27	2 27	9 35	5 ♓ 6'41"
30 MO	22:32:19	28 18	5 14	11 39	20 46	1 26	11 47	3 28	2 28	9 35	5 ♓ 6'41"
31 TU	22:36:15	2 ♒ 2	6 49	12 37	21 16	1 32	11 49	3 28	2 28	9 35	5 ♓ 6'41"

INGRESSES :

7	♀ → ♐ 17:23
11	☿ → ♐ 3:13
14	♃ → ♓ 6:26
17	⊕ → ♒ 21:56
21	☿ → ♑ 12:59
26	♀ → ♑ 16:27
30	☿ → ♒ 11: 1

ASPECTS (HELIOCENTRIC +MOON(TYCHONIC)) :

1	☿ □ ♆	2:37	8	☿ ☌ A	11:49	14	☿ ☌ ♇	12:59		☿ ✶ ♃	18:19		♀ ✶ ♅	20:50
	☿ △ ♅	10: 1	9	♀ ✶ ♆	4:47		♀ □ ♄	20:24	22	☿ ✶ ♅	15:10	30	☽ ☍ ♂	21:55
2	☽ ☍ ♂	12:39		♀ □ ♅	18:34	15	☿ □ ♄	4:16	24	☽ ☌ ♆	8:43	31	☿ ☌ ♆	2:47
	♀ ☌ ☋	14:37	10	☽ ☍ ♆	18:38		☿ ☌ ♀	13:58	25	☿ △ ♄	4:51			
4	☿ ✶ ♄	4:50	11	☿ □ ♃	0:39		☽ ☌ ♂	15:17	26	☽ ☌ ♃	18:48			
5	☽ ☍ ☿	9:20		☿ ✶ ♆	23:38	16	☿ ✶ ♂	2:39		☽ ☌ ♅	23:25			
6	☽ ☍ ♀	9:25	12	☿ □ ♅	7:36		♀ ✶ ♂	17:22	27	♀ ✶ ♃	10:43			
	♂ ✶ ♇	19: 0		☽ ☍ ♃	14:13	19	☽ ☌ ♇	22:52		☿ □ ♂	13:14			
7	☽ ☍ ♇	5:10		☽ ☍ ♅	19:44	20	⊕ ☌ ♆	9:57		☽ ☍ ♄	16: 3			
	♀ □ ♃	7:47	13	☽ ☌ ♄	8:37		☽ ☌ ♀	21: 6		⊕ ✶ ♇	20:24			
	☿ ✶ ⊕	11:54		♀ ☌ ♇	17:12	21	☽ ☌ ☿	16:11	28	☿ ⚼ ☊	16:38			

Master Jesus and the death of the Virgin Mary.

21 Sun at 3° Leo: The Raising of Lazarus from the dead. At this event Lazarus received the seven gifts of the Holy Spirit. The seven breaths plant the seeds for the Tree of Life within Lazarus. Mary's birth Moon (5° Leo) stands close by the Sun at the return of Lazarus from the dead. Why was her life so intimately intertwined with Lazarus, as shown by these two eyes of God, Sun and Moon? (See here and the 24th)

24 Full Moon: Sun at the Royal Star Regulus (5° of the Lion) opposite Moon 5° Aquarius. Note this is the location of the Moon (a New Moon at that time) at the raising of Lazarus marking the completion of a spiritual initiation of the heart (Leo). Also we find here the Moon at the birth of the Nathan Mary, contrasting to her Death-Moon position at this month's New Moon (on the 9th). Mary's *birth* Moon stands in the heart of hearts at 5° Leo, very close to the (*birth*) Sun at the Raising of Lazarus. This is the opposite of the New Moon on the 9th when Mary's *death* Moon cradles the *death* Sun of Lazarus. Sun and Moon weave together from the 9th to the 30th of this month. This month's Moon cycle (New—Full) arouses the memory of Nathan Mary, she who represents purity. We open to the mystery of the heart and the relationship of Mary to this initiation of Lazarus.

28 Sun 10½° Leo: Healing of the Nobleman's Son (Aug 3, 30). The "nobleman" Selathiel's dependence on Zorobabel (King) caused his self, which is intrinsically the nature of the Sun, to become moon-like; he lost his true self. This was the background to the illness of his son, Joel. Selathiel's faith in Christ restored his selfhood to its true sun-like nature, which restored health to his son who was later renamed Jesse (John 4:46, *Chron*, 165, 239). We may ask: Is my "I" in vertical alignment with my star, or have I succumbed to powers of this world?

30 Sun 12° Leo: Death of the Nathan Mary (See 9th, 21st and 24th).

SEPTEMBER

The month begins with an inferior conjunction between the **Sun** and **Mercury** on the 3rd. The waxing crescent **Moon** joins **Mars** and **Venus** on the 10th, in front of Spica, an important star at 29° of Virgo (the Sheaf of Wheat in the Virgin's hand). We should be able to see this visible in the West in the twilight of early evening.

The **Sun** moves into Virgo on the 17th. The Full **Moon** of the 22nd includes Jupiter with the **Moon**, so take time before and after the 22nd to watch the **Moon** move across **Jupiter** in the Fishes. After this, **Jupiter** will be visible in the night sky for the rest of the year. **Saturn** disappears into the glare of the **Sun** this month, while **Venus** and **Mars** will be visible in the western sky at sunset.

Mercury stations direct on the 13th (retrograde since August 21st), and **Pluto** stations direct on the 15th (retrograde since April).

✶ ✶ ✶

3   Sun conjunct Mercury 16° of the Lion. This is the same degree we find the position of the Moon during the time of the Baptism of Jesus in the Jordan River by John the Baptist—September 23, 29 C.E. It marks the descent of the Cosmic Christ into the body of the Nathan Jesus. We can imagine this moment as the arrival of the Sun King, the birthing of new forces for the heart of humanity. The Sun/Mercury conjunction acts as a focus point for the mind. Take into your focus the words, "This is my beloved Son in whom I am well pleased." Now take into your open heart these words, "This is my beloved Self in whom the I AM is well pleased." Allow these words to become your mantra and your inspiration for your actions throughout the day.

8   New Moon in 21° of the Lion. On August 12, 30 C.E., the Sun was also at 21° of the Lion. It was the day Jesus sharply reproached the Pharisees for their misinterpretation of the Law. So vehement was the reaction of the Pharisees that they attempted to cast Jesus from the top of a steep hill. "Suddenly, however, Jesus stopped, stood still, and with the help of Angelic beings passed—as if invisible—through the midst of the crowd to his escape" (Luke 4:29–30). The planet Uranus was in this degree from the time of the Crucifixion to Whitsun. Both of these indications remind us of how the Spirit is capable of overcoming and defying the laws of material nature and gravity. Equally significant to these two indicators is the quality of a courageous heart, the fearlessness to face the shadow of death.

12   Mercury turns direct at 11° of the Lion. At the 11th degree of the Lion lives the memory of the Sun's passage over it on August 3, 30 C.E. The memory is the event of the Healing of the Nobleman's Son of Capernaum (John 4:46–54). In this instance Jesus heals from a distance, once again superseding the laws of physicality.

17   The Sun moves from the Lion into the Virgin, sign of the Sophia! It is a day worth meditating on all you know of this Divine Being. Fill yourself up with the feelings of gratitude and peace. Take her image into the sacred well of your heart and be nourished.

19   Jupiter conjunct Uranus at 4° of the Fishes. See the article by William Bento herein. This degree has been saturated with memories of miracles performed by the Christ. The first was the Transformation of Water into Wine at the Wedding at Cana (John 2:4–11). During that time the Moon was conjunct Jupiter at this degree. It was the first of miracles performed by the Christ. In it we can sense the mystery of a new

SIDEREAL GEOCENTRIC LONGITUDES : SEPTEMBER 2010 Gregorian at 0 hours UT

DAY	☉	☽	☊	☿	♀	♂	♃	♄	⛢	♆	♇
1 WE	13 ♌ 35	4 ♉ 57	15 ♐ 7R	18 ♌ 25R	28 ♍ 53	25 ♍ 55	6 ♓ 6R	9 ♍ 14	4 ♓ 31R	2 ♒ 6R	7 ♐ 57R
2 TH	14 33	17 54	15 7D	17 29	29 44	26 34	5 59	9 21	4 29	2 4	7 56
3 FR	15 31	1 ♊ 14	15 7	16 31	0 ♎ 35	27 13	5 52	9 28	4 27	2 3	7 56
4 SA	16 29	15 0	15 8R	15 34	1 25	27 53	5 45	9 35	4 25	2 1	7 56
5 SU	17 27	29 13	15 7	14 39	2 14	28 32	5 38	9 42	4 22	2 0	7 55
6 MO	18 25	13 ♋ 52	15 4	13 46	3 2	29 11	5 31	9 49	4 20	1 58	7 55
7 TU	19 24	28 52	14 59	12 58	3 50	29 51	5 23	9 56	4 18	1 57	7 55
8 WE	20 22	14 ♌ 6	14 51	12 15	4 36	0 ♎ 30	5 16	10 3	4 16	1 55	7 54
9 TH	21 20	29 24	14 42	11 38	5 22	1 10	5 8	10 10	4 13	1 54	7 54
10 FR	22 18	14 ♍ 34	14 32	11 8	6 8	1 50	5 1	10 17	4 11	1 52	7 54
11 SA	23 17	29 26	14 23	10 46	6 52	2 29	4 53	10 24	4 9	1 51	7 54
12 SU	24 15	13 ♎ 53	14 15	10 33	7 35	3 9	4 45	10 32	4 6	1 49	7 54
13 MO	25 14	27 51	14 10	10 29D	8 17	3 49	4 37	10 39	4 4	1 48	7 54
14 TU	26 12	11 ♏ 19	14 7	10 34	8 59	4 29	4 30	10 46	4 1	1 46	7 54
15 WE	27 10	24 19	14 6	10 48	9 39	5 9	4 22	10 53	3 59	1 45	7 54D
16 TH	28 9	6 ♐ 56	14 7D	11 11	10 18	5 49	4 14	11 1	3 57	1 43	7 54
17 FR	29 7	19 15	14 7R	11 44	10 56	6 29	4 6	11 8	3 54	1 42	7 54
18 SA	0 ♍ 6	1 ♑ 20	14 5	12 25	11 33	7 9	3 58	11 15	3 52	1 40	7 54
19 SU	1 4	13 16	14 2	13 15	12 9	7 50	3 50	11 23	3 50	1 39	7 54
20 MO	2 3	25 8	13 56	14 12	12 43	8 30	3 42	11 30	3 47	1 38	7 54
21 TU	3 2	6 ♒ 58	13 47	15 17	13 16	9 10	3 34	11 37	3 45	1 36	7 55
22 WE	4 0	18 50	13 36	16 28	13 48	9 51	3 26	11 45	3 42	1 35	7 55
23 TH	4 59	0 ♓ 44	13 22	17 45	14 18	10 32	3 18	11 52	3 40	1 34	7 55
24 FR	5 58	12 44	13 8	19 8	14 47	11 12	3 10	11 59	3 37	1 32	7 55
25 SA	6 56	24 49	12 54	20 36	15 14	11 53	3 2	12 7	3 35	1 31	7 56
26 SU	7 55	7 ♈ 1	12 42	22 7	15 40	12 34	2 54	12 14	3 33	1 30	7 56
27 MO	8 54	19 22	12 32	23 43	16 4	13 14	2 46	12 21	3 30	1 29	7 56
28 TU	9 53	1 ♉ 52	12 25	25 21	16 26	13 55	2 38	12 29	3 28	1 27	7 57
29 WE	10 52	14 35	12 21	27 1	16 46	14 36	2 30	12 36	3 25	1 26	7 57
30 TH	11 51	27 33	12 19	28 44	17 5	15 17	2 22	12 44	3 23	1 25	7 58

INGRESSES :

2	♀ → ♎ 7:20	20	☽ → ♒ 9:52
	☽ → ♊ 21:47	22	☽ → ♓ 22:30
5	☽ → ♋ 1:17	25	☽ → ♈ 10:13
7	☽ → ♌ 1:47	27	☽ → ♉ 20:26
	♂ → ♎ 5:36	30	☽ → ♊ 4:28
9	☽ → ♍ 0:56		☿ → ♍ 17:32
11	☽ → ♎ 0:55		
13	☽ → ♏ 3:47		
15	☽ → ♐ 10:43		
17	☽ → ♑ 21:19		
	☉ → ♍ 21:34		

ASPECTS & ECLIPSES :

1	☉ □ ☽ 17:20	11	☽ ☌ ♂ 5:14	23	☽ ☌ ♃ 5: 4
3	☽ ☍ ♇ 11:45		☽ ☌ ♀ 12:53		☽ ☌ ⛢ 5:51
	☉ ☌ ☿ 12:34	15	☉ □ ☽ 5:48		☉ ☍ ☽ 9:16
4	☽ ☌ ☋ 0:13	16	☽ ☌ ♇ 1:50		☽ ☍ ♄ 22:30
7	☽ ☍ ♆ 4:51		☽ ☌ ☊ 13:55	26	☉ □ ♇ 0:20
	☽ ☌ ☿ 21:12	19	♃ ☌ ⛢ 1:24		☽ ☍ ♂ 11:26
8	☽ ☌ P 3:58	20	☽ ☌ ♆ 13: 8		☽ ☍ ♀ 17:24
	☉ ☌ ☽ 10:28	21	☽ ☌ A 7:56	30	☽ ☍ ♇ 18:53
9	☽ ☍ ⛢ 7:34		☉ ☍ ♃ 11:35		
	☽ ☍ ♃ 8:57		☉ ☍ ⛢ 16:55		
	☽ ☌ ♄ 17: 8		☽ ☍ ☿ 18:41		

SIDEREAL HELIOCENTRIC LONGITUDES : SEPTEMBER 2010 Gregorian at 0 hours UT

DAY	Sid. Time	☿	♀	⊕	♂	♃	♄	⛢	♆	♇	Vernal Point
1 WE	22:40:12	5 ♒ 52	8 ♑ 24	13 ♒ 35	21 ♎ 46	1 ♓ 37	11 ♍ 51	3 ♓ 29	2 ♒ 28	9 ♐ 36	5 ♓ 6'40"
2 TH	22:44: 9	9 48	9 59	14 33	22 16	1 43	11 53	3 30	2 29	9 36	5 ♓ 6'40"
3 FR	22:48: 5	13 51	11 34	15 31	22 46	1 48	11 55	3 30	2 29	9 36	5 ♓ 6'40"
4 SA	22:52: 2	18 2	13 9	16 29	23 16	1 54	11 57	3 31	2 30	9 37	5 ♓ 6'40"
5 SU	22:55:58	22 20	14 44	17 27	23 46	1 59	11 59	3 32	2 30	9 37	5 ♓ 6'40"
6 MO	22:59:55	26 46	16 18	18 25	24 16	2 5	12 1	3 32	2 30	9 37	5 ♓ 6'40"
7 TU	23: 3:51	1 ♓ 20	17 53	19 24	24 46	2 10	12 3	3 33	2 31	9 38	5 ♓ 6'40"
8 WE	23: 7:48	6 3	19 28	20 22	25 16	2 16	12 5	3 34	2 31	9 38	5 ♓ 6'40"
9 TH	23:11:44	10 54	21 3	21 20	25 46	2 21	12 7	3 34	2 31	9 38	5 ♓ 6'39"
10 FR	23:15:41	15 55	22 38	22 19	26 17	2 26	12 9	3 35	2 32	9 39	5 ♓ 6'39"
11 SA	23:19:38	21 4	24 13	23 17	26 47	2 32	12 11	3 36	2 32	9 39	5 ♓ 6'39"
12 SU	23:23:34	26 23	25 48	24 15	27 17	2 37	12 13	3 36	2 32	9 39	5 ♓ 6'39"
13 MO	23:27:31	1 ♈ 51	27 23	25 14	27 48	2 43	12 15	3 37	2 33	9 40	5 ♓ 6'39"
14 TU	23:31:27	7 28	28 58	26 12	28 18	2 48	12 17	3 37	2 33	9 40	5 ♓ 6'39"
15 WE	23:35:24	13 13	0 ♒ 33	27 10	28 49	2 54	12 19	3 38	2 34	9 40	5 ♓ 6'39"
16 TH	23:39:20	19 5	2 8	28 9	29 19	2 59	12 21	3 39	2 34	9 41	5 ♓ 6'38"
17 FR	23:43:17	25 6	3 43	29 7	29 50	3 5	12 23	3 39	2 34	9 41	5 ♓ 6'38"
18 SA	23:47:13	1 ♉ 12	5 18	0 ♓ 6	0 ♏ 21	3 10	12 25	3 40	2 35	9 41	5 ♓ 6'38"
19 SU	23:51:10	7 23	6 53	1 5	0 52	3 16	12 27	3 41	2 35	9 42	5 ♓ 6'38"
20 MO	23:55: 7	13 39	8 28	2 3	1 22	3 21	12 29	3 41	2 35	9 42	5 ♓ 6'38"
21 TU	23:59: 3	19 57	10 3	3 2	1 53	3 27	12 31	3 42	2 36	9 42	5 ♓ 6'38"
22 WE	0: 3: 0	26 16	11 38	4 0	2 24	3 32	12 33	3 43	2 36	9 43	5 ♓ 6'38"
23 TH	0: 6:56	2 ♊ 35	13 13	4 59	2 55	3 38	12 35	3 43	2 36	9 43	5 ♓ 6'37"
24 FR	0:10:53	8 52	14 49	5 58	3 26	3 43	12 37	3 44	2 37	9 43	5 ♓ 6'37"
25 SA	0:14:49	15 5	16 24	6 56	3 57	3 49	12 39	3 45	2 37	9 44	5 ♓ 6'37"
26 SU	0:18:46	21 14	17 59	7 55	4 28	3 54	12 41	3 45	2 37	9 44	5 ♓ 6'37"
27 MO	0:22:42	27 17	19 34	8 54	4 59	4 0	12 43	3 46	2 38	9 45	5 ♓ 6'37"
28 TU	0:26:39	3 ♋ 13	21 9	9 53	5 31	4 5	12 45	3 46	2 38	9 45	5 ♓ 6'37"
29 WE	0:30:36	9 1	22 45	10 52	6 2	4 11	12 47	3 47	2 39	9 45	5 ♓ 6'37"
30 TH	0:34:32	14 41	24 20	11 51	6 33	4 16	12 49	3 48	2 39	9 46	5 ♓ 6'36"

INGRESSES :

6	☿ → ♓ 17: 5
12	☿ → ♈ 15:56
14	♀ → ♒ 15:41
17	♂ → ♏ 7:44
	☿ → ♉ 19:19
	⊕ → ♓ 21:33
22	☿ → ♊ 14:10
27	☿ → ♋ 10:54

ASPECTS (HELIOCENTRIC +MOON(TYCHONIC)) :

1	☿ ✶ ♇ 22:47	8	☿ □ ♇ 17:49	16	☽ ☌ ♇ 5:17	20	☽ ☌ ♆ 15: 7		☽ ☌ ⛢ 5:59		☿ △ ♃ 3:36
3	♀ △ ♄ 5:33	9	☽ ☍ ♃ 4:40		♀ ☌ ♆ 6:35		♀ ✶ ♇ 18:45		☿ □ ⊕ 10:50		☽ ☍ ♂ 7:12
	☿ ☌ ⊕ 12:34		☿ ☍ ♄ 5:57		☿ ☌ ☊ 17:56	21	☽ ☌ ♀ 7:12		☽ ☍ ♄ 23:47		☿ △ ♂ 10:19
	☽ ☍ ♇ 14:41		☽ ☍ ⛢ 6:34	17	☿ ✶ ⊕ 18:54		☿ ☌ P 10:35	24	♃ ☌ ⛢ 3: 1		♀ □s ☊ 11: 4
5	☿ △ ♂ 8:51		☽ ☌ ♄ 20: 8		☿ ☍ ♂ 20:22		⊕ ☌ ♃ 11:20		☿ ☍ ♇ 3:18	29	☿ △ ⊕ 9:22
6	☽ ☍ ♀ 4:24	10	☽ ☍ ☿ 3:14	18	☿ □ ♆ 5:22		⊕ ☌ ⛢ 16:39		♂ △ ⛢ 14: 6		☿ ✶ ♄ 16: 0
	♀ ☌ A 7:50	11	☿ ✶ ♀ 20:17		☿ ✶ ♃ 7:48	22	♂ □ ♆ 9:25		☿ □ ♄ 14:31	30	☽ ☍ ♇ 22: 6
	♂ ☌ ☋ 23:16	12	☽ ☌ ♂ 23:55		☿ ✶ ⛢ 9:37	23	☿ △ ♆ 0: 5		♂ △ ♃ 16:12		
7	☿ ☌ ♃ 4:24	13	☿ ✶ ♆ 3: 1		⊕ △ ♂ 12:47		☿ □ ♃ 4: 3	25	☿ △ ♀ 6:48		
	☽ ☍ ♆ 5:45		♀ □ ♂ 9:16		☿ □ ♀ 21:23		☿ □ ⛢ 4:20	27	⊕ □ ♇ 20:42		
	☿ ☌ ⛢ 11:25	14	☿ △ ♇ 9:17	19	☿ △ ♄ 19:33		☽ ☌ ♃ 5:50	28	☿ △ ⛢ 2:16		

community—one that is not bound by blood, but by love. The second miracle was the Feeding of the Five Thousand, which followed his Sermon on the Mount wherein he taught the Lord's Prayer (John 6:5–15 & Mark 6:35–44). Late in the night that followed the third miracle occurred. Jesus Walked on the Water and demonstrated the power of faith to his apostles (Matt. 14:25–33). The second and third miracle happened while Venus was in the 4th degree of the Fishes.

21 The Sun in the 4th degree of the Virgin opposes Jupiter and Uranus. This continues to intensify the mood of the great Jupiter/Uranus conjunction. In it we may find the miraculous forces needed to transform our communities from the fears of scarcity to the joys of blessed relatedness one to another. We may also find the magical salvation that lies in the words of the Lord's Prayer. With these words we may be fed in our soul/spirit nature, and thereby gain the strength to transform our communities into beacons of light in this dark time.

> All of you together are like the heavenly constellations.
> You represent what is imperishable in the world,
> and in the future. This you bear within you.
> Just as the stars encircle and transmute the world,
> so you too will encircle and transmute the world,
> and the gaze of human beings will turn to you as to the stars.
> You will be to them as the stars, because I ray out within you,
> And they will be illumined through you.
> (J. von Halle, *The Lord's Prayer*)

These were the words the Christ delivered as a preparation to receive the Lord's Prayer. These words are no less relevant today than they were nearly two thousand years ago. The storm the apostles experienced on Peter's boat is no less apparent in our current state of the world. We are all in the midst of an economic tsunami, shaking our earthly securities and drenching us with uncertainties about the fate of our future. Yet these heavenly memories can be our sign of hope, our stars by which we navigate into a new world paradigm. We need only remember that it is possible to walk on water, or put in anthroposophic terms, it is possible to enter into the etheric world and unite ourselves with the source of life.

23 Full Moon in the Fishes at 6°. The theme of the Jupiter/Uranus conjunction in the Fishes is further amplified by the Full Moon in this sign. The above-mentioned miracles continue to pervade the psychic mantle of the Earth. As a means to deepen our relationship with the last mentioned miracle—Walking on Water—we may take up the following verse by Rudolf Steiner:

> Quiet I bear within me,
> I bear within myself
> Forces that make me strong.
> Now will I be imbued
> With their glowing warmth,
> Now will I permeate myself
> With the power of my will.
> And I will feel how quiet pours itself
> Through all my being,
> When I strengthen myself
> To find quiet as a very force
> Within me
> Through the might of my striving.
> (*Guidance in Esoteric Training*)

OCTOBER

We begin with the **Sun** conjunct **Saturn** in Virgo the 1st. **Venus** is conjunct **Mars** in Libra on the 2nd with this pair visible in the evenings to the west until **Venus** stations retrograde on the 9th, disappearing into the **Sun**'s radiance around the 16th, culminating in the inferior conjunction of the **Sun** and **Venus** on the 29th.

The New **Moon** of the 7th also includes **Saturn** in the mix on the edge of Virgo. Then the slim waxing crescent moves on to conjunct **Venus** and **Mars** on the 9th, perhaps barely visible in the western sky at sunset or near to these two gems on the 10th. The **Sun** makes a superior conjunction with **Mercury** on the 17th. **Jupiter** is visible as the sky darkens each night this month (through the end of the year). Catch the waning gibbous **Moon** as she joins **Jupiter** (and his invisible companion **Uranus**) on the 20th in Pisces, visible in the southeastern sky as the sky darkens. This day also marks retrograde **Jupiter**'s ingress into Aquarius (the Waterman).

October 2010—Commentary on planetary activity in relationship to Christology.

★ ★ ★

1   The Sun conjunct Saturn 13° of the Virgin. The births of the two Jesus children have planetary conjunctions upon this degree. The birth of the Solomon Jesus on March 5, 6 B.C.E., had the Moon conjunct Pluto at this degree, whereas the birth of the Nathan Jesus on December 6, 2 B.C.E., had Jupiter conjunct the Ascendant at the 13th degree of the Virgin. At the Baptism event, which could be conceived as the birth of the Cosmic Christ, Mercury was positioned at this degree. Just think how apropos to have the Cosmos accentuate Virgin births in this sign! The Sun conjunct Saturn asks of us to take seriously these historic phenomenal events. What will we give birth to?

2   Mercury at 4° of the Virgin opposite Uranus at 4° of the Fishes. See the commentary for September 19 and 21. Mercury invites the conversation of miracles past, present and future.

3   Venus conjunct Mars 18° of the Scales. At the end of the Temptation in the Wilderness (November 30, 29 C.E.) Mars was in the very same position. This can be imagined as a triumphant moment wherein the Christ Will prevailed and the adversaries' activity subsided. Today the joining of Venus at this degree adds a dimension of soul balance to our considerations. The wooden sculpture created by Rudolf Steiner known as the "Representative of Humanity" comes to mind as a pertinent image to carry throughout the day. Between Lucifer and Ahriman the Christ figure stands upright and in complete equipoise. May we stand as upright and as peaceful as this figure suggests to us.

7   New Moon at 20° of the Virgin. The Sun was at this degree on September 15, 29 C.E., when a prelude to the great Transfiguration took place. "Around midnight, Jesus said to Eliud that he would reveal himself, and—turning toward heaven—he prayed. A cloud of light enveloped them both and Jesus became radiantly transfigured" (*Chron.*, p. 199). What does it mean to be radiantly transfigured? Is this not an indication that we are all sons and daughters of light?

17 The Sun conjunct Mercury at 29° of the Virgin. This degree is where the bright star Spica shines. Spica designates the Virgin's hand holding the sheaf of wheat or in some versions, the bunch of grapes. It is a clear symbolic representation of the substances of Earth that have for ages been used as sacraments, the bread and the wine. These

SIDEREAL GEOCENTRIC LONGITUDES : OCTOBER 2010 Gregorian at 0 hours UT

DAY	☉	☽	☊	☿	♀	♂	♃	♄	♅	♆	♇
1 FR	12 ♍ 50	10 ♊ 49	12 ♐ 19R	0 ♍ 28	17 ♎ 21	15 ♎ 59	2 ♓ 15R	12 ♍ 51	3 ♓ 21R	1 ♒ 24R	7 ♐ 58
2 SA	13 49	24 27	12 19	2 14	17 36	16 40	2 7	12 58	3 18	1 23	7 59
3 SU	14 48	8 ♋ 27	12 18	4 0	17 49	17 21	1 59	13 6	3 16	1 22	7 59
4 MO	15 47	22 51	12 14	5 46	18 0	18 2	1 52	13 13	3 14	1 21	8 0
5 TU	16 46	7 ♌ 36	12 8	7 34	18 8	18 44	1 44	13 21	3 11	1 20	8 1
6 WE	17 45	22 36	11 59	9 21	18 14	19 25	1 37	13 28	3 9	1 19	8 1
7 TH	18 44	7 ♍ 44	11 49	11 8	18 19	20 7	1 29	13 35	3 7	1 18	8 2
8 FR	19 43	22 48	11 37	12 55	18 20	20 48	1 22	13 43	3 4	1 17	8 3
9 SA	20 43	7 ♎ 39	11 26	14 42	18 20R	21 30	1 15	13 50	3 2	1 16	8 3
10 SU	21 42	22 9	11 17	16 28	18 17	22 12	1 8	13 58	3 0	1 15	8 4
11 MO	22 41	6 ♏ 11	11 11	18 14	18 12	22 54	1 1	14 5	2 58	1 14	8 5
12 TU	23 41	19 44	11 7	19 59	18 4	23 35	0 54	14 12	2 55	1 13	8 6
13 WE	24 40	2 ♐ 50	11 5	21 43	17 54	24 17	0 47	14 20	2 53	1 12	8 7
14 TH	25 39	15 30	11 5	23 28	17 42	24 59	0 41	14 27	2 51	1 11	8 8
15 FR	26 39	27 50	11 5	25 11	17 27	25 42	0 34	14 34	2 49	1 11	8 9
16 SA	27 38	9 ♑ 56	11 4	26 54	17 10	26 24	0 28	14 42	2 47	1 10	8 10
17 SU	28 38	21 51	11 2	28 36	16 50	27 6	0 22	14 49	2 45	1 9	8 11
18 MO	29 37	3 ♒ 42	10 57	0 ♎ 17	16 28	27 48	0 16	14 56	2 43	1 9	8 12
19 TU	0 ♎ 37	15 33	10 50	1 58	16 4	28 30	0 10	15 3	2 41	1 8	8 13
20 WE	1 36	27 27	10 40	3 38	15 38	29 13	0 4	15 10	2 39	1 7	8 14
21 TH	2 36	9 ♓ 26	10 28	5 18	15 10	29 55	29 ♒ 59	15 18	2 37	1 7	8 15
22 FR	3 36	21 34	10 15	6 57	14 41	0 ♏ 38	29 53	15 25	2 35	1 6	8 16
23 SA	4 35	3 ♈ 50	10 3	8 35	14 9	1 20	29 48	15 32	2 33	1 6	8 17
24 SU	5 35	16 16	9 51	10 13	13 36	2 3	29 43	15 39	2 31	1 5	8 18
25 MO	6 35	28 52	9 42	11 50	13 2	2 46	29 38	15 46	2 29	1 5	8 19
26 TU	7 35	11 ♉ 38	9 36	13 26	12 27	3 29	29 33	15 53	2 27	1 4	8 21
27 WE	8 34	24 35	9 33	15 2	11 52	4 11	29 29	16 0	2 25	1 4	8 22
28 TH	9 34	7 ♊ 45	9 32	16 38	11 15	4 54	29 24	16 7	2 23	1 3	8 23
29 FR	10 34	21 7	9 32D	18 13	10 39	5 37	29 20	16 14	2 22	1 3	8 25
30 SA	11 34	4 ♋ 45	9 33	19 47	10 2	6 20	29 16	16 21	2 20	1 3	8 26
31 SU	12 34	18 39	9 33R	21 21	9 26	7 4	29 12	16 28	2 18	1 3	8 27

INGRESSES :

2 ☽ → ♋ 9:35
4 ☽ → ♌ 11:41
6 ☽ → ♍ 11:44
8 ☽ → ♎ 11:34
10 ☽ → ♏ 13:19
12 ☽ → ♐ 18:44
15 ☽ → ♑ 4:15
17 ☽ → ♒ 16:29
☿ → ♎ 19:54
18 ☉ → ♎ 9:11
20 ☽ → ♓ 5: 8
♃ → ♒ 18:24
21 ♂ → ♏ 2:37
22 ☽ → ♈ 16:32
25 ☽ → ♉ 2: 8
27 ☽ → ♊ 9:55
29 ☽ → ♋ 15:41
31 ☽ → ♌ 19:15

ASPECTS & ECLIPSES :

1 ☉ ☌ ♄ 0:41
☽ ☌ ☋ 2:40
☉ □ ☽ 3:51
☿ ☍ ♃ 22:35
2 ☿ ☍ ♅ 14:21
3 ♀ ☌ ♂ 21:55
4 ☽ ☍ ♆ 13:51
5 ☿ □ ♇ 6: 5
6 ☽ ☌ P 13:39
☽ ☍ ♃ 14:10
☽ ☍ ♅ 16:41
7 ☽ ☌ ☿ 6: 7
☽ ☌ ♄ 9:22
☉ ☌ ☽ 18:43
8 ☿ ☌ ♄ 11:34
9 ☽ ☌ ♀ 17:33
10 ☽ ☌ ♂ 0: 5
13 ☽ ☌ ♇ 9:55
☽ ☌ ☊ 15:32
14 ☉ □ ☽ 21:26
17 ☉ ☌ ☿ 1: 3
☽ ☌ ♆ 18:48
18 ☽ ☌ A 18:28
20 ☽ ☌ ♃ 5:14
☽ ☌ ♅ 10:24
21 ☽ ☍ ♄ 11:44
22 ♂ □ ♆ 15:44
23 ☉ ☍ ☽ 1:35
☽ ☍ ☿ 10:35
☽ ☍ ♀ 19: 6
25 ☽ ☍ ♂ 7:47
☿ ☌ ♀ 13:16
28 ☽ ☍ ♇ 1:10
☽ ☌ ☋ 3:13
29 ☉ ☌ ♀ 1: 9
30 ☉ □ ☽ 12:45
31 ☽ ☍ ♆ 21: 0

SIDEREAL HELIOCENTRIC LONGITUDES : OCTOBER 2010 Gregorian at 0 hours UT

DAY	Sid. Time	☿	♀	⊕	♂	♃	♄	♅	♆	♇	Vernal Point
1 FR	0:38:29	20 ♋ 11	25 ♒ 55	12 ♓ 50	7 ♏ 4	4 ♓ 22	12 ♍ 51	3 ♓ 48	2 ♒ 39	9 ♐ 46	5 ♓ 6'36"
2 SA	0:42:25	25 31	27 30	13 49	7 36	4 27	12 53	3 49	2 40	9 46	5 ♓ 6'36"
3 SU	0:46:22	0 ♌ 42	29 6	14 48	8 7	4 33	12 55	3 50	2 40	9 47	5 ♓ 6'36"
4 MO	0:50:18	5 44	0 ♓ 41	15 47	8 39	4 38	12 57	3 50	2 40	9 47	5 ♓ 6'36"
5 TU	0:54:15	10 36	2 16	16 46	9 10	4 44	12 59	3 51	2 41	9 47	5 ♓ 6'36"
6 WE	0:58:11	15 18	3 52	17 45	9 42	4 49	13 1	3 52	2 41	9 48	5 ♓ 6'36"
7 TH	1: 2: 8	19 52	5 27	18 44	10 14	4 55	13 3	3 52	2 41	9 48	5 ♓ 6'36"
8 FR	1: 6: 5	24 16	7 3	19 43	10 46	5 0	13 5	3 53	2 42	9 48	5 ♓ 6'35"
9 SA	1:10: 1	28 32	8 38	20 43	11 17	5 6	13 7	3 54	2 42	9 49	5 ♓ 6'35"
10 SU	1:13:58	2 ♍ 41	10 14	21 42	11 49	5 11	13 9	3 54	2 43	9 49	5 ♓ 6'35"
11 MO	1:17:54	6 41	11 49	22 41	12 21	5 17	13 11	3 55	2 43	9 49	5 ♓ 6'35"
12 TU	1:21:51	10 35	13 25	23 41	12 53	5 22	13 13	3 55	2 43	9 50	5 ♓ 6'35"
13 WE	1:25:47	14 22	15 0	24 40	13 25	5 28	13 15	3 56	2 44	9 50	5 ♓ 6'35"
14 TH	1:29:44	18 3	16 36	25 39	13 57	5 33	13 17	3 57	2 44	9 50	5 ♓ 6'35"
15 FR	1:33:40	21 38	18 11	26 39	14 29	5 39	13 19	3 57	2 44	9 51	5 ♓ 6'34"
16 SA	1:37:37	25 7	19 47	27 38	15 2	5 44	13 21	3 58	2 45	9 51	5 ♓ 6'34"
17 SU	1:41:34	28 31	21 23	28 38	15 34	5 50	13 23	3 59	2 45	9 51	5 ♓ 6'34"
18 MO	1:45:30	1 ♎ 51	22 58	29 37	16 6	5 55	13 25	3 59	2 45	9 52	5 ♓ 6'34"
19 TU	1:49:27	5 7	24 34	0 ♈ 37	16 38	6 0	13 27	4 0	2 46	9 52	5 ♓ 6'34"
20 WE	1:53:23	8 18	26 10	1 36	17 11	6 6	13 29	4 1	2 46	9 52	5 ♓ 6'34"
21 TH	1:57:20	11 26	27 46	2 36	17 43	6 11	13 31	4 1	2 47	9 53	5 ♓ 6'34"
22 FR	2: 1:16	14 30	29 21	3 36	18 16	6 17	13 33	4 2	2 47	9 53	5 ♓ 6'33"
23 SA	2: 5:13	17 32	0 ♈ 57	4 35	18 49	6 22	13 35	4 3	2 47	9 53	5 ♓ 6'33"
24 SU	2: 9: 9	20 31	2 33	5 35	19 21	6 28	13 37	4 3	2 48	9 54	5 ♓ 6'33"
25 MO	2:13: 6	23 27	4 9	6 35	19 54	6 33	13 39	4 4	2 48	9 54	5 ♓ 6'33"
26 TU	2:17: 3	26 21	5 45	7 35	20 27	6 39	13 41	4 4	2 48	9 54	5 ♓ 6'33"
27 WE	2:20:59	29 13	7 21	8 34	20 59	6 44	13 43	4 5	2 49	9 55	5 ♓ 6'33"
28 TH	2:24:56	2 ♏ 3	8 56	9 34	21 32	6 50	13 45	4 6	2 49	9 55	5 ♓ 6'33"
29 FR	2:28:52	4 52	10 32	10 34	22 5	6 55	13 47	4 6	2 49	9 55	5 ♓ 6'32"
30 SA	2:32:49	7 40	12 8	11 34	22 38	7 1	13 49	4 7	2 50	9 56	5 ♓ 6'32"
31 SU	2:36:45	10 27	13 44	12 34	23 11	7 6	13 51	4 8	2 50	9 56	5 ♓ 6'32"

INGRESSES :

2 ☿ → ♌ 20:40
3 ♀ → ♓ 13:39
9 ☿ → ♍ 8:22
17 ☿ → ♎ 10:34
18 ⊕ → ♈ 9: 9
22 ♀ → ♈ 9:42
27 ☿ → ♏ 6:35

ASPECTS (HELIOCENTRIC +MOON(TYCHONIC)) :

1 ⊕ ☍ ♄ 0:41
☿ ☊ ☊ 15: 8
3 ☿ ☍ ♆ 9:16
4 ☿ □ ♂ 16: 2
☽ ☍ ♆ 16: 2
☿ △ ♇ 19:57
5 ☽ ☌ ☿ 7: 4
♀ ☌ ♅ 23:56
6 ♀ ☌ ♃ 15:17
☽ ☍ ♅ 17:52
☽ ☍ ♃ 19:30
☽ ☍ ♀ 19:57
7 ☽ ☌ ♄ 8:28
9 ♀ □ ♇ 17:46
10 ☿ ☍ ♅ 7:15
☿ ☍ ♃ 15:15
11 ☽ ☌ ♂ 11:15
♀ △ ♂ 12: 5
☿ □ ♇ 19:16
♀ ☍ ♄ 21: 3
12 ♂ ⚹ ♄ 16: 3
☿ ☌ ♄ 16:47
☿ ⚹ ♂ 16:54
13 ☿ ☍ ♀ 7:11
☽ ☌ ♇ 13:10
17 ☿ ☍ ⊕ 1: 3
☽ ☌ ♆ 22: 4
18 ☿ △ ♆ 6:37
20 ☿ ⚹ ♇ 12: 0
☽ ☌ ♅ 13:10
☽ ☌ ♃ 17:28
21 ⊕ ⚹ ♆ 4:14
☽ ☍ ♄ 8: 8
22 ☽ ☌ ♀ 17:33
24 ♀ ⚹ ♆ 3:41
☽ ☍ ☿ 10:36
25 ☿ ☌ ☋ 0:59
26 ☽ ☍ ♂ 17: 4
28 ☽ ☍ ♇ 3:55
☿ □ ♆ 6:28
⊕ △ ♇ 8:23
♀ △ ♇ 14:42
☿ △ ♅ 17:25
29 ♀ ☌ ⊕ 1: 9
☿ △ ♃ 18:11

substances graced the table at the Last Supper, the bread signifying the body of Christ and the wine signifying the blood of Christ. The sacrament of communion offered on Holy Thursday underscores the need to embody the Christ in us, both as individuals and as a community. With the current Sun/Mercury conjunction, our thoughts can easily embrace the idea of the healing sacrament. It should also be noted that the Sun had just moved one degree past Spica on the day of the Baptism. Did this not foretell the significance of the incarnating Christ into the body of Jesus? Did it not highlight the reality of the "Not I, but Christ in me"?

18 The Sun moves from the Virgin into the Scales. See above commentary regarding the Baptism.

21 Mars enters the Scorpion and Jupiter enters the Waterbearer. On the first day of the Temptation in the Wilderness the Sun entered the sign of the Scorpion. Given the ensuing events endured by Jesus in the Wilderness it is not difficult to imagine the sting of the Scorpion in effect. The Moon entered the Scorpion just prior to the appearance of Jesus in the garden on the day of Resurrection, signifying again the victory over the great temptation—death!

When the Sun entered the Waterbearer on January 19, 31 C.E., Jesus healed the paralyzed man who had been ill for thirty-eight years (John 5:1–15). In the evening John the Baptist's body was buried at Juttah in the vault of Zecharias. The latter event has its significance in the legendary association with John the Baptist as the initiate of the Waterbearer.

23 The Full Moon in 5° of the Ram. Jupiter was at 5° of the Ram at the time of John the Baptist's beheading. Although departed from the earthly plane, Steiner indicates he overshadowed the disciples as a guiding power of wisdom. This may well be affirmed by realizing that the Moon's Ascending Node (Portal to the Angelic realm) was at 5° of the Ram at Whitsun.

25 Mercury conjunct Venus at 13° of the Scales. When the Sun was at this degree on October 6 in 30 and in 31 C.E., healings took place. In 30 C.E., Jesus healed the blind youth of Manahem who had the gift of prophecy. In 31 C.E., Jesus healed the man born blind. Why do both healings at this degree involve blindness? This is indeed a mystery question. Let us approach it by asking ourselves what is the nature of seeing? If the eyes are the windows of the soul into the world, what is the nature of the blinds put upon them? Healing blindness may be considered an act of reconnecting the soul with the world. If such is the case, then we might say in today's world that the need is great for healing the blindness of humanity. We desperately need to reconnect. Let us begin with encounters of soul to soul filled with interest and love.

29 The Sun conjunct Venus in 11° of the Scales. This planetary aspect has been regarded as an opportunity for initiation, an opportunity to give and receive love. We find this degree on the horizon of three Christological events:

The Ascendant of the birth of the Solomon Jesus

The Ascendant of the death of John the Baptist

The Descendant of the moment of Jesus Christ's Resurrection

These events follow a sequence of birth, death and rebirth, reminding us of cycle of incarnations.

NOVEMBER

Early risers, see the waning crescent **Moon** join **Saturn** on the 4th, just two days before the New **Moon**. **Venus** emerges as the Morning Star this month around the 12th as glittering star in the east before sunrise and remaining thus through the end of the year. **Venus** stations direct on the 19th (in the Scales) as does **Jupiter** (in Aquarius). **Jupiter** continues to be visible this month, with the **Moon** joining **Jupiter** on the 16th as waxing gibbous, visible looking south after sunset. The **Sun** enters Scorpio on the 17th and **Mercury** conjuncts **Mars** farther on in Scorpio on the 20th, possibly just visible in the west just as the **Sun** sets.

★ ★ ★

6   New Moon in 19° of the Scales. See October 3 commentary. This New Moon is within one degree of the Venus/Mars conjunction that took place last month. It echoes the end of the forty days of Temptation in the Wilderness.

9   Pluto conjunct the Moon's Ascending Node in 9° of the Archer. In a remarkable way this aspect also has its ties to the end of the forty days of Temptation in the Wilderness. This is approximately where the Sun conjunct Pluto was at the time.

17 The Sun moves from the Scales into the Scorpion.

20 Mercury conjunct Mars in 22° of the Scorpion. It was with the Sun at 22° of the Scorpion on November 13, 30 C.E., that an extraordinary public demonstration occurred. Robert Powell wrote in the *Chronicle of the Living Christ* (1996), "at around nine in the morning, as Jesus and the disciples were approaching Nain, they met a funeral procession emerging from the city gate. Jesus commanded the coffin bearers to stand still and set the coffin down. He raised his eyes to heaven and spoke the words recorded in Matthew 11:25–30. There then occurred the miraculous raising from the dead of the youth of Nain –the twelve-year-old Martialis, son of the widow Maroni" as described in Luke 7:11–17. Jesus addressed the widow with the words "weep not." And to the youth of Nain he said, "arise." The power of his words was irrefutably stronger than grief and death. They were spoken from a place of compassion and conviction. We could do well to remember these words –"Weep Not, Arise!"

21 Full Moon in 5° of the Bull. From the perspective of the Ancient Indian astrologers, the 5th degree of the Bull begins the lunar zodiac. There shines the cluster of seven stars, the Pleiades. Those stars were regarded as the seven wives of the Holy Rishis. From them all wisdom was reflected to humanity. The Moon was in this degree during the Healing of the Paralyzed Man who had been ill for thirty-eight years by Jesus Christ at the Pool of Bethesda (John 5:1–15).

SIDEREAL GEOCENTRIC LONGITUDES : NOVEMBER 2010 Gregorian at 0 hours UT

DAY	☉	☽	☊	☿	♀	♂	♃	♄	♅	♆	♇
1 MO	13 ♎ 34	2 ♌ 49	9 ♐ 31R	22 ♎ 55	8 ♎ 50R	7 ♏ 47	29 ♒ 8R	16 ♍ 35	2 ♓ 17R	1 ♒ 2R	8 ♐ 29
2 TU	14 34	17 15	9 27	24 28	8 15	8 30	29 5	16 42	2 15	1 2	8 30
3 WE	15 34	1 ♍ 52	9 21	26 0	7 40	9 13	29 2	16 49	2 14	1 2	8 32
4 TH	16 34	16 35	9 13	27 33	7 7	9 57	28 58	16 56	2 12	1 2	8 33
5 FR	17 34	1 ♎ 18	9 5	29 4	6 35	10 40	28 56	17 2	2 10	1 2	8 35
6 SA	18 34	15 52	8 57	0 ♏ 36	6 5	11 24	28 53	17 9	2 9	1 2	8 36
7 SU	19 35	0 ♏ 10	8 50	2 7	5 36	12 7	28 50	17 16	2 8	1 2	8 38
8 MO	20 35	14 6	8 45	3 37	5 10	12 51	28 48	17 22	2 6	1 2D	8 39
9 TU	21 35	27 38	8 43	5 8	4 45	13 35	28 46	17 29	2 5	1 2	8 41
10 WE	22 35	10 ♐ 45	8 42D	6 37	4 23	14 18	28 44	17 35	2 4	1 2	8 42
11 TH	23 36	23 28	8 43	8 7	4 2	15 2	28 42	17 42	2 2	1 2	8 44
12 FR	24 36	5 ♑ 52	8 44	9 36	3 44	15 46	28 41	17 48	2 1	1 2	8 46
13 SA	25 36	18 0	8 45	11 4	3 29	16 30	28 40	17 55	2 0	1 2	8 47
14 SU	26 37	29 58	8 46R	12 32	3 15	17 14	28 38	18 1	1 59	1 2	8 49
15 MO	27 37	11 ♒ 50	8 44	14 0	3 5	17 58	28 38	18 7	1 58	1 3	8 51
16 TU	28 38	23 42	8 41	15 27	2 56	18 42	28 37	18 14	1 57	1 3	8 52
17 WE	29 38	5 ♓ 38	8 37	16 53	2 50	19 26	28 36	18 20	1 56	1 3	8 54
18 TH	0 ♏ 39	17 41	8 31	18 19	2 47	20 10	28 36	18 26	1 55	1 4	8 56
19 FR	1 39	29 55	8 24	19 44	2 46D	20 55	28 36D	18 32	1 54	1 4	8 58
20 SA	2 40	12 ♈ 22	8 17	21 8	2 47	21 39	28 36	18 38	1 53	1 4	9 0
21 SU	3 40	25 3	8 11	22 32	2 51	22 23	28 37	18 44	1 53	1 5	9 1
22 MO	4 41	7 ♉ 57	8 6	23 54	2 58	23 8	28 37	18 50	1 52	1 5	9 3
23 TU	5 41	21 5	8 3	25 16	3 6	23 52	28 38	18 56	1 51	1 6	9 5
24 WE	6 42	4 ♊ 26	8 2	26 36	3 17	24 37	28 39	19 2	1 50	1 6	9 7
25 TH	7 43	17 57	8 2D	27 55	3 30	25 22	28 40	19 7	1 50	1 7	9 9
26 FR	8 43	1 ♋ 39	8 3	29 12	3 45	26 6	28 42	19 13	1 49	1 8	9 11
27 SA	9 44	15 31	8 5	0 ♐ 28	4 2	26 51	28 43	19 19	1 49	1 8	9 13
28 SU	10 45	29 30	8 6	1 41	4 22	27 36	28 45	19 24	1 48	1 9	9 15
29 MO	11 45	13 ♌ 37	8 6R	2 52	4 43	28 21	28 47	19 30	1 48	1 10	9 17
30 TU	12 46	27 50	8 6	4 1	5 6	29 6	28 49	19 35	1 48	1 10	9 19

INGRESSES :

2 ☽ → ♍ 20:57
4 ☽ → ♎ 21:52
5 ☿ → ♏ 14:34
6 ☽ → ♏ 23:43
9 ☽ → ♐ 4:16
11 ☽ → ♑ 12:34
14 ☽ → ♒ 0: 4
16 ☽ → ♓ 12:42
17 ☉ → ♏ 8:41
19 ☽ → ♈ 0: 9
21 ☽ → ♉ 9:15
23 ☽ → ♊ 16: 4
25 ☽ → ♋ 21: 6
26 ☿ → ♐ 15: 8
28 ☽ → ♌ 0:50
30 ☽ → ♍ 3:38

ASPECTS & ECLIPSES :

2 ☽ ☍ ♃ 19:22
3 ☽ ☍ ♅ 0:35
☽ ☌ P 17:15
4 ☽ ☌ ♄ 0:33
5 ☽ ☌ ♀ 8:22
6 ☉ ☌ ☽ 4:50
☿ □ ♆ 6:48
7 ☽ ☌ ☿ 3:43
☽ ☌ ♂ 21:41
9 ♇ ☌ ☊ 17: 7
☽ ☌ ☊ 20:12
☽ ☌ ♇ 20:12
13 ☉ □ ☽ 16:37
14 ☽ ☌ ♆ 2:10
15 ☽ ☌ A 11:48
16 ☽ ☌ ♃ 9:54
☽ ☌ ♅ 16:35
18 ☽ ☍ ♄ 1:29
☉ □ ♆ 10: 0
19 ☽ ☍ ♀ 5:31
20 ☿ ☌ ♂ 18:52
21 ☉ ☍ ☽ 17:26
23 ☽ ☍ ♂ 5:20
☽ ☍ ☿ 8:24
24 ☽ ☌ ☋ 6:25
☽ ☍ ♇ 8:22
25 ☿ □ ♃ 14:17
28 ☿ □ ♅ 2:24
☽ ☍ ♆ 2:48
☉ □ ☽ 20:35
29 ♂ □ ♃ 14:49
30 ☽ ☍ ♃ 1:39
☽ ☍ ♅ 6:39
☽ ☌ P 18:46

SIDEREAL HELIOCENTRIC LONGITUDES : NOVEMBER 2010 Gregorian at 0 hours UT

DAY	Sid. Time	☿	♀	⊕	♂	♃	♄	♅	♆	♇	Vernal Point
1 MO	2:40:42	13 ♏ 13	15 ♈ 20	13 ♈ 34	23 ♏ 44	7 ♓ 12	13 ♍ 53	4 ♓ 8	2 ♒ 50	9 ♐ 56	5 ♓ 6'32"
2 TU	2:44:38	15 58	16 57	14 34	24 18	7 17	13 55	4 9	2 51	9 57	5 ♓ 6'32"
3 WE	2:48:35	18 43	18 33	15 34	24 51	7 23	13 57	4 10	2 51	9 57	5 ♓ 6'32"
4 TH	2:52:32	21 27	20 9	16 34	25 24	7 28	13 59	4 10	2 52	9 57	5 ♓ 6'32"
5 FR	2:56:28	24 12	21 45	17 34	25 57	7 34	14 1	4 11	2 52	9 58	5 ♓ 6'32"
6 SA	3: 0:25	26 57	23 21	18 35	26 31	7 39	14 3	4 12	2 52	9 58	5 ♓ 6'31"
7 SU	3: 4:21	29 42	24 57	19 35	27 4	7 45	14 5	4 12	2 53	9 58	5 ♓ 6'31"
8 MO	3: 8:18	2 ♐ 28	26 33	20 35	27 38	7 50	14 7	4 13	2 53	9 59	5 ♓ 6'31"
9 TU	3:12:14	5 15	28 10	21 35	28 11	7 56	14 9	4 13	2 53	9 59	5 ♓ 6'31"
10 WE	3:16:11	8 3	29 46	22 36	28 45	8 1	14 11	4 14	2 54	9 59	5 ♓ 6'31"
11 TH	3:20: 7	10 52	1 ♉ 22	23 36	29 19	8 7	14 13	4 15	2 54	10 0	5 ♓ 6'31"
12 FR	3:24: 4	13 43	2 59	24 36	29 52	8 12	14 15	4 15	2 54	10 0	5 ♓ 6'31"
13 SA	3:28: 1	16 35	4 35	25 37	0 ♐ 26	8 18	14 17	4 16	2 55	10 1	5 ♓ 6'30"
14 SU	3:31:57	19 29	6 11	26 37	1 0	8 23	14 19	4 17	2 55	10 1	5 ♓ 6'30"
15 MO	3:35:54	22 25	7 48	27 37	1 34	8 29	14 21	4 17	2 56	10 1	5 ♓ 6'30"
16 TU	3:39:50	25 24	9 24	28 38	2 8	8 34	14 23	4 18	2 56	10 2	5 ♓ 6'30"
17 WE	3:43:47	28 26	11 1	29 38	2 42	8 40	14 25	4 19	2 56	10 2	5 ♓ 6'30"
18 TH	3:47:43	1 ♑ 30	12 37	0 ♉ 39	3 16	8 45	14 27	4 19	2 57	10 2	5 ♓ 6'30"
19 FR	3:51:40	4 37	14 14	1 39	3 50	8 51	14 29	4 20	2 57	10 3	5 ♓ 6'30"
20 SA	3:55:36	7 48	15 50	2 40	4 24	8 56	14 31	4 21	2 57	10 3	5 ♓ 6'29"
21 SU	3:59:33	11 3	17 27	3 40	4 59	9 2	14 33	4 21	2 58	10 3	5 ♓ 6'29"
22 MO	4: 3:30	14 22	19 4	4 41	5 33	9 7	14 35	4 22	2 58	10 4	5 ♓ 6'29"
23 TU	4: 7:26	17 45	20 40	5 41	6 7	9 13	14 37	4 22	2 58	10 4	5 ♓ 6'29"
24 WE	4:11:23	21 13	22 17	6 42	6 42	9 18	14 39	4 23	2 59	10 4	5 ♓ 6'29"
25 TH	4:15:19	24 46	23 54	7 43	7 16	9 24	14 41	4 24	2 59	10 5	5 ♓ 6'29"
26 FR	4:19:16	28 24	25 31	8 43	7 51	9 29	14 43	4 24	2 59	10 5	5 ♓ 6'29"
27 SA	4:23:12	2 ♒ 8	27 7	9 44	8 25	9 35	14 45	4 25	3 0	10 5	5 ♓ 6'28"
28 SU	4:27: 9	5 58	28 44	10 45	9 0	9 40	14 47	4 26	3 0	10 6	5 ♓ 6'28"
29 MO	4:31: 5	9 55	0 ♊ 21	11 45	9 35	9 46	14 49	4 26	3 1	10 6	5 ♓ 6'28"
30 TU	4:35: 2	13 58	1 58	12 46	10 9	9 51	14 51	4 27	3 1	10 6	5 ♓ 6'28"

INGRESSES :

7 ☿ → ♐ 2:34
10 ♀ → ♉ 3:29
12 ♂ → ♐ 5:27
17 ⊕ → ♉ 8:40
☿ → ♑ 12:20
26 ☿ → ♒ 10:21
28 ♀ → ♊ 18:47

ASPECTS (HELIOCENTRIC +MOON(TYCHONIC)) :

1 ☽ ☍ ♆ 0: 2
☿ ⚹ ♄ 5:56
3 ☽ ☍ ♅ 3:45
☽ ☍ ♃ 9: 3
☽ ☌ ♄ 19:44
4 ☿ ☌ A 11:10
5 ☿ ☌ ♂ 19:13
6 ☽ ☍ ♀ 14: 4
8 ☿ ⚹ ♆ 3:34
☿ □ ♅ 15: 6
9 ☽ ☌ ♂ 1: 2
☽ ☌ ☿ 17:37
☽ ☌ ♆ 22:35
☿ □ ♃ 23:46
10 ☿ ☌ ♇ 16:35
11 ♀ □ ♆ 22:56
12 ☿ □ ♄ 4:34
♀ ⚹ ♅ 19:13
14 ☽ ☌ ♆ 5:57
15 ♀ ⚹ ♃ 10:48
16 ☽ ☌ ♅ 21:21
17 ☽ ☌ ♃ 6: 7
♂ ⚹ ♆ 10:15
☿ △ ⊕ 14: 7
☽ ☍ ♄ 17:34
18 ☿ ⚹ ♅ 21:45
19 ♀ △ ♄ 3:48
♂ □ ♅ 21:18
20 ⊕ □ ♆ 7: 3
☿ ⚹ ♃ 8:39
21 ⊕ ⚹ ♅ 16:24
22 ☿ △ ♄ 1:33
☽ ☌ ♀ 23: 9
23 ♀ ☌ ☊ 18: 3
24 ☽ ☍ ♂ 4:13
☽ ☍ ♇ 10: 3
☿ △ ♀ 13:24
☿ ⚻ ☊ 15:59
26 ⊕ ⚹ ♃ 20: 0
27 ☿ ☌ ♆ 5:28
28 ☽ ☍ ♆ 5:57
☽ ☍ ☿ 15:14
☿ ⚹ ♂ 21:38
29 ☿ ⚹ ♇ 1: 7
♂ □ ♃ 9:12
☿ □ ⊕ 14:39
♂ ☌ ♇ 21:53
30 ☽ ☍ ♅ 11: 8
♀ △ ♆ 15:39
☽ ☍ ♃ 20:20

DECEMBER

On the 1st, the waning crescent **Moon** hangs with **Saturn** in the Virgin and **Venus** to the left in the Scales. With the New **Moon** only 4 days later, early risers will see this one!

Uranus stations direct on the 6th (retrograde since July 5th, traveling only 3° the entire period). **Mercury** stations retrograde on the 11th, stationing direct again on the 31st.

The **Sun** enters Sagittarius (the Archer) on the 16th and **Jupiter** reenters Pisces (the Fishes) on the 17th.

Jupiter continues to be visible at night, with "hidden" **Uranus** nearby. The waxing **Moon** joins these two on the 13th in Pisces, visible in the south west sky after sunset and moving to the western horizon around midnight. **Mars** and **Mercury** are hidden in the glow of the **Sun**, with **Mars** trailing the **Sun** as it sets in the west. **Mercury** does too, until the inferior conjunction of **Sun** and **Mercury** on the 20th. **Saturn** gains the **Moon** again at the end of the month on the 28th, this time as waning half **Moon**.

✸ ✸ ✸

5   New Moon in 19° of the Scorpion. The Sun at this position on November 10, 30 C.E., reveals Christ's activity as primarily one of healing. In *Chronicle of the Living Christ* by Robert Powell we read the following: "This morning, in Capernaum, Jesus was approached by the Roman centurion Cornelius, whose servant was desperately ill. Jesus praised Cornelius for his faith and healed the servant from afar (Matthew 8:5–13 and Luke 7:1–10). Next, Jesus went to a leper's hut and healed the leper, as described in Mark 1:40–45. Leaving the leper's hut, he went to an inn in the Valley of the Doves, south of Capernaum, where he met Maroni, the widow of Nain, who begged him to come and heal her twelve-year-old son. In the afternoon, he returned to Capernaum and taught in the synagogue as the Sabbath began. Suddenly a man who was possessed ran in and caused a great commotion. Jesus healed him (Mark 1:21–28). Seeing this, the Pharisees—utterly astounded—gave up their plan to lay hands on Jesus."

6   Mercury conjunct Pluto in 10° of the Archer, and Uranus turns direct. With regard to the conjunction see the commentary listed for November 9th. With regard to the turning direct motion of Uranus refer back to the article by William Bento. Uranus represents the capacity to see the future. We might ask ourselves how and what do we see of the future.

10 Mercury turns retrograde in 11° of the Archer. See commentary written for November 9th.

14 Mercury conjunct Mars conjunct Pluto in 10° of the Archer. This triple conjunction amplifies the memory and seeming recapitulation of the Temptations in the Wilderness. In 29 C.E., it was the trial of Jesus Christ. Today it is the collective trial of humanity as a whole.

16 The Sun at 30° of the Scorpion in a square to Jupiter at 30° of the Waterbearer. The Sun moves from the Scorpion into the Archer. See the article written by David Tresemer, particularly the section referred to the "Globe of Light." It is quite striking to see that the Jupiter degree of the time of the Temptation in the Wilderness was also at 30° of the Waterbearer.

17 Jupiter reenters the Fishes.

18 Conjunct the Galactic Center, the Sun at 2° of the Archer is in a square to Uranus at 2° of the Fishes. This square coupled with the square of December 16 establishes a zone

SIDEREAL GEOCENTRIC LONGITUDES : DECEMBER 2010 Gregorian at 0 hours UT

DAY		☉	☽	☊	☿	♀	♂	♃	♄	♅	♆	♇
1	WE	13 ♏ 47	12 ♍ 6	8 ♐ 4R	5 ♐ 6	5 ♎ 31	29 ♏ 51	28 ♒ 52	19 ♍ 40	1 ♓ 47R	1 ♒ 11	9 ♐ 21
2	TH	14 48	26 23	8 1	6 8	5 58	0 ♐ 36	28 54	19 46	1 47	1 12	9 23
3	FR	15 49	10 ♎ 36	7 57	7 6	6 26	1 21	28 57	19 51	1 47	1 13	9 25
4	SA	16 49	24 41	7 54	7 59	6 56	2 6	29 0	19 56	1 47	1 14	9 27
5	SU	17 50	8 ♏ 34	7 52	8 47	7 28	2 51	29 3	20 1	1 47	1 15	9 29
6	MO	18 51	22 12	7 50	9 29	8 1	3 36	29 7	20 6	1 47	1 16	9 31
7	TU	19 52	5 ♐ 31	7 49	10 4	8 35	4 21	29 10	20 11	1 47	1 17	9 33
8	WE	20 53	18 31	7 50D	10 32	9 11	5 7	29 14	20 16	1 47D	1 18	9 35
9	TH	21 54	1 ♑ 12	7 51	10 51	9 49	5 52	29 18	20 20	1 47	1 19	9 37
10	FR	22 55	13 36	7 52	11 1	10 27	6 38	29 22	20 25	1 47	1 20	9 39
11	SA	23 56	25 46	7 53	11 1R	11 7	7 23	29 27	20 30	1 47	1 21	9 41
12	SU	24 57	7 ♒ 46	7 55	10 50	11 48	8 9	29 31	20 34	1 48	1 22	9 43
13	MO	25 58	19 39	7 55	10 28	12 30	8 54	29 36	20 39	1 48	1 23	9 45
14	TU	26 59	1 ♓ 31	7 55R	9 55	13 13	9 40	29 41	20 43	1 48	1 24	9 47
15	WE	28 0	13 27	7 55	9 10	13 58	10 26	29 46	20 47	1 49	1 26	9 50
16	TH	29 1	25 31	7 54	8 14	14 43	11 11	29 51	20 51	1 49	1 27	9 52
17	FR	0 ♐ 2	7 ♈ 47	7 53	7 8	15 29	11 57	29 57	20 55	1 50	1 28	9 54
18	SA	1 3	20 19	7 52	5 55	16 17	12 43	0 ♓ 3	20 59	1 50	1 29	9 56
19	SU	2 4	3 ♉ 9	7 51	4 36	17 5	13 29	0 8	21 3	1 51	1 31	9 58
20	MO	3 5	16 18	7 51	3 13	17 54	14 15	0 14	21 7	1 52	1 32	10 0
21	TU	4 6	29 47	7 51	1 51	18 44	15 1	0 21	21 11	1 52	1 34	10 2
22	WE	5 7	13 ♊ 32	7 51D	0 30	19 34	15 47	0 27	21 15	1 53	1 35	10 5
23	TH	6 8	27 33	7 51	29 ♏ 15	20 26	16 33	0 33	21 18	1 54	1 36	10 7
24	FR	7 10	11 ♋ 44	7 51	28 7	21 18	17 19	0 40	21 22	1 55	1 38	10 9
25	SA	8 11	26 1	7 51R	27 7	22 11	18 5	0 47	21 25	1 56	1 39	10 11
26	SU	9 12	10 ♌ 21	7 51	26 17	23 5	18 51	0 54	21 28	1 57	1 41	10 13
27	MO	10 13	24 39	7 50	25 38	23 59	19 37	1 1	21 32	1 58	1 43	10 15
28	TU	11 14	8 ♍ 53	7 50	25 10	24 54	20 23	1 9	21 35	1 59	1 44	10 17
29	WE	12 15	22 59	7 50D	24 52	25 50	21 10	1 16	21 38	2 0	1 46	10 20
30	TH	13 16	6 ♎ 57	7 50	24 44	26 46	21 56	1 24	21 41	2 1	1 47	10 22
31	FR	14 17	20 45	7 51	24 46D	27 43	22 42	1 32	21 43	2 3	1 49	10 24

INGRESSES :

1 ♂ → ♐ 5: 2
2 ☽ → ♎ 6: 5
4 ☽ → ♏ 9: 8
6 ☽ → ♐ 13:59
8 ☽ → ♑ 21:41
11 ☽ → ♒ 8:25
13 ☽ → ♓ 20:55
16 ☽ → ♈ 8:49
☉ → ♐ 23:11
17 ♃ → ♓ 13: 9
18 ☽ → ♉ 18: 9
21 ☽ → ♊ 0:23
22 ☿ → ♏ 9:26
23 ☽ → ♋ 4:10
25 ☽ → ♌ 6:39
27 ☽ → ♍ 8:59
29 ☽ → ♎ 12: 0
31 ☽ → ♏ 16:16

ASPECTS & ECLIPSES :

1 ☽ ☌ ♄ 12:47
2 ☽ ☌ ♀ 16:42
3 ♂ □ ♅ 13:56
☿ ☌ ☊ 21:57
5 ☉ ☌ ☽ 17:34
6 ☿ ☌ ♇ 1:13
☽ ☌ ♂ 21:45
7 ☽ ☌ ☊ 4:12
☽ ☌ ♇ 7:23
☽ ☌ ☿ 8:39
11 ☽ ☌ ♆ 11: 8
♂ ☌ ☊ 16:24
13 ☽ ☌ A 8:34
☉ □ ☽ 13:57
☽ ☌ ♃ 20:15
14 ☽ ☌ ♅ 0:33
♂ ☌ ♇ 4: 8
☿ ☌ ♂ 4: 9
☿ ☌ ♇ 4: 9
15 ☽ ☍ ♄ 14:42
16 ☿ ☌ ☊ 7:44
☉ □ ♃ 21:46
17 ☽ ☍ ♀ 15:48
18 ☉ □ ♅ 18:45
20 ☉ ☌ ☿ 1:22
☿ □ ♅ 23:30
21 ☽ ☍ ☿ 3:18
☉ ☍ ☽ 8:12
☽ ●● T 8:18
☽ ☌ ☋ 14: 7
☽ ☍ ♇ 17:59
22 ☿ □ ♃ 0:57
☽ ☍ ♂ 4: 5
24 ☉ ☌ ☊ 16:11
25 ☽ ☍ ♆ 9:27
☽ ☌ P 12:11
27 ☉ ☌ ♇ 0:59
☽ ☍ ♃ 10:48
☽ ☍ ♅ 12:19
28 ☉ □ ☽ 4:17
☽ ☌ ♄ 21:39
29 ♂ □ ♄ 15:28
31 ☽ ☌ ♀ 13:10

SIDEREAL HELIOCENTRIC LONGITUDES : DECEMBER 2010 Gregorian at 0 hours UT

DAY		Sid. Time	☿	♀	⊕	♂	♃	♄	♅	♆	♇	Vernal Point
1	WE	4:38:59	18 ♒ 9	3 ♊ 35	13 ♉ 47	10 ♐ 44	9 ♓ 57	14 ♍ 53	4 ♓ 28	3 ♒ 1	10 ♐ 7	5 ♓ 6'28"
2	TH	4:42:55	22 27	5 12	14 48	11 19	10 2	14 55	4 28	3 2	10 7	5 ♓ 6'28"
3	FR	4:46:52	26 53	6 49	15 49	11 54	10 8	14 57	4 29	3 2	10 7	5 ♓ 6'28"
4	SA	4:50:48	1 ♓ 28	8 26	16 50	12 29	10 13	14 59	4 30	3 2	10 8	5 ♓ 6'28"
5	SU	4:54:45	6 11	10 3	17 50	13 4	10 19	15 1	4 30	3 3	10 8	5 ♓ 6'27"
6	MO	4:58:41	11 3	11 40	18 51	13 39	10 24	15 3	4 31	3 3	10 8	5 ♓ 6'27"
7	TU	5: 2:38	16 4	13 17	19 52	14 14	10 30	15 5	4 31	3 3	10 9	5 ♓ 6'27"
8	WE	5: 6:34	21 14	14 54	20 53	14 49	10 35	15 7	4 32	3 4	10 9	5 ♓ 6'27"
9	TH	5:10:31	26 33	16 31	21 54	15 25	10 41	15 9	4 33	3 4	10 9	5 ♓ 6'27"
10	FR	5:14:28	2 ♈ 1	18 8	22 55	16 0	10 46	15 11	4 33	3 5	10 10	5 ♓ 6'27"
11	SA	5:18:24	7 38	19 45	23 56	16 35	10 52	15 13	4 34	3 5	10 10	5 ♓ 6'27"
12	SU	5:22:21	13 23	21 23	24 57	17 11	10 57	15 15	4 35	3 5	10 10	5 ♓ 6'26"
13	MO	5:26:17	19 17	23 0	25 58	17 46	11 3	15 17	4 35	3 6	10 11	5 ♓ 6'26"
14	TU	5:30:14	25 17	24 37	26 59	18 22	11 8	15 19	4 36	3 6	10 11	5 ♓ 6'26"
15	WE	5:34:10	1 ♉ 23	26 14	28 0	18 57	11 14	15 21	4 37	3 6	10 11	5 ♓ 6'26"
16	TH	5:38: 7	7 35	27 52	29 1	19 33	11 19	15 23	4 37	3 7	10 12	5 ♓ 6'26"
17	FR	5:42: 3	13 51	29 29	0 ♊ 2	20 8	11 25	15 25	4 38	3 7	10 12	5 ♓ 6'26"
18	SA	5:46: 0	20 9	1 ♋ 6	1 3	20 44	11 30	15 27	4 38	3 7	10 12	5 ♓ 6'26"
19	SU	5:49:57	26 28	2 44	2 4	21 20	11 36	15 29	4 39	3 8	10 13	5 ♓ 6'25"
20	MO	5:53:53	2 ♊ 47	4 21	3 5	21 56	11 41	15 31	4 40	3 8	10 13	5 ♓ 6'25"
21	TU	5:57:50	9 4	5 59	4 6	22 32	11 47	15 33	4 40	3 9	10 13	5 ♓ 6'25"
22	WE	6: 1:46	15 18	7 36	5 7	23 8	11 52	15 35	4 41	3 9	10 14	5 ♓ 6'25"
23	TH	6: 5:43	21 26	9 13	6 9	23 44	11 58	15 37	4 42	3 9	10 14	5 ♓ 6'25"
24	FR	6: 9:39	27 29	10 51	7 10	24 20	12 3	15 39	4 42	3 10	10 14	5 ♓ 6'25"
25	SA	6:13:36	3 ♋ 25	12 28	8 11	24 56	12 9	15 40	4 43	3 10	10 15	5 ♓ 6'25"
26	SU	6:17:32	9 13	14 6	9 12	25 32	12 14	15 42	4 44	3 10	10 15	5 ♓ 6'25"
27	MO	6:21:29	14 52	15 43	10 13	26 8	12 20	15 44	4 44	3 11	10 15	5 ♓ 6'24"
28	TU	6:25:26	20 22	17 21	11 14	26 44	12 25	15 46	4 45	3 11	10 16	5 ♓ 6'24"
29	WE	6:29:22	25 42	18 58	12 15	27 20	12 31	15 48	4 46	3 11	10 16	5 ♓ 6'24"
30	TH	6:33:19	0 ♌ 53	20 36	13 16	27 57	12 36	15 50	4 46	3 12	10 16	5 ♓ 6'24"
31	FR	6:37:15	5 54	22 13	14 18	28 33	12 42	15 52	4 47	3 12	10 17	5 ♓ 6'24"

INGRESSES :

3 ☿ → ♓ 16:24
9 ☿ → ♈ 15:13
14 ☿ → ♉ 18:34
16 ⊕ → ♊ 23: 9
17 ♀ → ♋ 7:38
19 ☿ → ♊ 13:23
24 ☿ → ♋ 10: 6
29 ☿ → ♌ 19:52

ASPECTS (HELIOCENTRIC +MOON(TYCHONIC)) :

1 ☽ ☌ ♄ 4:40
♀ □ ♅ 13: 8
2 ⊕ △ ♄ 2:50
♃ □ ♇ 21:51
4 ☿ ☌ ♅ 15:31
5 ♀ ☍ ♇ 1:17
♀ □ ♃ 4:11
☿ □ ♇ 19:34
☿ ☌ ♃ 20:49
6 ☿ □ ♀ 4:26
☿ □ ♂ 14:12
☿ ☍ ♄ 19:19
7 ☽ ☌ ♇ 8:28
☽ ☍ ♀ 16:17
☽ ☌ ♂ 16:46
☿ ⚹ ⊕ 22: 3
♀ ☍ ♂ 22:11
8 ♀ □ ♄ 3:12
♂ □ ♄ 12:33
10 ☿ ⚹ ♆ 4:34
11 ☿ △ ♇ 10:38
☽ ☌ ♆ 14:36
12 ☿ △ ♂ 17:13
13 ☿ ☌ ☊ 17:11
☿ ⚹ ♀ 20:24
14 ☽ ☌ ♅ 6:12
☽ ☌ ♃ 19:30
15 ☽ ☍ ♄ 3:47
☿ □ ♆ 6:40
☿ ⚹ ♅ 12:31
16 ☿ ⚹ ♃ 14:33
17 ☿ △ ♄ 5:59
18 ☿ ☌ P 9:48
20 ⊕ △ ♆ 1: 7
☿ △ ♆ 1:19
☿ ☌ ⊕ 1:22
♀ △ ♅ 4:37
☿ □ ♅ 7: 9
21 ☿ ☍ ♇ 4:26
☿ □ ♃ 10:34
⊕ □ ♅ 13:31
☽ ☍ ♇ 18:16
22 ☿ □ ♄ 1: 5
☽ ☌ ☿ 5:26
☽ ☍ ♂ 17:12
23 ☿ ☍ ♂ 10: 0
☽ ☌ ♀ 22:19
24 ♀ △ ♃ 18:54
25 ☿ △ ♅ 5:20
☽ ☍ ♆ 11:58
26 ☿ △ ♃ 12:59
27 ♀ ⚹ ♄ 0:19
⊕ ☍ ♇ 0:59
☿ ⚹ ♄ 3:48
☿ ☌ ♀ 5:14
♀ ☌ P 16:18
☽ ☍ ♅ 17: 0
28 ☽ ☍ ♃ 6: 2
☽ ☌ ♄ 11:43
☿ ☌ ☊ 14:19
29 ⊕ □ ♃ 6:42
30 ☿ ☍ ♆ 11: 0
31 ☿ △ ♇ 21:38

of tension with the predominant aspect of the year—Jupiter/Uranus conjunction. It may be read as a time of struggle between powers of good and evil to take hold of the new set of cosmic energies being made available to humanity at this time.

20 Sun conjunct Mercury in 4° of the Archer. The Sun was within a degree of this current conjunction when Jesus responded to a scribe who declared his wish to follow him. Jesus replied, "Foxes have holes, and birds of the air have nests; but the Son of Man has nowhere to lay his head" (Matthew 8:19–20). In an uncanny way Jesus intimates that there is no safe haven for those who wish to follow him. One must be firm in their resolve to do so. Only this resolve can assure that your needs can be met. This is demonstrated on the same day (November 26, 30 C.E.) when Jesus instructed Peter to row his boat out upon the lake and to cast out the nets. The result was a great shoal of fish filled the nets. So great was the catch that their net was breaking and they needed to call their partners in the other boat to help them. So great was the load that both boats were almost sinking from the weight of the catch (Luke 5:4–7).

21 Full Moon 5° of the Twins. As the time of high tension grew in the spring of 32 C.E., Jesus continued his teachings. When the Sun passed through the 5th degree of the Twins in May 26th of that year he was able to walk through the barriers put before him by the Pharisees and enter the synagogue. There he taught in parables.

27 Sun conjunct Pluto in 11° of the Archer. Once again we arrive at the sensitive memory of the end of the forty days of Temptation in the Wilderness endured by the Christ. It was indeed this very configuration that signified the conclusion to a series of events tantamount to a descent through Hell. With the agony put aside, the extraordinary blessings of angels descended upon the Christ. Anne Catherine Emmerich described how the twelve angels of the twelve apostles served him heavenly food. These twelve angels were accompanied in turn by the seventy-two angels of the seventy-two disciples.

29 Mars at 21° of the Archer square Saturn at 21° of the Virgin. The Mars activates memories of the Sun position that occurred at the raising from the dead of Jairus's daughter (Matthew 9:23–25 and Mark 5:35–43 and Luke 8:49–56). It also activates the memory of the position of Mercury at the beheading of John the Baptist. Saturn activates memories of the Sun position on September 13, 30 C.E., when Jesus reproached the Rechabites for their severe interpretation of the Law; and on September 13, 32 C.E., when Jesus told the shepherds that he was the one the three kings followed the stars to meet.

30 Mercury turns direct in 25° of the Scorpion. See John 9:1–11. The story of the healing of the man born blind has within it a secret teaching. Not all illnesses are results of sins of the past, but some, as is the case with the man born blind, are so that a new vision may emerge...a vision that demonstrates the workings of God. It is in this instance that Christ says, "As long as I am in the world, I am the light of the world." May we all see this light!

EPITAPH:
"THOUGH MY SOUL MAY SET IN DARKNESS"

ABOUT THE CONTRIBUTORS

 **Daniel Andreev** (1906-1959) was born in Berlin. His father was the well-known Russian writer Leonid Andreev. His mother Alexandra Veligorsky died during childbirth. Daniel's father, overcome with grief, gave up Andreev to Alexandra's sister Elizabeth Dobrov, who lived in Moscow. It was a critical event in Daniel Andreev's life, for in contrast to many of the Russian intelligentsia at the time, the family maintained its Russian Orthodox faith. Daniel's childhood included contact with persons such as his godfather Maxim Gorky. Daniel was conscripted as a noncombatant in the Soviet Army in 1942, and after the war he returned to writing fiction and poetry. He was arrested in 1947, along with his wife and many of his relatives and friends, and sentenced to twenty-five years in prison, while his wife received twenty-five years of labor camp. All of his previous writing were destroyed. With the rise of Khrushchev, Andreev's case was reviewed and his sentence reduced to ten years. He was released to his waiting wife in 1957, his health ruined following a heart attack in prison. While in prison, he had written the first drafts of *The Rose of the World* and *Russian Gods* (a collection of poetry), as well as *The Iron Mystery,* a play in verse. Andreev spent the last two years of his life finishing these works. Andreev's wife Alla, realizing the negative reception the books would get from the Soviet authorities, hid them until the mid-1970s, but didn't publish them until Gorbachev and glasnost. The first edition of *The Rose of the World* (100,000 copies) quickly sold out, and since then several editions have been equally popular in Russia.

 **William Bento**, Ph.D., has worked in the field of human development for more than thirty years. He is a recognized pioneer and a published author in psychosophy (soul wisdom) and astrosophy (star wisdom) and travels extensively as a speaker, teacher, and consultant. He currently resides in Citrus Heights, California. Dr. Bento is the Associate Dean of Academic Affairs at Rudolf Steiner College, Fair Oaks, California and works as a transpersonal clinical psychologist at the Center for Living Health in Gold River, California. His involvement in guiding social therapy seminars for Camphill Communities has been well received over the last two decades. He is coauthor of *Signs in the Heavens: A Message for Our Time* and author of *Lifting the Veil of Mental Illness: An Approach to Anthroposophical Psychology*. His forthcoming book is *Psychosophy: A Primer for an Extended Anthroposophical Psychology,* to be published by SteinerBooks.

CLAUDIA MCLAREN LAINSON is a teacher and Therapeutic Educator. She has been working in the field of Anthroposophy since 1982, when she founded her first Waldorf program in Boulder, Colorado. She lectures nationally on various topics related to spiritual science, human development, the evolution of consciousness and the emerging Christ and Sophia mysteries of the twenty-first century. Claudia is the founder of Windrose Farm and Academy near Boulder. Windrose is a biodynamic farm and academy for collaborative work in anthroposophic courses, therapeutic education, cosmic and sacred dance and nature-based educational programs. Claudia most recently founded the School for the Sophia Mysteries at Windrose.

SALLY NURNEY has been interested in astrology all her life, beginning her research with her "Sun sign" in elementary school. After several years of travel and exploration, she arrived at The StarHouse in Boulder, Colorado, in 1997 and quickly transitioned to the Sidereal perspective of reading the stars. Along with her studies in the Path of the Ceremonial Arts, she has deepened her direct understanding of the stars through research with David Tresemer at The StarHouse and study with Brian Gray at the Rudolf Steiner College in Fair Oaks, California. She currently lives in the Rocky Mountain foothills near the StarHouse of Boulder.

ROBERT POWELL, Ph.D., is an internationally known lecturer, author, eurythmist, and movement therapist. He is founder of the Choreocosmos School of Cosmic and Sacred Dance, and cofounder of the Sophia Foundation of North America. He received his doctorate for his thesis *The History of the Zodiac*, available as a book from Sophia Academic Press. His published works include *The Sophia Teachings*, a six-tape series (Sounds True Recordings), as well as *Elijah Come Again: A Prophet for Our Time; The Mystery, Biography, and Destiny of Mary Madgalene; Divine Sophia—Holy Wisdom; The Most Holy Trinosophia and the New Revelation of the Divine Feminine; Chronicle of the Living Christ; Christian Hermetic Astrology; The Christ Mystery; The Sign of the Son of Man in the Heavens; The Morning Meditation in Eurythmy;* and the yearly *Journal for Star Wisdom* (previously *Christian Star Calendar*). He translated the spiritual classic *Meditations on the Tarot* and co-translated Valentin Tomberg's *Lazarus, Come Forth!* Robert is also coauthor with Kevin Dann of *Christ & the Maya Calendar: 2012 & the Coming of the Antichrist;* and coauthor with Lacquanna Paul of *Cosmic Dances of the Zodiac* and *Cosmic Dances of the Planets.* He teaches a gentle form of healing movement: the sacred dance of eurythmy, as well as the cosmic dances of the planets and signs of the zodiac. Through the Sophia Grail Circle, Robert facilitates sacred celebrations dedicated to the Divine Feminine. He offers workshops in Europe, Australia, and North America, and with Karen Rivers, cofounder of the Sophia Foundation, leads pilgrimages to the world's sacred sites: 1996, Turkey; 1997, the Holy Land; 1998, France; 2000, Britain; 2002, Italy; 2004, Greece; 2006, Egypt; 2008, India. Visit www.sophiafoundation.org.

 **Ellen Schalk** was born in Stuttgart shortly before the Nazis came to power in Germany and, as a teenager, experienced the ravages wrought by World War II. She encountered Anthroposophy while in high school. After the war, she studied mathematics, geography, and geology at the Technical College in Stuttgart. Later, through her anthroposophic studies, she made the acquaintance of Ernst Bindel, whom Rudolf Steiner had suggested to teach mathematics at the original Waldorf school in Stuttgart. In 1961, Ernst Bindel invited her to teach mathematics at the Waldorf school, where she became a teacher. On sabbatical leave from the school in 1976, she met Werner Greub and became interested in his research into the historical and geographical background of the Grail events, which he later published in his book *Wolfram von Eschenbach and the Reality of the Grail*. Through her studies, and encouraged by Werner Greub, she penetrated more deeply into the mysteries of the stellar script of the Parsifal story. She now lives in a retirement community in Stuttgart and loves to play piano and flute, as well as sometimes playing the organ on special occasions at the Christian Community chapel in her community.

 **Robert Schiappacasse** has been a student of Rudolf Steiner's Anthroposophy for more than thirty years. He developed a deep interest humanity's relationship to the world of the stars and, in 1977, began studies with Willi Sucher, a pioneer researcher in the field of Astrosophy, or star wisdom. He presents at conferences and workshops on star wisdom themes and other anthroposophic topics. He is coauthor with David Tresemer and William Bento of the book *Signs in the Heavens: A Message for our Time*, about the comets Hyakutake and Hale-Bopp and their crossing of the mysterious and ominous star Algol at the end of the twentieth century. Robert most recently worked with David Tresemer on the book *Star Wisdom and Rudolf Steiner: A life Seen through the Oracle of the Solar Cross*. He also coauthored with David Tresemer the articles "The Chain Reaction Experiment"; "The Signature of Saturn in Christ Jesus' Life"; and "The Signature of Pluto in the Events of Christ Jesus' Life."

 **David Tresemer**, Ph.D., has a doctorate in psychology. In 1990, he cofounded the StarHouse in Boulder, Colorado, for community gatherings and workshops (www.TheStarHouse.org) and cofounded, with his wife Lila, the Healing Dreams Retreat Centre in Australia (www.healingdreams.com.au). He has also founded the Star Wisdom website (www.StarWisdom.org), which offers readings from the Oracle of the Solar Crosses, an oracle relating to the heavenly imprint received on one's day of birth. Dr. Tresemer has written in many areas, including *The Scythe Book: Mowing Hay, Cutting Weeds, and Harvesting Small Grains with Hand Tools* and a book on mythic theater, *War in Heaven: Accessing Myth Through Drama*. With his wife, he also coauthored several plays produced in the U.S., including *My Magdalene* (winner of Moondance 2004, Best Script). With William Bento and Robert Schiappacasse, he wrote *Signs in the Heavens: A Message for Our Time*.

www.ingramcontent.com/pod-product-compliance
Lightning Source LLC
Chambersburg PA
CBHW080346170426
43194CB00014B/2707